SECOND EDITION

Rules for Writers
A CONCISE HANDBOOK

Diana Hacker

A BEDFORD BOOK
ST. MARTIN'S PRESS ◆ NEW YORK

Acknowledgments

The American Heritage Dictionary of the English Language, from the entry
    under "prevent." Copyright © 1978 by Houghton Mifflin Company. Reprinted
    by permission.
Russell Baker, from "From Song to Sound: Bing and Elvis." Copyright © 1977
    by The New York Times Company, and from "Poor Russell's Almanac," copy-
    right © 1972 by The New York Times Company. Reprinted by permission.
Alan Brinkley, from *Voices of Protest: Huey Long, Father Coughlin, and the
    Great Depression.* Copyright © 1982 by Alan Brinkley. Reprinted by permis-
    sion of Alfred A. Knopf, Inc.
Jane Brody, from *Jane Brody's Nutrition Book.* Copyright © 1981 by Jane E.
    Brody. Reprinted by permission of W. W. Norton & Company, Inc.
Roger Caras, from "What's a Koala?" Copyright 1983 by Roger Caras. First
    appeared in *Geo* Magazine, May 1983. Reprinted by permission of Roberta
    Pryor, Inc.
Bruce Catton, from "Grant and Lee: A Study in Contrasts," *The American
    Story,* Earl Schenck Miers, editor. © 1956 by Broadcast Music, Inc. Reprinted
    by permission of the U.S. Capitol Historical Society.
Napoleon A. Chagnon, from *Yanomamo: The Fierce People.* Reprinted by per-
    mission of Holt, Rinehart and Winston, Publishers.

(Continued on page 474)

Preface
for Instructors

When I began writing this book, I had been teaching long enough to know just what I wanted in a handbook. Like many of my colleagues, I teach five classes a semester, each with twenty-five students of varying abilities, so there is all too little time for individualized grammar lessons. I wanted a handbook so clear and accessible that my students could learn from it on their own. I had in mind a book that would give students what they seem to prefer — straightforward, unambiguous rules — but without suggesting that rules are absolutes or that writing well is simply a matter of following the rules.

Further, though I preferred a brief, quick reference, I wanted a handbook comprehensive enough to address the full range of problems that crop up in my students' drafts. And because my students have such a wide range of abilities, I hoped for a book that would be useful for all of them, offering a little help or a lot of help depending on their needs.

Finally, I envisioned a handbook that would support the philosophy of composition that I work so hard to convey in the classroom. Writing is a process, I tell my students, and revision is central to that process. Revision is not a punishment for failing to get things right the first time. Nor is it a perfunctory clean-up exercise. It occurs right on the pages of a rough draft, often messily, with cross-outs and insertions, and it requires an active mind, a mind willing to look at a draft from the point of view of the reader, to spot problems, and to choose solutions.

With these aims in mind, then, I began writing this book. And it was with them in mind that I rewrote it again and again, with each draft edging closer to my vision. Now, three years after its initial publication, I have revised *Rules for Writers* once again, this time in light of suggestions passed along to me from the book's users — both faculty and students. Because *Rules for Writers* has now been tested in the classroom, the second edition comes even closer than the first to fulfilling my original aims. Here are its principal features.

Comprehensive coverage and compact format. To make *Rules for Writers* useful as a quick reference, I have limited myself within each section to the essentials: straightforward rules backed up by concise explanations, realistic examples, and brief comments on examples. In its coverage, however, the book is complete. It is a guide to the full range of conventions of grammar, punctuation, mechanics, and usage as well as to the writing process, paragraphs, style, diction, logic, the research paper, business letters, and résumés.

Hand-edited sentences. Most examples appear as they would in a rough draft, with handwritten revisions made in color over typeset faulty sentences. Unlike the usual technique of printing separate incorrect and correct versions of a sentence, hand-edited sentences highlight the revision, allowing students to grasp both the error and its correction at a glance. Further, hand-edited sentences mimic the process of revision as it should appear in the students' own drafts.

An organization reflecting the writing process. *Rules for Writers* moves from the whole paper and paragraphs through sentence rhetoric and diction to grammar, punctuation, and mechanics. This organization puts the stages of the writing process in context, thereby showing students when — as well as how — to revise and edit their drafts.

An emphasis on rules. As its title suggests, *Rules for Writers* focuses on rules rather than on grammatical abstractions. Although abstract section headings such as "parallelism" and "agreement" are understandable to instructors, they are not always clear to students. Rules such as "Balance parallel ideas" and "Make subjects and verbs agree" are clearer because they both identify the problem and tell students what to do about it.

Handbooks are by their very nature prescriptive, but that does not mean they must be unbending. Like other modern handbooks, *Rules for Writers* alerts students to levels of formality, rhetorical options, and current standards of usage. It distinguishes between rules intended as rhetorical advice and those that are more strictly matters of right and wrong.

A problem-solving approach to errors. Where relevant, *Rules for Writers* attends to the linguistic and social causes of errors and to the effects of errors on readers. The examples of errors in the text are realistic, most having been drawn from student papers and local newspapers. The text treats these errors as problems to be solved, often in light of rhetorical considerations, not as violations of a moral code. Instead of preaching at students, it shows them why problems occur, how to recognize them, and how to solve them.

Full explanations for students who need them. Because *Rules for Writers* highlights rules and examples, it provides quick answers for students who need nothing more. But students who need more help will find it. Throughout the text, they will find extra help in full explanations following rules, in analytical comments pegged to examples, and in cross-references to descriptions of key grammatical concepts.

A unique section on standard English.   Part VI, Editing for Standard English, is devoted to written errors caused by the speech patterns of nonstandard or nonnative English. Students who need help with such matters as omitted -*s* and -*ed* endings will find a description of important differences between standard and nonstandard English. Speakers of English as a second language will find advice on when to use — and when not to use — the articles *a, an,* and *the.*

Extensive exercises, some with answers.   At least one exercise set accompanies nearly every section of the book. Most sets begin with five lettered sentences whose answers appear at the back of the book so that students may test their understanding independently. The sets then continue with ten numbered sentences whose answers appear only in the Instructor's Edition, so that instructors may use the exercises in class or assign them as homework. In addition, a full set of alternate exercises is available in an 8½″ × 11″ workbook, either for duplication or for student purchase.

Preface to the second edition

Response to the first edition of *Rules for Writers* has been gratifying. Instructors report that their students can indeed learn from the book on their own, as I had hoped they would. And *Rules for Writers* has earned praise in the publishing world for its superior design. At the 1985 New England Book Show, the judges presented it with a Special Merit Award, remarking that it was "a real pleasure to see a small paperback containing complex reference material designed with taste, clarity, and simplicity."

In planning the second edition of *Rules for Writers,* I had the help of many instructors who have tested the book in their classrooms. Sixty-nine instructors responded to a detailed questionnaire, and twenty-nine reviewers commented extensively on the first edition and on the evolving drafts of the second. It became clear to me early on that my challenge was to expand the book where necessary, but without limiting its usefulness as a quick reference.

Those of you who are familiar with the first edition will find that the central reference sections — Parts III – IX — remain brief. In the chapters dealing with the whole paper and the research paper, however, which are rarely used strictly for reference, you will find numerous additions that make the book more useful as a classroom text. Here is a summary of what is new.

Fuller coverage of the whole paper. Part I of *Rules for Writers* now surveys the writing process more fully. Prewriting in particular is discussed in greater detail. New to this edition are a list of one hundred writing topics, an expanded section on audience analysis, more techniques for generating ideas, a fuller discussion of the thesis statement, and examples of both formal and informal outlining. The section on drafting now includes student examples of introductions and conclusions and a brief discussion of writer's block. As for revision, the second edition contains a discussion of peer review, a checklist, and a new section on revising and editing on a word processor. The sample essay now provides examples of both global and sentence-level revisions.

Stronger reference sections. Numerous small improvements throughout Parts III – IX strengthen *Rules for Writers* as a reference. In Part III, Revising Sentences, I have reworked the sections on coordination and subordination and dangling modifiers and have expanded the coverage of parallelism, mixed constructions, and shifts. Part IV, Changing Words, contains a new section on sexist English and a more positive treatment of figurative language.

Part V, Editing for Grammar, contains fuller coverage of fragments, pronoun-antecedent agreement, and pronoun reference. In addition, Chapter 27 on verbs has been substantially reworked. It now includes material on irregular verbs (formerly Chapter 30) and a chart of tenses. In the first edition of *Rules for Writers*, Part VI, Editing for Standard English, dealt primarily with dialect interference. Now, with the addition of rules on the use of the articles *a*, *an*, and *the*, it also addresses an interference problem that faces many speakers of English as a second language.

In Parts VII – IX — Editing for Punctuation, Editing for Mechanics, and Grammar Basics — you will find minor improvements, most notably in the sections on commas, semicolons, and quotation marks. You will also find a new section on the use of the dictionary, illustrated with a sample entry.

Two full chapters on the research paper. Part X has been substantially revised to make the research paper material more useful both as a reference and as a classroom text. The material is now divided into two chapters (one on researching, the other on writing the paper), and the alternative documentation styles are clearly separated from MLA's preferred style of in-text citation. In addition to both new and old MLA style, the second edition also includes the APA style of in-text citations and references plus a list of style manuals in other disciplines.

To make the research paper chapters more useful as a classroom text, I have included further advice on matters most troublesome to students: choosing and narrowing a topic, planning a search strategy, integrating quotations, and avoiding plagiarism both at the note-taking and the drafting stages of the writing process. I have also added a section on revision that features a detailed checklist.

Expanded ancillary package. An $8\frac{1}{2}'' \times 11''$ workbook, *Exercises to Accompany Rules for Writers*, provides instructors with a full set of alternate exercises for a variety of possible uses: as homework, as quizzes, as independent study, or as support for a writing center. The workbook also reprints the exercises in *Rules for Writers*, allowing a variety of uses for those exercises as well. Instructors who have adopted *Rules for Writers* may duplicate any of these exercises simply by photocopying them, and the workbooks are also available for student purchase.

Selected alternate exercises appear on a disk. The software program asks students to edit the sentences on the computer screen, not simply to retype them with corrections or to choose among a set of alternatives.

Diagnostic tests covering common sentence and punctuation errors are now included in a manual, *Instructional Resources to Accompany Rules for Writers*. In addition, the manual contains answers to the book's exercises and to the alternate exercises.

Also available is an Instructor's Edition containing answers to all of the book's exercises.

Acknowledgments

No author can possibly anticipate the many ways in which a variety of students might respond to a text: Where might students be confused? How much explanation is enough? What is too intimidating? Do the examples appeal to a range of students? Are they free of stereotypes? To help me answer such questions, nearly one hundred professors from more than eighty colleges and universities contributed useful insights based on their varied experiences in the classroom.

For their many helpful suggestions, I would like to thank an unusually perceptive group of reviewers: Victoria Aarons, Trinity University (Texas); Lucien Agosta, Kansas State University; Patricia Bizzell, College of the Holy Cross; Santi Buscemi, Middlesex Community College; Thomas Copeland, Youngstown State University; Richard Fulkerson, East Texas State University; Linda Gajdusek, San Francisco State University; George Hanson, University of California (San Diego); Dorothy Harris, Okaloosa-Walton Junior College; Sandra Hastings, Seattle Central Community College; Frank Hubbard, Cleveland State University; Brian Kennedy, Miami University (Ohio); Edward Kline, University of Notre Dame; Eileen Klink, California State University (Long Beach); Joyce Magnotto, Prince Georges Community College; Helen Malin, Dillard University; Michael Matthews, Tarrant County Junior College; Stuart Millner, Suffolk University; Shirley Morahan, Northeast Missouri State University; Lyle Morgan, Pittsburgh State University; Carolyn O'Hearn, University of Texas (El Paso); Ann Raimes, Hunter College; Michael Robertson, Lafayette College; Eleanor Robinson, Niagara County Community College; Jeanne C. Ryan, Cleveland State University; Faye Schuett, Tulsa Junior College; Carol Slade, Columbia University; Thomas Whissen, Wright State University; and Suellyn Winkle, Sante Fe Community College.

For helping me to see the strengths and deficiencies of the first edition, thanks go to the many instructors who took the time to answer a detailed questionnaire: Margaret L. Allison, Eyal Amiran, T. M. Antrim, Philip Auslander, Laurine Blankenau, Neville Britto, Lurene Brooks, Arline Burgmeier, Charles Cagle, Michael Cass, Edward Chadwick, Lila Chalpin, Cynthia Chapman, Sue Coody, Herbert Crook, Mary-Ellen Cummings, Karen R. Dhar, Charles B. Dodson, Ren Draya, Karen G. Druliner, Linda Dunleavy, J. L. Funston, Jeff Glauner, Dennis Goldsberry, John M. Hansen, Dorothy P. Harris, Claire-Marie Hart, Clyde Haupt, Pauline Havens, Shannon T. Hiatt, Allan M. Hikida, Dorothy M. Hill, Jean Hodgin, Rich Ives, Anne Jackets, Richard Keller, David G. Kent, Anne Kingan, Karen E. Kirk, Carolyn Kyler, Elizabeth Larsen, Nancy J. Levine, E. D. Lister, Susan Lyons, Mary Mackey, John Magee, Joyce Magnotto, John Markley, John W. Martin, Marie E. McAllister, Linda McDanal, Brian E. Michaels, John D. Mitchell, Deirdre Neilen, Thomas B. O'Grady, E. Suzanne Owens, William Peirce, Rita Phipps, Ellen Pryor, Steven S. Reynolds, Barbara Rippey, Elizabeth S. Scott, Marcia Seabury, Eugene R. Senff, Michael Shelden, Sheila Simonson, David M. Smith, Gwen Towey, J. M. Valenti, and Wanda Van Goor.

Special thanks are due to the people at Bedford Books: to Charles Christensen for his creativity and his wise and expert counsel; to Joan Feinberg for setting a standard of excellence and nudging me toward it, always with intelligence, grace, and good humor; to Elizabeth Schaaf for guiding the book so expertly through production; to Julie Shevach for orchestrating the review program and editing the Glossary; and to Mary Lou Wilshaw for handling permissions and reviewing all stages of proofs.

For their assistance with the research paper chapters, I would like to thank William Peirce, who drafted the chapters, and Lloyd Shaw and Charmaine Boyd, who served as consultants. For bringing consistency and grace to the final manuscript—no small task in a handbook—copyeditor Barbara Flanagan receives my highest praise.

I am also grateful to Claire Seng-Niemoeller for designing clean, uncluttered pages that highlight the book's hand-edited sentences. In presenting the Special Merit Award at the 1985 New England Book Show, one of the judges remarked that the handbook "is a true designer's book, gracefully fit for its plain purpose."

Finally, a note of thanks goes to my parents and to Joseph and Marian Hacker, Robert Hacker, Tom Henderson, Robbie and Austin Nichols, Betty Renshaw, Greg Tarvin, and the Dougherty family for their support and encouragement; and to the many students over the years who have taught me that errors, a natural by-product of the writing process, are simply problems waiting to be solved.

D. H.
Prince Georges Community College

Introduction
for Students

Though it is small enough to hold in your hand, *Rules for Writers* will answer nearly all of your questions about the rules of English. It is brief only because it limits itself to the essentials: straightforward rules, concise explanations, and clear examples.

The plan of the book

A glance at the table of contents will show you that *Rules for Writers* is organized to reflect the writing process. Advice about the whole paper and paragraphs comes first (Parts I and II), followed by strategies for revising sentences for clarity and style (Parts III and IV) and editing them for problems with grammar, punctuation, and mechanics (Parts V–VIII).

The book ends with several special reference sections. Part IX, Grammar Basics, defines key grammatical terms and concepts. Part X, Special Types of Writing, offers advice on the research paper, logic, business letters, and résumés. Following Part X is a Glossary of Usage, which lists alphabetically many common problems in word choice.

How to find information

When you are revising a paper that has been marked by your instructor, tracking down information is simple. If your instructor marks problems with a number such as *16* or a number and letter such as *12c,* you can turn directly to the appropriate section of the handbook. Just flip through the colored tabs on the upper corners of the pages until you find the number in question. The number *16,* for example, leads you to the rule "Tighten wordy sentences," and 12c takes you to the subrule "Repair dangling modifiers." If your instructor uses an abbreviation such as *w* or *dm* instead of a number, consult the list of abbreviations and symbols inside the back cover of the book, where you will find the name of the problem (*wordy; dangling modifier*) and the number of the section to consult.

When consulting the handbook on your own, you may find information in several ways. The alphabetical index at the back is perhaps the most reliable way to find what you're looking for. As you become familiar with the overall plan of the book, however, you can also make use of the full table of contents at the beginning of the book or of the brief table of contents inside the front cover. And as you become accustomed to the headings at the tops of the pages next to the colored tabs, you may be able to find information simply by flipping through the pages.

Many sections of the handbook contain cross-references to other sections of the book. Most of these will lead you to specific sections in Part IX, Grammar Basics, where you will find a discussion of grammatical concepts and terminology necessary for understanding many of the rules in the rest of the book. Whenever the book uses a grammatical term that you don't fully understand, you can also track down its meaning by consulting the list of grammatical terms inside the back cover.

The process of revision

Rules for Writers shows you how to improve sentences the way practicing writers do it — by working directly on a rough draft version of the paper. Instead of making corrections as you recopy sentences and paragraphs, try marking up your drafts with cross-outs and insertions. This technique gives you better control over your sentences, and it saves you time as well. To see what a marked-up draft looks like, turn to pages 46 – 47 or flip through the central sections of this book, which are illustrated with sentences that look just like those in a carefully revised draft.

How to use this book for self-study

In a composition class, most of your time should be spent writing. Therefore it is unlikely that you will want to study all of the chapters in this book in detail. Instead you should focus on the problems that tend to crop up in your own writing. Your instructor (or your college's writing center) will be glad to help you design an individualized program of self-study.

Rules for Writers has been designed so that you can learn from it on your own. By providing answers to some of the exercise sentences, it allows you to test your understanding of the material. Most exercise sets begin with five sentences lettered from *a* to *e* and conclude with ten sentences numbered from *1* to *10*. Answers to the five lettered sentences appear in an appendix at the end of the book. Extra practice exercises are available in two forms: in a workbook, *Exercises to Accompany Rules for Writers*, or on a software disk. The software provides you with one or two possible revisions for all sentences, and it gives explanations as well.

Contents

Part II

Part III

Part IV

Part VI

Part VII

Part VIII

| EDITING FOR MECHANICS | 279 |

Part X

SPECIAL TYPES OF WRITING   353

Writing and Revising the Whole Paper

Since it's not possible to think about everything all at once, most experienced writers take a paper through stages. They begin by generating ideas and sketching a plan. When they feel ready to attempt an initial draft, they rough it out imperfectly, concentrating more on content than on style, grammar, and mechanics. If possible, they then get away from the draft for a while.

For the experienced writer, revising is rarely a one-step process. The larger elements of writing generally receive attention first — the focus, organization, paragraphing, content, and overall strategy. Improvements in sentence structure, word choice, grammar, punctuation, and mechanics come later.

Of course the writing process will not always occur for you quite as simply as just described. While revising, for example, you may need to generate more ideas and draft new material. Or while drafting, you may discover an interesting new approach to your topic that demands a revised plan. Although you should generally move from planning to drafting to revising, be prepared to circle back to earlier stages whenever the need arises.

1

Generate ideas and sketch a plan.

Before attempting a first draft, spend some time creating ideas. Mull over your subject while listening to music or driving to work, jot down inspirations on scratch paper, and explore your insights with anyone willing to listen. At this stage you should be collecting information and experimenting with ways of focusing and organizing it to best reach your readers.

1a Assess the writing situation.

Begin by taking a look at the writing situation in which you find yourself. The key elements of the writing situation include your subject, the sources of information available to you, your purpose, your audience, and constraints such as length and format.

Subject

Frequently your subject will be given to you. In a psychology class, for example, you may be asked to explain Bruno Bettelheim's Freudian analysis of fairy tales. Or in a course on the history of filmmaking, you may be assigned an essay on the political impact of D. W. Griffith's silent film *The Birth of a Nation*. In the business world, your assignment may be to draft a quarterly sales report or craft a diplomatic letter to a customer who has complained about your firm's computer software.

Sometimes you will be free to choose your own subject. Then you will be wise to select a subject that you already know something about or one that you can reasonably investigate in the time you have. Students in composition classes have written successfully on all of the subjects listed below, most of which were later narrowed into topics suitable for essays of 500 – 750 words. By browsing through the lists, perhaps you can pick up some ideas of your own.

Education: computers in the classroom, an inspiring teacher, sex education in junior high school, magnet schools, a learning disability such as dyslexia, programmed instruction, parochial schools, teacher certification, a local program to combat adult illiteracy, creative means of funding a college education

Careers and the workplace: working in an emergency room, the image versus the reality of a job such as lifeguarding, a police officer's workday, advantages of flex-time for workers and employers, company-sponsored day care, mandatory drug testing by employers, sexual or racial discrimination on the job, the psychological effects of unemployment, the rewards of a part-time job such as camp counseling

Families: an experience with adoption, a portrait of a family member who has aged well, the challenges facing single parents, living with an alcoholic parent, a portrait of an ideal parent, growing up in a large family, the problems of split custody, an experience with child abuse, the depiction of male-female relationships in a popular TV series, expectations versus the reality of marriage, overcoming sibling rivalry, the advantages or disadvantages of being a twin

Health: a vegetarian diet, weight loss through hypnotism, a fitness program for the elderly, reasons not to smoke, the rights of smokers or nonsmokers, overcoming an addiction, lithium as a treatment for depression, the side effects of a particular treatment for cancer, life as a diabetic, the benefits of an aerobic exercise such as swimming

Sports and hobbies: an unusual sport such as free-fall parachuting, surviving a wilderness program, bodybuilding, a sport from another culture, the philosophy of karate, the language of sports announcers, pros and cons of banning boxing, coaching a Little League team, cutting the costs of an expensive sport such as skiing, a portrait of a favorite sports figure, sports for the handicapped, the discipline required for a sport such as gymnastics, the rewards of a hobby such as woodworking

The arts: working behind the scenes at a theater, censorship of rock and roll lyrics, photography as an art form, the Japanese tea ceremony, the influence of African art on Picasso, the appeal of a local art museum, a portrait of a favorite musician or artist, performing as a musician, a high school for the arts, the colorization of black-and-white films, science fiction as a serious form of literature, a humorous description of romance novels or hard-boiled detective thrillers

Social justice: an experience with racism or sexism, affirmative action, reverse discrimination, making public transportation accessible for the physically handicapped, an experience as a juror, a local program to aid the homeless, discrimination against homosexuals, pros and cons of a national drinking age of twenty-one

Death and dying: working on a suicide hotline, the death of a loved one, a brush with death, caring for terminally ill patients, the Buddhist view of death, explaining death to a child, passive euthanasia, death with dignity, an out-of-body experience

Violence and crime: an experience with a gun, a wartime experience, violence on television news programs, visiting a friend in prison, alternative sentencing for first offenders, victims' rights, a successful program to eliminate violence in a public high school, violence between parents and children or between husband and wife

Nature and ecology: safety of nuclear power plants, solar energy, wind energy, air pollution in our national parks, grizzly bears in Yellowstone, communication among dolphins, organic gardening, backpacking in the Rockies, marine ecology, an experimental farming technique, cleaning up Boston Harbor, the preservation of beaches in Delaware

Many of these subjects are too broad. Part of your challenge as a writer will be whittling broad subjects down to manageable topics. If you are limited to a few pages, for example, you could not possibly do justice to a subject as broad as "sports for the handicapped." You would be wise to restrict your paper to a topic more manageable in the space allowed — perhaps a description of the Saturday morning athletic program your college offers for handicapped children.

Sources of information

Where will your facts, details, and examples come from? Can your topic be illustrated by personal experience, or will you need to search out relevant information?

You can develop many topics wholly through personal experience, depending of course on your own life experiences. For instance, the students who wrote about lifeguarding, learning disabilities, weight loss through hypnotism, and free-fall parachuting all spoke with the voice of experience, as did those who wrote about flex-time, coaching a Little League team, and company-sponsored day care. When narrowing their subjects, these students chose to limit themselves to information they had at hand. For example, instead of writing about company-sponsored day care in general — a subject that would have required a great deal of research — one student limited her discussion to the successful day care center at the company for which she worked.

To develop many subjects, however, you must move beyond personal experience. Other possible sources of information include direct observation, interviews or questionnaires, and reading. Direct observation is an excellent means of collecting information about a wide range of subjects: perhaps male-female relationships on "Cheers," the language of sports announcers, or the appeal of a local art museum. For such subjects, do not rely on your memory alone; your information will be fresher and more detailed if you actively collect it, with a notebook or tape recorder in hand. As writer Stuart Chase advises young journalists assigned to report on their city's water system, "You will write a better article if you heave yourself out of a comfortable chair and go down in tunnel 3 and get soaked."

Interviews and questionnaires can also supply you with detailed and interesting information on a variety of subjects. A nursing student interested in the care of terminally ill patients might interview nurses at a hospice; a political science major might speak with a local judge to learn about alternative sentencing for first offenders; a future teacher might conduct a telephone survey on the use of computers in area classrooms. It is a good idea to tape interviews to preserve any lively quotations that you might want to weave into your essay. Keep questionnaires simple and specify a deadline to ensure that you get a reasonable number of responses.

Reading will be your primary source of information for many college assignments across the curriculum. These assignments will generally be one of two kinds: analytical assignments that call for a close reading of one book, essay, or literary work; or research assignments that send you to the library to consult a variety of sources on a particular topic. For analytical papers, you can usually assume that your reader is familiar with the work and has a copy of it at hand. You select details from the work not to inform readers but to support an interpretation. When you quote from the work, page references are often sufficient. For research papers, on the other hand, you cannot assume that your reader is familiar with your sources or has them close at hand. This means that you must formally document all quoted and paraphrased material (see 51 and 52). When in doubt about the need for formal documentation, consult your instructor.

Purpose

Your purpose will often be dictated by the specific writing situation that faces you. Perhaps you have been asked to take minutes for a club meeting, to draft a letter requesting payment from a client, or to describe the results of a biology experiment. Even though your overall purpose is fairly obvious in such situations, a close look at that purpose can help you make a variety of necessary decisions. How detailed should the minutes be? Is your purpose to summarize the meeting or to establish a careful record of discussion in case future controversies arise? How firmly should your letter request payment? Do you need the money at all costs, or do you hope to get it without risking loss of the client's business? How technical is the biology report expected to be?

In many writing situations, part of your challenge will be discovering a purpose. Consider, for example, the topic of magnet schools — schools that draw students from different neighborhoods because of features such as advanced science classes or late-afternoon day care. Your purpose could be to inform parents of the options available in your county. Or you might argue that the county's magnet schools are not promoting racial integration as had been planned. Or you might propose that the board of education create a magnet high school for the arts on your college campus.

Although no precise guidelines will lead you to a purpose, you can begin by asking whether you hope to inform readers, to persuade them, to entertain them, or to call them to action. And such questions will lead you to another important question: Just who are those readers?

Audience

Audience analysis can often lead you to an effective strategy for reaching your readers. One writer, whose purpose was to persuade teenagers not to smoke, jotted down the following observations about her audience:

> dislike lectures, especially from older people
> have little sense of their own mortality
> are concerned about physical appearance and image
> want to be socially accepted
> have limited budgets

This analysis led the writer to focus more on the social aspects of smoking (she pointed out, for instance, that kissing a smoker is like licking an ashtray) than on the health risks. Her audience analysis also warned her against adopting a preachy tone that her readers might find offensive. Instead of lecturing to her audience, she decided to draw examples from her own experience as a hooked smoker: burning holes in her best sweater, driving in zero-degree weather late at night in search of an open tavern to buy cigarettes, rummaging through ashtrays for stale butts, and so on. The result was an essay that reached its readers instead of alienating them.

Of course in some writing situations the audience will not be neatly defined for you. Nevertheless, many of the choices you make as you write will reflect your sense of your audience — how familiar with your subject you assume them to be, for example — so it is best to make conscious decisions at the outset. The following questions will help you make decisions about your audience.

How well informed are your readers about the subject?

How interested and attentive are they likely to be?

What values do they hold dear?

Will they resist any ideas in the essay?

How close a relationship with them can you assume?

How sophisticated are they as readers? Do they have large vocabularies? Can they process long and complex sentences?

When your audience is so unknown that you can't honestly answer such questions, you must still make decisions about these matters, even if this means creating an audience that is in some sense a fiction.

In college composition classes, you are rarely presented with a real audience. Your instructor will read the paper, of course, and may even be a member of the group you hope to reach, but you should not consider him or her to be your sole audience. Instead, decide what group of people might reasonably be informed, persuaded, entertained, or called to action by what you have to say. Then aim your paper in their direction.

Length and format

Writers seldom have complete control over length and format. Journalists usually write within strict word limits set by their editors, businesspeople routinely aim for conciseness, and most college assignments specify an approximate length.

Certain formats also may be required by your writing situation. Specific formats are frequently used in the business world for documents such as letters, memos, reports, budget analyses, and personnel records. In the academic world, you may need to learn precise conventions for lab reports, critiques, research papers, and so on.

For most undergraduate papers, a standard format is acceptable (see 46). The conventions for research papers are discussed in 52.

EXERCISE 1–1

Choose one of the subject areas mentioned on pages 3–5 and add at least five subjects to those already on the list. If other members of your class have also done this exercise, pool the results.

EXERCISE 1–2

Narrow five of the following subjects into topics that would be manageable for an essay of two to five pages.

1. Working behind the scenes at a theater
2. A sport from another culture
3. Violence between parents and children
4. The advantages or disadvantages of being a twin
5. An experience with adoption
6. The side effects of a particular treatment for cancer
7. Computers in the classroom
8. Parochial schools
9. Performing as a musician
10. An experience with racism or sexism

EXERCISE 1–3

Which of the following subjects might be illustrated wholly by personal experience? For the others, suggest possible sources of information: direct observation, interviews, questionnaires, or reading.

1. The problems of split custody
2. Working in an emergency room
3. Backpacking in the Rockies
4. The influence of African art on Picasso
5. Violence on television news programs
6. The discipline required for a sport such as gymnastics
7. Photography as an art form
8. Affirmative action
9. A local program to aid the homeless
10. Visiting a friend in prison

EXERCISE 1 – 4

Suggest a possible purpose and audience for five of the following subjects.

1. A vegetarian diet
2. Cutting the costs of an expensive sport such as skiing
3. The challenges facing single parents
4. Advantages of flex-time for workers and employers
5. Growing up in a large family
6. Pros and cons of a national drinking age of twenty-one
7. Science fiction as a serious form of literature
8. An unusual sport such as free-fall parachuting
9. A police officer's workday
10. Working on a suicide hotline

1b Experiment with ways of getting started.

Instead of just plunging into a first draft, experiment with one or more techniques for exploring your subject—perhaps listing, clustering, branching, or asking questions. Whatever technique you turn to, the goal is the same: to generate a wealth of ideas. At this early stage of the writing process, you should aim for quantity, not necessarily quality, of ideas. If an idea proves to be off the point, trivial, or too farfetched, you can always throw it out later.

Listing

You might begin by simply listing ideas, putting them down in the order in which they occur to you — a technique sometimes known as "brainstorming." Here, for example, is a list one student writer jotted down:

Lifeguarding — an ideal summer job?

> my love of swimming and lying in the sun
>
> hired by Powdermill Village, an apartment complex
>
> first, though, there was a test
>
> two weeks of training — grueling physical punishment plus book work
>
> I passed. The work was over — or so I thought.
>
> greeted by manager; handed a broom, hose, bottle of disinfectant
>
> scrubbing bathrooms, cleaning the pool, clearing the deck of dirt and leaves
>
> little kids breaking every pool rule in the book — running on deck, hanging on buoyed ropes, trying to drown each other
>
> spent most of my time blowing the whistle
>
> working the evening shift no better — adults smuggling in gin and tonics, sexual advances from married men
>
> by end of day, a headache and broom-handled hands

The ideas appear here in the order in which they first occurred to the writer. Later she felt free to rearrange them, to cluster them under general categories, to delete some, and to add others. In other words, she treated her initial list as a source of ideas and a springboard to new ideas, not as a formal outline.

Clustering and branching

Unlike listing, the techniques of clustering and branching highlight relationships among ideas. To cluster ideas, write your topic in the center of a sheet of paper, draw a circle around it, and surround that with related ideas connected to it with lines. If some of the satellite ideas lead to more specific clusters, write them down as well. The writer of the following diagram was exploring ideas for an essay on home uses for computers.

To use the branching technique, put the main idea at the top of a page and then list major supporting ideas beneath it, leaving plenty of space between each one. To the right of each major idea, branch out to minor ideas, drawing lines to indicate the connections. If minor ideas lead to even more specific ideas, continue branching. Here, for example, is a branching diagram for an essay describing an innovative magnet high school called "School without Walls."

School without Walls—an attractive option

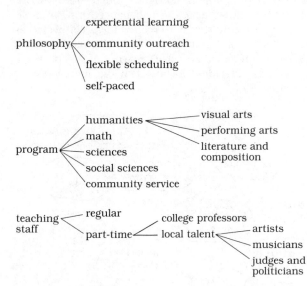

philosophy
- experiential learning
- community outreach
- flexible scheduling
- self-paced

program
- humanities
  - visual arts
  - performing arts
  - literature and composition
- math
- sciences
- social sciences
- community service

teaching staff
- regular
- part-time — local talent
  - college professors
  - artists
  - musicians
  - judges and politicians

Asking questions

By asking relevant questions, you can generate many ideas — and you can make sure that you have adequately surveyed your subject. When gathering material for a story, journalists routinely ask themselves Who? What? When? Where? Why? and How? In addition to helping journalists get started, these questions ensure that they will not overlook an important fact: the date of a prospective summit meeting, for example, or the exact location of a neighborhood burglary.

Whenever you are writing about events, whether current or historical, the journalist's questions are one way to get started. One student, whose subject was the reaction in 1915 to D. W. Griffith's silent film *The Birth of a Nation*, began exploring her topic with this set of questions:

Who objected to the film?

What were the objections?

When were protests first voiced?

Where were protests most strongly expressed?

Why did protesters object to the film?

How did protesters make their views known?

In the academic world, scholars often generate ideas with discipline-specific questions: one set of questions for analyzing short stories, another for evaluating experiments in social psychology, still another for reporting field experiences in anthropology. If you are writing in a particular discipline, try to discover the questions that scholars typically explore. These are frequently presented in textbooks as checklists.

EXERCISE 1–5

Generate a list of at least fifteen items for one of the subjects listed on pages 3–5.

EXERCISE 1–6

Using the technique of clustering or branching, explore one of the subjects listed on pages 3–5 (or one of the subjects you produced in Exercise 1–2).

1c Settle on a tentative focus.

The focus of an essay is its central idea. For many types of writing, the central idea can be asserted in one sentence, a generalization preparing readers for the supporting details that will follow in the paper. Such a sentence, which ordinarily appears in the opening paragraph, is called a *thesis*. A successful thesis — like those below, all taken from student essays — points both the writer and the reader in a definite direction.

> All too often, authors of historical fiction assault our sensibilities and insult our intelligence by framing scenes with pornography.

> One of the most difficult working assignments within the police community is training dogs for K-9 narcotic detection.

> Two types of musicians play percussion instruments — drummers and percussionists — and they are as different as Quiet Riot and the New York Philharmonic.

Frequently a thesis sentence outlines the major sections of the essay, a technique known as *blueprinting.* The following thesis sentence prepares readers for a three-part survey of the roles a Vietnamese woman is expected to fulfill as she grows up.

> From the moment her mind is mature enough to understand commands, to the day she is married off, to the time when she bears children, a Vietnamese woman continuously tries to establish a good name as a diligent daughter, a submissive wife, and an altruistic mother.

It is a good idea to formulate a thesis early in the writing process, perhaps by jotting it on scratch paper, by putting it at the head of a rough outline, or by attempting an introductory paragraph. But be prepared to reformulate the thesis, if necessary, as your drafts evolve. Keep in mind that a thesis should be

1. more general than the material supporting it,
2. limited enough to be supported in the space allowed, and
3. an accurate reflection of the true thrust of the paper.

Because a thesis must prepare readers for facts and details, it cannot itself be a fact. It must always be a generalization demanding proof or further development.

TOO FACTUAL	The first polygraph was developed by Dr. John A. Larson in 1921.
REVISED	Because the polygraph has not been proved reliable, even under the most controlled conditions, its use by private employers should be banned.

Although a thesis must be a generalization, it must not be *too* general. You will need to narrow the focus of any thesis that you cannot adequately develop in the space allowed. Unless you were writing a book or a very long research paper, the following thesis would be too broad:

TOO BROAD	Many drugs are now being used successfully to treat mental illnesses.

You would need to restrict the thesis, perhaps like this:

REVISED	Despite its risks and side effects, lithium is currently the most effective treatment for depression.

For some types of writing, it may be difficult or impossible to express the central idea in a thesis sentence; or it may be unwise or unnecessary to put a thesis sentence in the paper itself. A personal narrative, for example, may have a focus too subtle to be capsulized in a single sentence, and such a sentence might ruin the story. Strictly informative writing, like that found in many business memos, may be difficult to summarize in a thesis. In such instances, do not try to force the central idea into a thesis sentence. Instead, think in terms of an overriding purpose, which may or may not be stated directly in the paper itself.

1d Sketch a tentative plan.

Once you have generated some ideas and formulated a tentative thesis, you may want to construct an outline. The outline might be informal, consisting of the thesis and its major supporting ideas:

> Hawaii is losing its cultural identity.
>
> — pure-blooded Hawaiians increasingly rare
> — native language diluted
> — natives forced off ancestral lands
> — little emphasis on native culture in schools
> — customs exaggerated and distorted by tourism

For complex writing tasks, however, a formal outline provides a clearer blueprint. The following formal outline brought order to the complexities of a difficult subject, proposed methods for limiting and disposing of nuclear waste.

> Thesis: Although various methods for limiting or disposing of nuclear wastes have been proposed, each has serious drawbacks.
>
> I. Limiting nuclear waste: partitioning and transmutation
>   A. The process is complex and costly.
>   B. Radiation exposure to nuclear workers would increase.
>
> II. Antarctic ice sheet disposal
>   A. Our understanding of the behavior of ice sheets is too limited.
>   B. An international treaty prohibits disposal in Antarctica.
>
> III. Space disposal
>   A. The risk of an accident and resulting worldwide disaster is great.
>   B. The cost is prohibitive.
>   C. The method would be unpopular at home and abroad.
>
> IV. Seabed disposal
>   A. Scientists have not yet solved technical difficulties.

B. We do not fully understand the impact of such disposal on the ocean's ecology.

V. Deep underground disposal
   A. There is much political pressure against the plan from citizens who do not want their states to become nuclear dumps.
   B. Geologists disagree about the safest disposal sites.

In constructing a formal outline, keep the following guidelines in mind:

1. Put the thesis at the top.
2. Make items at the same level of generality as parallel as possible.

   In the sample outline, all the Roman numerals state methods of limiting or disposing of nuclear waste, and all the capital letters state drawbacks. *Caution:* If your material cannot honestly be presented in perfectly parallel fashion, do not force it.

3. Use sentences unless phrases are clear.

   In the sample outline, phrases were clear enough for the major categories, but the writer felt that sentences were necessary in stating the drawbacks of each method.

4. Use the conventional system of numbers and letters for the levels of generality.

   I.
      A.
      B.
         1.
         2.
            a.
            b.
               (1)
               (2)
                  (a)
                  (b)
   II.

5. Always use at least two subdivisions for a category.

    If a subject is divided, logically it must have at least two parts. When you are tempted to use a 1 without a 2 or an *a* without a *b*, either incorporate the idea into the level of generality immediately above it or omit it entirely.

6. Limit the number of major sections in the outline.

    If the list of roman numerals grows too long, find some way of clustering the items into more general categories. In the sample outline, for example, the writer might have decided to treat the two methods for limiting nuclear wastes separately, in which case he could have reduced the major sections to two:

   I. Limiting nuclear wastes
     A. Partitioning
     B. Transmutation
  II. Disposing of nuclear wastes
     A. Antarctic ice sheet disposal
     B. Space disposal
     C. Seabed disposal
     D. Deep underground disposal

7. Be flexible.

    Do not feel that if you have two points under roman numeral I you must have an equal number of points beneath the other roman numerals. Also, do not assume that every bit of material that will come up in the paper itself must be specifically covered in the outline. In the sample outline, for example, the writer does not attempt to describe the various methods of disposing of nuclear wastes, though such descriptions will certainly appear in the paper.

EXERCISE 1–7

Organize the following list of items into two rough outlines, each with a different thesis. If some items do not support the thesis, eliminate them; if you can think of other items that do, add them.

Topic: The growing influence of computers on our daily lives

Automatic banks
Personal computers installed in every dorm room in colleges
Computers in grade schools
Computer literacy as a job requirement in many fields
Computers in scholarship
Computer games
Isolation of many "hackers"
Mechanization of society
Fear of computers
Robots
Liberal arts education made obsolete by computers
Computer cash registers in stores
Robot actors at EPCOT Center and Disney World
Revenge of computers as the subject for science fiction films
Computer dating
Computers eliminating jobs
Computers eliminating tedious work

2

Rough out an initial draft.

As long as you treat an initial draft as a rough draft, you can focus your attention on ideas and organization, knowing that problems with sentence structure and word choice can always be dealt with later.

2a Attempt an introduction, a body, and a conclusion.

The introduction announces the main point; the body develops it, usually in several paragraphs; the conclusion drives it home. You can begin drafting, however, at any point. If you find it difficult to introduce a paper that you have not yet written, you can write the body first and save the introduction for later.

The introduction

For most writing tasks, your introduction will be a paragraph of 50 to 150 words. Perhaps the most common strategy is to open the paragraph with a few sentences that engage the reader and to conclude it with a statement of the essay's main point. The sentence stating the main point is called a *thesis* (see 1c). In the following examples, the thesis has been italicized.

> To the Australian aborigines, the Dreamtime was the time of creation. It was then that the creatures of the earth, including man, came into being. There are many legends about that mystical period, but unfortunately, the koala does not fare too well in any of them. *Slow-witted though it is in life, the koala is generally depicted in myth and folklore as a trickster and a thief.*   —Roger Caras, "What's a Koala?"

> When I was sixteen, I married and moved to a small town to live. My new husband nervously showed me the house he had rented. It was after dark when we arrived there, and I remember wondering why he seemed so apprehensive about my reaction to the house. I thought the place seemed shabby but potentially cozy and quite livable inside. The morning sun revealed the reason for his anxiety by exposing the squalor outdoors. Up to that point, my contact with any reality but that of my own middle-class childhood had come from books. *The next four years in a small Iowa town taught me that reading about poverty is a lot different from living with it.*
> —Julie Reardon, a student

Ideally, the sentences leading to the thesis should hook the reader, perhaps with one of the following:

a startling statistic or unusual fact

a vivid example

a description

a paradoxical statement

a quotation or bit of dialogue

a question

an analogy

a joke or an anecdote

Such hooks are particularly important when you cannot assume your reader's interest in the subject. Hooks are less necessary in scholarly essays and other writing aimed at readers with a professional interest in the subject.

Although the thesis frequently appears at the end of the introduction, it can just as easily appear at the beginning. Much work-related writing, in which a straightforward approach is most effective, commonly begins with the thesis.

> *Flex-time scheduling, which has proved its effectiveness at the Library of Congress, should be introduced on a trial basis at the main branch of the Montgomery County Public Library.* By offering flexible work hours, the library can boost employee morale, cut down on absenteeism, and expand its hours of operation. — David Warren, a student

In narrative and descriptive writing, it is not always necessary to have an explicitly stated thesis. (See 1c.) However, an introduction without a thesis should clearly suggest the purpose and direction of the essay to follow. For example, even though a thesis has not been directly stated in the following introduction, readers understand that they are about to hear a gripping story:

> At the Coast Guard Training Center in Alameda, California, our instructors stressed that we still had much to learn about the sea's moods and temperaments. Our training, they said, was only inadequate preparation for what could happen to us in open water. "The ocean humbles even the

most experienced skipper!" warned one teacher ominously. He often spoke of the *Edmund Fitzgerald*, an ore carrier which had foundered in a winter storm on Lake Superior. Even though the ship was over seven hundred feet from stem to stern and equipped with the latest technology, she went down in less than a sweep of the radar's antenna. But it made no difference to me. After all, those men on the *Fitzgerald* were only civilians; I was a Coast Guardsman. After fifteen weeks at the Center, after long hours delving into the art of navigation and piloting, I could deal with any emergency. Steering— "wheeling" as we called it—was my forte. Several times, in fact, in less-than-perfect conditions, I had brought ships through narrow entrances in the breakwall. I could handle any ship of any tonnage. There was nothing that I couldn't do.

—Jonathan Schilk, a student

The body

As you begin drafting the body of the essay, keep your pre-writing materials — lists, diagrams, outlines, and so on — close at hand. In addition to helping you get started, such notes and blueprints will encourage you to keep moving. With notes close by, you won't need to pause so frequently, staring at a blank page in search of ideas. Writing tends to flow better when it is drafted relatively quickly, without many stops and starts. The trick, of course, is to relax—to overcome the fear that grips many of us as we face that blank page.

At one time or another, we all experience writer's block. But if writer's block is a chronic problem for you, consider whether you're being too hard on yourself. Do you demand that your sentences all be stylish and perfectly grammatical right from the start? Do you expect your ideas to emerge full-blown, like Athena from the head of Zeus?

Professional writers are not so tough on themselves. Jacques Barzun, for example, lets his rough-draft sentences be "as stupid" as they wish. Joan Didion acknowledges that she discovers ideas *as she writes;* for her, writing is a way of learning, not just a means of revealing already known truths.

As Didion puts it, "I write entirely to find out what I'm thinking, what I'm looking at, what I see and what it means." Later, of course, she revises.

The conclusion

The conclusion should echo the main idea, without dully repeating it. Often the concluding paragraph can be relatively short. By the end of the essay, readers should already understand your main point; your conclusion simply drives it home and perhaps suggests its significance.

In addition to echoing your main idea, a conclusion might summarize the essay's key points, pose a question for future study, offer advice, or propose a course of action. To end an essay detailing the social skills required of a bartender, one writer concludes with some advice:

> If someone were to approach me one day looking for the secret to running a good bar, I suppose I would offer the following advice: Get your customers to pour out their ideas at a greater rate than you pour out the liquor. You will both win in the end.   —Kathleen Lewis, a student

To make the conclusion memorable, consider including a detail, example, or image from the introduction to bring readers full circle; a quotation or bit of dialogue; an anecdote; or a humorous, witty, or ironic comment. To end a narrative describing a cash register holdup, one student uses an anecdote that includes some dialogue:

> It took me a long time to get over that incident. Countless times I found myself gasping as someone "pointed" a dollar bill at me. On one such occasion, a jovial little man buying a toy gun for his son came up to me and said in a Humphrey Bogart impression, "Give me all your money, Sweetheart." I didn't laugh. Instead, my heart skipped a beat, for I had heard those words before.   —Diana Crawford, a student

Whatever concluding strategy you choose, avoid introducing new ideas at the end of an essay. Also avoid apologies and other limp, indeterminate endings. The essay should end crisply, preferably on a positive note.

Do not become discouraged if the perfect conclusion eludes you at the rough-draft stage of the writing process. Because the conclusion is so closely tied to the rest of the essay in both content and tone, you may well decide to rework it (or even replace it) as your drafts evolve.

2b Keep your audience in mind.

As they head into a draft, writers frequently forget their audience. Consider, for example, one dentist's postcard reminder to his patients, sent out twice yearly:

> It is the custom of this office to notify patients on record, for periodical examination of the mouth. This service is rendered to safeguard previous work and to ensure future good health and appearance. May I suggest you call.

Not surprisingly, the dentist got a better response when he decided to address his audience directly:

> Things to do today:
>   1. Floss.
>   2. Call your dentist.
> It's time again for your regular dental checkup, so please call today for an appointment.

The new version, simple and clear, is easier to read. And it has a human voice behind it, one that speaks out directly, person to person, in a tone appropriate to the dentist's audience.

Keeping your audience in mind will help you adopt an appropriate tone. It will also help you make a variety of other choices. Assume, for example, that you are writing an instruction booklet for machinists at Caterpillar Tractor Company. You are considering two ways of structuring a sentence, both of which are perfectly grammatical. In light of your audience, which one do you choose?

> Move the control lever to the reverse position after the machine stops.

> After the machine stops, move the control lever to the reverse position.

Once you've envisioned machinists with the control lever in front of them, ready to pull it, you'll choose the second version because it is safer. Not everyone reads instructions all the way through before putting them into action, so some readers of the first version will move the lever while the machine is still running. The second version ensures that machinists will stop the machine first.

In addition to considering your specific audience, keep in mind the needs of readers in general. Most readers appreciate a writer who

> respects their intelligence,

> gives them real content,

> presents the message as simply as the subject allows,

> refuses to waste their time, and

> provides a touch of human interest wherever possible.

2c Keep the facts in mind.

If you do not have in mind a rich assortment of specific facts, examples, and details, you will almost certainly get stuck in the middle of a draft. Or you will find yourself simply repeating generalizations, moving forward without really advancing. Whether your facts come from personal experience, from direct observation, from interviews, or from written sources, you'll be better able to keep them in mind if you have first jotted them down. (See 1b.) Keep any notes close at hand as you begin writing.

Having the facts at hand will make a great difference in the quality of the draft you produce. Consider, for example, the following two sentences, taken from drafts written by different students. You'll have no difficulty deciding which student had the facts at hand.

> First and foremost, the hamburgers that are sold in the cafeteria's machines are dry in texture and cold to the taste.

> When I turned to the machine, I decided to try a sizzling hamburger, lean and juicy. Instead out came a small dry patty so cold that the fat was congealed in tiny globs on top of the meat.

The second writer is reporting specific and vivid facts. The first writer needs to head back to the cafeteria for another look, perhaps another taste, this time with a notebook in hand.

EXERCISE 2–1

Write introductory paragraphs for essays on two different subjects, perhaps selected from the lists on pages 3–5. Either begin or end your introduction with a thesis statement.

EXERCISE 2–2

Write the first draft of an essay of approximately 500 words, perhaps using one of the subjects on pages 3–5.

3

Make global revisions: Think big.

Revising is not just a matter of moving words around and correcting grammar. It involves much larger changes, global improvements that can be quite dramatic. Whole paragraphs might be dropped, others added. Material once stretched over two or three paragraphs might be condensed into one. Entire sections could be rearranged. Even the content may change dramatically, for the process of writing stimulates thought.

Major revising can be difficult, sometimes even painful. You might discover, for example, that an essay's first three pages are nothing but padding, that its central argument tilts the wrong way, and that you sound like a stuffed shirt throughout. But the sheer fact that you can see such problems in your writing is a sign of hope. Those opening paragraphs can be dropped, the argument's slant realigned, the voice made more human.

3a Get some distance, perhaps with the help of reviewers.

Many of us resist global revisions because we find it difficult to distance ourselves from a draft. We tend to review our work from our own, not from our audience's, perspective.

To distance yourself from a draft, begin by putting it aside for a while, preferably overnight or even longer. When you return to it, try to play the role of your audience as you read. Mark any places where your readers are likely to be confused, misled, or annoyed; look too for sentences and paragraphs that are not likely to persuade.

If at all possible, enlist the help of reviewers — persons willing to play the role of audience for you. Possible reviewers include peers, such as family members, friends, and other students; and professionals, such as professors, trained writing-center tutors, and practicing writers. Ask your reviewers to focus on the larger issues of writing, not on the fine points. If they are at first captivated by fine points such as grammar and spelling — and many peer reviewers are — remind them that you are not ready to think about such matters. For the moment you are interested in their response to the essay as a whole. The following checklist may help them get started.

Checklist for reviewers

1. Does the essay have a clear purpose? Is it aimed at an appropriate audience? (See 1a.)
2. Is the opening paragraph interesting? Does it focus clearly on a main idea? (See 2a.)
3. Is the supporting material persuasive? Where might material be deleted? Which ideas need further development?
4. Can readers follow the structure? Are the ideas ordered effectively?
5. Do the paragraphs reflect logical or natural divisions? Does each paragraph have a clear topic sentence? (See 5a.)
6. Are any paragraphs too long or too short for easy reading?
7. Are the parts proportioned sensibly? Do major ideas receive enough attention?
8. Is the point of view consistent and appropriate? (See 3c.)
9. Is the overall tone appropriate? (See 3d.)
10. Is the essay worth reading? If so, why?

3b Improve the unity, organization, and development.

A draft is unified when it focuses on a clear main point and does not stray from that point. To check for unity, compare the paper's introduction, particularly its thesis sentence, with the body of the paper. Do they match? If not, one or the other must be adjusted. Either rebuild the introduction to fit the body of the paper or keep the introduction and delete any sentences or paragraphs that stray from its point.

To review the organization of a draft, scan the thesis sentence and the topic sentences of the paragraphs in the body of the paper. (Topic sentences, as you probably know, express the main idea of a paragraph.) Are the divisions logical? Are the paragraphs arranged in the most effective order?

Restructuring a paper can be as simple as moving a few sentences from one paragraph to another or switching the order of paragraphs. Often, however, the process is more complex. Topic sentences may require major revision, and whole sections of the paper may need to be torn apart and rebuilt. If such major restructuring becomes necessary, it is a good idea to revise the preliminary outline or to construct a new one. Divisions in the outline can become topic sentences in the restructured paper. (See 5a.)

In reviewing the development of a draft, consider whether any material should be deleted or added. Look first for sentences and paragraphs that can be cut — those that are off the point or that simply repeat generalizations or give undue emphasis to minor ideas. Cuts may also be necessitated by any word limits within which you may be working, such as those imposed by a college assignment or by the realities of the business world, where readers are often pressed for time.

If any paragraphs or sections of the paper are developed too skimpily, you will need to add material. This necessity will take you back to the beginning of the writing process: listing specifics, perhaps clustering them, and then roughing out new sentences and paragraphs. Many writers deliberately overwrite a first draft, filling it out with more details than they will probably need, to prevent their having to produce new material later. Cutting and rearranging is almost always easier than beginning again from scratch.

3c If necessary, adjust the point of view.

If the point of view of a draft shifts confusingly or if it seems not quite appropriate for your purpose, audience, and subject matter, consider adjusting it.

There are three basic points of view to choose from: the first person (*I* or *we*), the second person (*you*), and the third person (*he/she/it/one* or *they*). Each point of view is appropriate in at least some contexts, and you may need to experiment before discovering which one best suits your needs.

The third-person point of view

Much academic and professional writing is best presented from the third-person point of view (*he/she/it/one* or *they*), which puts the subject in the foreground. The *I* point of view is usually inappropriate in such contexts because, by focusing attention on the writer, it pushes the subject into the background. Consider, for example, one student's first-draft description of the behavior of a species of frog that he had observed in the field:

> Each frog that *I* was able to locate in trees remained in its given tree during the entirety of *my* observation period. However, *I* noticed that there was considerable movement within the home tree.

Here the *I* point of view is distracting, as the student himself noticed when he began to revise his report. His revision focuses more on the frogs, less on himself:

> Each frog located in a tree remained in that tree throughout the observation period. The frogs moved about considerably, however, within their home trees.

Just as the first-person pronoun *I* can draw too much attention to the writer, the second-person pronoun *you* can focus unnecessarily on the reader. One biology manual, for example, in an exercise meant to focus on the skeletal system, shifts the attention instead to the reader:

> Give at least two functions of the backbone from *your* reading.

This exercise would be clearer and more direct if presented without the distraction of the *you* point of view:

> What are two functions of the backbone?

Although the third-person point of view is often a better choice than the *I* or *you* point of view, it is by no means trouble-free. Writers who choose it can run into problems when they want to use singular pronouns in an indefinite sense. For example, when Miss Piggy says that a reason for jogging is "to improve *one's* emotional health and make *one* feel better about *oneself*," one wishes she wouldn't use quite so many *one*'s, doesn't one? The trouble is that American English, unlike British English, does not allow this pronoun to echo unselfconsciously throughout a sentence. The repetitions sound stuffy.

Some years ago Americans would have said "to improve a person's emotional health and to make *him* feel better about *himself*," with the understanding that *him* really meant *him or her*. Today, however, this use of *him* is offensive to many readers and is best avoided. On the other hand, "to make *him or her* feel better about *himself or herself*" is distinctly awkward. So what is poor Miss Piggy to say?

Her only hope, it turns out, is a flexible and inventive mind. She might switch to the plural: *Joggers run to improve their emotional health and to make them feel better about themselves.* Or she could restructure the sentence altogether: *Jogging improves a person's emotional health and self-image.* (See 22a.)

The second-person point of view

The *you* point of view, which puts the reader in the foreground, is appropriate if the writer is advising readers di-

The first-person point of view

If much of a writer's material comes from personal experience, the *I* point of view will prove most natural. It is difficult to imagine, for example, how James Thurber could have avoided the word *I* in describing his early university days:

> *I* passed all the other courses that *I* took at my university, but *I* could never pass botany. This was because all botany students had to spend several hours a week in a laboratory looking through a microscope at plant cells, and *I* could never see through a microscope. *I* never once saw a cell through a microscope. This used to enrage my instructor. [Italics added]
> — "University Days"

Thurber's *I* point of view puts the writer in the foreground, and since the writer is in fact the subject, this makes sense.

Writers who are aware that the first-person point of view is often inappropriate in academic writing sometimes overgeneralize the rule. Concluding that the word *I* is never appropriate, they go to extreme lengths to avoid it.

> Mama read with such color and detail that *one* could fancy *oneself* as the hero of the story.

Since the paper in which this sentence appeared was a personal reminiscence, the entire paper sounded more natural once the writer allowed himself to use the word *I:*

> Mama read with such color and detail that *I* could fancy *myself* as the hero of the story.

3d If necessary, modify the tone.

The tone of a draft expresses the writer's feelings about the subject and audience, so it is important to get it right. If the

Your comments about the physical layout of the story were, in fact, echoed by the staff here. The layout could not be changed, however, because it was typed under a tight deadline that allowed retyping only in cases of major errors of judgment.

Thank you for writing. Even though our newsletter has a limited circulation, we hope that Roger's open letter will elicit serious thought about the President's March 23 address on the Soviet Union and weapons in space.

Sincerely,

Robbie Nichols

EXERCISE 3 – 1

Make global revisions of the essay you wrote in Exercise 2 – 2. Use the checklist on page 30 as a guide.

4

Revise and edit sentences.

Most of the rest of this book offers advice on revising sentences for style and clarity and on editing them for grammar, punctuation, and mechanics. The process of revising and editing sentences should ordinarily occur right on the pages of an earlier draft, like this:

Finally ~~we decided~~ *deciding* that perhaps our dream needed ~~some~~ prompting, ~~and~~ we visited a fertility doctor and began the expensive, time-consuming round of procedures that held out ~~the~~ *some* promise of *our dream's fulfillment. Our efforts, however, were* ~~fulfilling our dream. All this was~~ to no avail/.

> *As*
> ~~and as~~ we approached the sixth year of our mar-
> *could no longer*
> riage, we ~~had reached the point where we couldn't~~
> even discuss our childlessness without becoming
> very depressed. We questioned why this had hap-
> *such a*
> pened to us~~,~~**.** Why had we been singled out for ~~this~~
> major disappointment?

The original paragraph was flawed by wordiness and an excessive reliance on structures connected with *and*. Such problems can be addressed through any number of acceptable revisions. The first sentence, for example, could have been changed like this:

> Finally we decided that perhaps our dream
> *After visiting*
> needed ~~some~~ prompting~~.~~ ~~and we visited~~ a fertility
> *we*
> doctor~~,~~ ~~and~~ began the expensive, time-consuming
> *promised hope*
> round of procedures that ~~held out the promise~~ of
> fulfilling our dream.

Though some writers might argue about the effectiveness of these improvements compared with the previous revision, most would agree that both versions are better than the original.

Some of the paragraph's improvements involve less choice and are not so open to debate. The hyphen in *time-consuming* is necessary; a noun must be substituted for the pronoun *this*, which was being used more loosely than grammar allows; and the question mark in the next-to-last sentence must be changed to a period.

As it details the various rules for revising and editing sentences, this handbook will suggest when an improvement is simply one among several possibilities and when it is more strictly a matter of right and wrong.

Revising and editing on a word processor

A word processor, as you probably know, is a computer equipped with software that allows writers to compose and revise text with ease. Although a word processor cannot think for you, it can certainly speed the revision process.

Let's assume that you have typed and saved your rough draft on a computer equipped with a word processing package such as WordPerfect or WordStar. You have printed a copy of the draft, reviewed it for global revisions, and marked it up to indicate where you need to add, delete, and move chunks of text. Once you have called up the text onto the computer's screen, you simply move the cursor to the place where you want to add, delete, or move text. Most word processing packages allow you to add text simply by typing it in and to delete text by hitting a delete key. Moving blocks of text is a bit more complicated, usually requiring several keystrokes, but with practice it too is relatively simple.

Some writers handle sentence-level revisions directly at the computer, but most prefer to print out a copy of the draft (called *hard copy*), mark it up, and then return to the computer. Once you've indicated changes on the hard copy, you can enter them into the computer in a matter of minutes. To proofread the final text, either read the words on the screen or, if this is too hard on your eyes, print a new copy and proofread the hard copy. Enter any necessary corrections into the computer, print a final copy, and you are done. If you want to preserve the final draft in the computer's memory, make sure to save it before you turn off the computer.

EXERCISE 4 – 1

Revise the draft of your essay from Exercise 3 – 1, looking carefully at your words and sentences for clarity and style. Check for errors in grammar, punctuation, and mechanics, consulting this handbook when necessary.

SAMPLE ESSAY

The essay on pages 41 – 44 was written by Gary Laporte for an English class assignment. Laporte thought about the assignment for several days, but he was unable to come up with a subject. He was still pondering the question when he watched a basketball playoff game on television. Besides interviewing the stars of each team, the sportscaster spoke with a ten-year-old fan whose ambition was to become a famous athlete. Why famous? thought Laporte. Why not a *good* athlete? Don't people who see games on TV understand that winning depends on good play and teamwork, not on competing with one another for fame and the camera's attention?

Laporte decided that television sports might make a good essay subject since he knew something about it. He jotted down ideas during breaks in the game and came up with the following list:

Cooperation should be focus, not competition

TV creates stars — cameras follow them, commentators interview them

TV doesn't show whole game, only most dramatic shots, slow-motion replays

More people admire sports stars than admire the President of U.S.

Sports stars make more money than President, also do commercials for money

Money becomes purpose of sport

Sports should represent American values — teamwork, shared enthusiasm — easier to see in live games where spectators participate

Cheering, choosing what to watch, buying beer & hot dogs, catching fly balls

Later, Laporte reread his list and concluded that his focus should be the effect of television on both athletes and spectators. With this focus in mind, he formulated a tentative thesis and sketched a rough outline:

> Although it is convenient, TV creates a distance between the sport and its fans and between the athletes and the team.
>
> — television's convenience to fans
> > — no need to travel and spend money
> > — ability to see more games
>
> — television's damage to sports
> > — creates distance between the sport and fans
> > — creates distance between the athletes and the team

Working from his list and outline, Laporte wrote a rough draft. He wrote quickly, focusing more on his ideas than on grammar, punctuation, and spelling. As you read his rough draft, which follows, consider what changes (aside from grammar, punctuation, and spelling) you would recommend.

LAPORTE'S ROUGH DRAFT

Sports on TV——A Win or a Loss?

Team sports are as much a part of Americain life as Mom and apple pie, and they have a good tendency to bring people together. They encourage team members to cooperate with one another, they also create shared enthusiasm among fans. Thanks to television, this togetherness now seems available to nearly all of us at the flick of a switch. We do not have to buy tickets, and travel to a

stadium, to see the World Series or the Super
Bowl, these games are on television. We can enjoy
the game in the comfort of our own living room.
After Thanksgiving or Christmas dinner, the whole
family may gather around the TV set to watch football together. It would appear that television
has done us a great service. But is this really
the case?

It is necessary to look at the differences
between live and televised sports. We can see
more games than if we had to attend each one in
person, and we can follow greater varieties of
sports. On the other hand, television creates a
distance between the sport and the fans and between athletes and the teams they play for.

The gap between a game and those who watch it
on television has two major aspects. One is that
the armchair audience sees only what the camera
shows. The advantage of this is that we get a
clear look at important plays; also, if we miss a
play, we can fall back on the commentator's explanation or the instant replay, which often shows us
exactly what happened in slow motion. The disadvantage is that we have no choice about what to
watch. If a viewer would rather follow someone in
the backfield than the quarterback or would rather

look at a batter warming up than a commercial,
they are out of luck. The other aspect of observ-
ing a game on television is that we miss all the
sights, sounds, and smells that link live viewers
with the players and one another. When a fly ball
comes over the fence, the television audience cannot try to catch it. The roar of cheers after a
touchdown is less exciting from the living room
sofa than when you are sitting in the bleachers.
Someone watching a televised game may feel silly
cheering at all, since there is no chance those
tiny figures on the screen will hear it.

TV creates a gap between athletes and their
teams, in addition. Traditionally, sports have
been viewed as arenas where teamwork is essential,
and the goals of the group overshadow personal ambition. TV cameras, however, find it more dramatic and more convenient to focus on individual
achievements than something as intangible as teamwork. Interviews with sports stars are often part
of a televised game. Athletes make more money
than the President of the United States, and they
appear in the media more often, and they are uni-
versally admired. In addition, sports stars have
the extra added benefit of endorsing products on
TV commercials for large bonus payments.

```
    Team sports are a major part of American
life.  All the more so since television has
brought them into most of our homes.  The chal-
lenge for sports fans is to support their favorite
teams in ways to encourage the best values repre-
sented by sports.  One way is to continue to at-
tend live games rather than watch games on
television.
```

Before beginning to revise this draft, Laporte brought it to class for a peer review session that had been scheduled by his instructor. Three of Laporte's classmates read the draft and responded to it, using the checklist for reviewers on page 30 as a guideline for their discussion. Here are some of their comments and suggestions:

> I like your details describing the distance between the spectator and the sport (in the third paragraph). You make me experience what you mean.

> Why did you put your thesis at the end of the second paragraph? Wouldn't it be more effective in the introduction?

> You talk about advantages to televised sports in the first and second paragraphs. Maybe this should all be in one place.

> You do a good job of acknowledging that TV does have its advantages.

> Your language seems too stiff in places. Does your audience really require such a formal approach?

> Two of your paragraphs are pretty long. Maybe you could tighten up the third paragraph, which seems wordy. The fourth paragraph probably needs to be divided.

You haven't convinced me that television separates the players from their team. An example or two would help.

You're tending to shift from the *we* point of view to the *they* point of view and back again. I'd use the *we* point of view because it is more personal. And after all, most of us are fans.

You seem to have two introductory paragraphs. Shouldn't you get to the point faster?

I like the way you pull the essay together in the concluding paragraph.

Notice that Laporte and his classmates were focusing on global matters, not on sentence-level revisions. Because the draft needed a fair amount of work, it made little sense to tinker with its sentences, some of which would be thrown out anyway. For an example of Laporte's global revisions, see page 46.

Once Laporte had written the second draft, he felt ready to devote his full attention to matters of style and correctness. He tightened wordy sentences, combined sentences for better flow, chose his words more carefully, and brought consistency to his style. Finally, with his handbook and dictionary close by, he corrected errors in grammar, punctuation, and spelling. For an example of Laporte's sentence-level revisions, see page 47.

Laporte's final draft appears on pages 48–50.

EXAMPLE OF GLOBAL REVISIONS

Sports on TV—A Win or a Loss?

Team sports are as much a part of Americain life as Mom and apple pie, and they have a good tendency to bring people together. They encourage team members to cooperate with one another, they also create shared enthusiasm among fans. Thanks to television, this togetherness now seems available to nearly all of us at the flick of a switch. We do not have to buy tickets, and travel to a stadium, to see the World Series or the Super Bowl, these games are on television. We can enjoy the game in the comfort of our own living room After Thanksgiving or Christmas dinner, the whole family may gather around the TV set to watch football together. It would appear that television has done us a great service. But is this really the case? *Although television does make sports more accessible, it also creates a distance between the sport and the fans and between athletes and the teams they play for.*

The advantage of television is that it provides sports fans with greater convenience.

[insert] ←

We can see more games than if we had to attend each one in person, and we can follow a greater variety of sports.

EXAMPLE OF SENTENCE-LEVEL REVISIONS

Televised
Sports ~~on TV~~ —A Win or a Loss?

Team sports, ~~are~~ as much a part of America~~n~~
tend
life as Mom and apple pie, ~~and they have a good~~
us
~~tendency~~ to bring ~~people~~ together.   They encourage
and
team members to cooperate with one another, they
Because of
~~also~~ create shared enthusiasm among fans. ~~Thanks~~
twist of a dial.
~~to~~ television, this togetherness now seems available ~~to nearly all of us~~ at the ~~flick of a switch.~~
~~It would appear that television has done us a~~
~~great service.~~ But is this really the case?   Al-
makes
though television ~~does make~~ sports more accessi-
their
ble, it also creates a distance between the sport
and the fans and between athletes and ~~the~~ teams.
~~they play for.~~

The advantage of television is that it provides sports fans with greater convenience.   We do
not have to buy tickets/ and travel to a stadium/
but
to see the World Series or the Super Bowl/ ~~these~~
any
~~games are on television.~~ ~~We~~ can enjoy the game in
rooms
the comfort of our own living ~~room~~.   We can see
more games than if we had to attend each one in
a   *variety*
person, and we can follow greater ~~varieties~~ of
sports.

LAPORTE'S FINAL DRAFT

Televised Sports--A Win or a Loss?

Team sports, as much a part of American life as Mom and apple pie, tend to bring us together. They encourage team members to cooperate with one another, and they create shared enthusiasm among fans. Because of television, this togetherness now seems available at the twist of a dial. But is this really the case? Although television makes sports more accessible, it also creates a distance between the sport and the spectator and between athletes and their teams.

The advantage of television is that it provides sports fans with greater convenience. We do not have to buy tickets and travel to a stadium to see the World Series or the Super Bowl but can enjoy any game in the comfort of our own living rooms. We can see more games than if we had to attend each one in person, and we can follow a greater variety of sports.

The price paid for this convenience, however, is high. Television changes the role of the fans who watch the game, making their participation more passive and distant. As television spectators, we see only what the camera shows. Yes, we do get a clearer look at important plays, and if we miss a detail, the commentator's explanation or the instant replay will fill us in. But we have no choice about what to watch. We cannot decide to follow the wide receiver rather than the quarterback or to watch a batter warming up rather than a commercial. Moreover, we miss all the sights, sounds, and smells that link live viewers with the players and with one another. When a fly ball comes over the fence, we cannot try to catch it. The roar of cheers after a touchdown is less exciting from the living room sofa than from the bleachers. We may feel silly cheering at all, since there is no chance those tiny figures on the screen will hear us.

The distance television has created between viewers and players does little more than reduce excitement and perhaps cheapen the experience of watching a game, but the unwholesome gap television creates between athletes and their teams threatens the foundation of team sports. Teamwork has always been paramount in team sports; the goals of the group have always overshadowed personal ambition. Television cameras, however, find it more dramatic to focus on individuals rather than on something as intangible as teamwork. In

addition, the economics of television advertising
and of team sports as big business create a situation in which players compete with one another for
astronomical salaries and the chance to endorse
products on television commercials.

Not surprisingly, the competition fostered by
television causes players to try to make themselves look good, sometimes at the expense of the
team. For example, a basketball player might take
--and miss--a difficult shot instead of passing
the ball to a teammate left unguarded closer to
the basket. Or a star hockey player might work
behind the scenes to keep a promising rookie from
replacing him.

Team sports are a major part of American
life, all the more so since television has brought
them into our homes. The challenge for sports
fans is to support their favorite teams in ways
that encourage the best values represented by
sports. One way to do this is to attend more live
games rather than watch games on television. Attendance at live games may give the teams, the
players, and the television networks the message
that teamwork, not individual achievement and financial success, is what matters most about
sports.

Writing and Revising Paragraphs

Except for special-purpose paragraphs, such as introductions and conclusions, paragraphs are clusters of information in support of an essay's main point. They correspond, at least roughly, to the divisions or subdivisions of an outline.

Ideally, paragraphs reflect the organization of the essay: one paragraph per point in short essays, a group of paragraphs per point in longer ones. Some ideas require more development than others, however, so it is best to be flexible. If an idea stretches to a length unreasonable for a paragraph, it should be divided, even if comparable points in the essay have been presented in single paragraphs.

Most readers feel comfortable with paragraphs ranging between 100 and 200 words. Shorter paragraphs force too much starting and stopping, and longer ones strain the reader's attention span. There are exceptions to this general rule, however. Paragraphs longer than 200 words frequently appear in scholarly writing, where they suggest seriousness and depth. Paragraphs shorter than 100 words occur in newspapers because of narrow columns; in informal essays to quicken the pace; and in business letters, where information is routinely scanned.

5

Focus on a main point.

A paragraph should be unified around a main point. The point should be clear to readers, and all sentences in the paragraph must relate to it.

5a State the main point in a topic sentence.

As readers move into a paragraph, they need to know where they are — in relation to the whole essay — and what to expect in the sentences to come. A good topic sentence, a one-sentence summary of the paragraph's main point, acts as a signpost pointing in two directions: backward toward the thesis of the essay and forward toward the body of the paragraph.

Like a thesis statement (see 1c), a topic sentence is more general than the material supporting it. Often the topic sentence comes first:

> *Nearly all living creatures manage some form of communication.* The dance patterns of bees in their hive help to point the way to distant flower fields or announce successful foraging. Male stickleback fish regularly swim upside-down to indicate outrage in a courtship contest. Male deer and lemurs mark territorial ownership by rubbing their own body secretions on boundary stones or trees. Everyone has seen a frightened dog put his tail between his legs and run in panic. We, too, use gestures, expressions, postures, and movement to give our words point. [Italics added]
> — Olivia Vlahos, *Human Beginnings*

Frequently the topic sentence is introduced by a transitional sentence linking it to earlier material. In the following paragraph, the topic sentence (italicized) has been delayed to allow for a transition.

> But flowers are not the only source of spectacle in the wilderness. *An opportunity for late color is provided by the berries of wildflowers, shrubs, and trees.* Baneberry presents its tiny white flowers in spring but in late summer bursts forth with clusters of red berries. Bunchberry, a ground-cover plant, puts out red berries in the fall, and the red berries of wintergreen last from autumn well into winter. In California, the bright red, fist-sized clusters of Christmas berries can be seen growing beside highways for up to six months of the year. [Italics added]
> — James Crockett et al., *Wildflower Gardening*

Occasionally the topic sentence may be withheld until the end of the paragraph — but only if the earlier sentences hang together so well that the reader perceives their direction, if not their exact point. The opening sentences of the following paragraph state facts, making them supporting material rather than topic sentences, but they strongly suggest a central idea. The topic sentence at the end is hardly a surprise.

> Tobacco chewing starts as soon as people begin stirring. Those who have fresh supplies soak the new leaves in water and add ashes from the hearth to the wad. Men, women, and children chew tobacco and all are addicted to it. Once there was a shortage of tobacco in Kaobawa's village and I was plagued for a week by early morning visitors who requested permission to collect my cigarette butts in order to make a wad of chewing tobacco. Normally, if anyone is short of tobacco, he can request a share of someone else's already chewed wad, or simply borrow the entire wad when its owner puts it down somewhere. *Tobacco is so important to them that their word for "poverty" translates as "being without tobacco."* [Italics added]
> — Napoleon A. Chagnon, *Yanomamo: The Fierce People*

Although it is generally wise to use topic sentences, at times they are unnecessary. A topic sentence is not needed if a paragraph continues developing an idea clearly introduced in a previous paragraph, if the details of the paragraph unmistakably suggest its main point, or if the paragraph appears in a narrative of events where generalizations might interrupt the flow of the story.

5b Do not stray from the point.

Sentences that do not support the topic sentence destroy the unity of a paragraph. If the paragraph is otherwise well focused, such offending sentences can simply be deleted or perhaps moved elsewhere. In the following paragraph describing the inadequate facilities in a high school, the information about the typing instructor (in italics) is clearly off the point.

> As the result of tax cuts, the educational facilities of Lincoln High School have reached an all-time low. Some of the books date back to 1970 and have long since shed their covers. The lack of lab equipment makes it necessary for four to five students to work at one table, with most watching rather than performing experiments. The few typewriters in working order have not been cleaned in so long that most letters come out blotchy and hard to read. There is only one self-correcting typewriter and no prospect of the school's ordering a word processor or computer anytime soon. *Also, the typing instructor left to have a baby at the beginning of the semester, and most of the students don't like the substitute.* As for the furniture, many of the upright chairs have become recliners, and the desk legs are so unbalanced that they play seesaw on the floor.

Sometimes the cure for a disunified paragraph is not as simple as deleting or moving material. Writers often wander into uncharted territory because they cannot think of enough evidence to support a topic sentence. Feeling that it is too soon to break into a new paragraph, they move on to new ideas for which the reader has not been prepared. When this happens, the writer is faced with a choice: Either find more evidence to support the topic sentence or adjust the topic sentence to mesh with the evidence that is available.

EXERCISE 5 – 1

Underline the topic sentence in the following paragraph and eliminate any material that does not clarify or develop the central idea.

A recent plan of the mayor's threatens to destroy one of the oldest and most successfully integrated neighborhoods in our city, replacing it with luxury condominiums and a shopping mall. This neighborhood, Thompson's Fields, was settled by a mixture of immigrants from Ireland, Italy, Poland, and Austria in the early part of the twentieth century. Over the years black and Hispanic families have also moved in and have become part of the community. When the mayor designated a five-block area along the neighborhood's main street as the location for a redevelopment program, the community decided to take the mayor to court. The mayor has hired the best urban planners and architects in the country to design and build three large skyscrapers along with parking facilities for the area. One woman has even moved to the city from California to work on the project. If the court accepts the case, the lawyer for the residents will be Ann Tyson, who grew up in Thompson's Fields. The residents have seen a great deal of change over the years, but they refuse to stand by while their homes are razed for some gentrification project that they will never enjoy.

6

Develop the main point.

Topic sentences are generalizations in need of support, so once you have written a topic sentence, ask yourself, "How do I know that this is true?" Your answer will suggest how to develop the paragraph.

6a   Flesh out skimpy paragraphs.

Though an occasional short paragraph is fine, particularly if it functions as a transition or emphasizes a point, a series of brief paragraphs suggests inadequate development. How much development is enough? That varies, depending on the writer's purpose and audience.

For example, when she wrote a paragraph attempting to convince readers that it is impossible to lose fat quickly, health columnist Jane Brody knew that she would have to present a great deal of evidence because many dieters want to believe the opposite. She did *not* write:

> When you think about it, it's impossible to lose — as many diets suggest — 10 pounds of *fat* in ten days, even on a total fast. Even a moderately active person cannot lose so much weight so fast. A less active person hasn't a prayer.

This three-sentence paragraph is too skimpy to be convincing. But the paragraph that Brody in fact wrote contains enough evidence to convince even skeptical readers:

> When you think about it, it's impossible to lose — as many diets suggest — 10 pounds of *fat* in ten days, even on a total fast. A pound of body fat represents 3,500 calories. To lose 1 pound of fat, you must expend 3,500 more calories than you consume. Let's say you weigh 170 pounds and, as a moderately active person, you burn 2,500 calories a day. If your diet contains only 1,500 calories, you'd have an energy deficit of 1,000 calories a day. In a week's time that would add up to a 7,000-calorie deficit, or 2 pounds of real fat. In ten days, the accumulated deficit would represent nearly 3 pounds of lost body fat. Even if you ate nothing at all for ten days and maintained your usual level of activity, your caloric deficit would add up to 25,000 calories. . . . At 3,500 calories per pound of fat, that's still only 7 pounds of lost fat.
> — Jane Brody, *Jane Brody's Nutrition Book*

6b Choose a suitable pattern of development.

Though paragraphs may be patterned in an almost infinite number of ways, certain patterns of development occur frequently, either alone or in combination: examples and illustrations, process, comparison and contrast, analogy, cause and effect, classification, and definition. There is nothing magical about these methods of development. They simply reflect the natural ways in which we think.

Examples and illustrations

Examples, perhaps the most common pattern of development, are appropriate whenever the reader might be tempted to ask, "For example?" Though examples are just selected instances, not a complete catalog, they are enough to suggest the truth of many topic sentences, as in the following paragraph.

> A passenger list of the early years of the Orient Express would read like a *Who's Who of the World,* from art to politics. Sarah Bernhardt and her Italian counterpart Eleonora Duse used the train to thrill the stages of Europe. For musicians there were Toscanini and Mahler. Dancers Nijinsky and Pavlova were there, while lesser performers like Harry Houdini and the girls of the Ziegfeld Follies also rode the rails. Violinists were allowed to practice on the train, and occasionally one might see trapeze artists hanging like bats from the baggage racks.
> — Barnaby Conrad III, "Train of Kings"

Illustrations are extended examples, frequently presented in story form. Because they require several sentences apiece, they are used more sparingly than examples. When well selected, however, they can be a vivid and effective means of developing a point. The writer of the following paragraph uses illustrations to demonstrate that Harriet Tubman, famous conductor on the underground railway for escaping slaves, was a master at knowing how and when to retreat.

> Part of Harriet Tubman's strategy of conducting was, as in all battle-field operations, the knowledge of how and when to retreat. Numerous allusions have been made to her moves when she suspected that she was in danger. When she feared the party was closely pursued, she would take it for a time on a train southward bound. No one seeing Negroes going in this direction would for an instant suppose them to be fugitives. Once on her return she was at a railway station. She saw some

men reading a poster and she heard one of them reading it aloud. It was a description of her, offering a reward for her capture. She took a southbound train to avert suspicion. At another time when Harriet heard men talking about her, she pretended to read a book which she carried. One man remarked, "This cannot be the woman. The one we want can't read or write." Harriet devoutly hoped the book was right side up.   — Earl Conrad, *Harriet Tubman*

Process

A process paragraph is patterned in time order, usually chronologically. A writer may choose this pattern either to describe a process or to show readers how to follow a process. The following paragraph, taken from a biography of Thomas Jefferson, describes the process of electing a president during the early years of the United States.

A presidential election in those days was neither simple nor direct. In each State the Electoral College voted for both offices, without designating which of the candidates was to get first place (the Presidency) and which second (the Vice-Presidency). The votes were then sent to the national capital to be counted. The candidate who had the highest number of votes was declared President and the next highest, Vice-President. If the two leading candidates had an equal number of votes, the election was to be decided in the House of Representatives, wherein each State cast one vote. Communication being slow and uncertain, it took several weeks for all the votes to come in from States so far apart as Georgia and Massachusetts.   — Saul K. Padover, *Jefferson*

Comparison and contrast

To compare two subjects is to draw attention to their similarities, although the word *compare* also has a broader meaning that includes a consideration of differences. To contrast is to focus only on differences.

Whether a comparison-and-contrast paragraph stresses similarities or differences, it may be patterned in one of two ways. The two subjects may be presented one at a time, block style, as in the following paragraph of contrast.

> So Grant and Lee were in complete contrast, representing two diametrically opposed elements in American life. Grant was the modern man emerging; beyond him, ready to come on the stage, was the great age of steel and machinery, of crowded cities and a restless burgeoning vitality. Lee might have ridden down from the old age of chivalry, lance in hand, silken banner fluttering over his head. Each man was the perfect champion of his cause, drawing both his strengths and weaknesses from the people he led.
>
> — Bruce Catton, "Grant and Lee: A Study in Contrasts"

Or a paragraph may proceed point by point, treating two subjects together, one aspect at a time. The following paragraph uses the point-by-point method to both compare and contrast.

> Wilson brought qualities as unusual as those of Theodore Roosevelt to American politics. The two men had much in common: cultivation, knowledge, literary skill, personal magnetism, relentless drive. But, where Roosevelt was unbuttoned and expansive, Wilson was reserved and cool; no one known to history ever called him "Woody" or "W.W." Both were lay preachers, but where Roosevelt was a revivalist, bullying his listeners to hit the sawdust trail, Wilson had the severe eloquence of a Calvinist divine. Roosevelt's egotism overflowed his personality; Wilson's was a hard concentrate within. Roosevelt's power lay in what he did, Wilson's in what he held in reserve.
>
> — Arthur M. Schlesinger, Jr., *The Age of Roosevelt: The Crisis of the Old Order*

Analogy

Analogies draw comparisons between items that appear to have little in common. They are used to make the unfamiliar seem familiar, to provide a concrete understanding of abstract topics, or to provoke fresh thoughts about a subject. In the following paragraph, physician Lewis Thomas draws an analogy between the behavior of ants and that of humans.

> Ants are so much like human beings as to be an embarrassment. They farm fungi, raise aphids as livestock, launch armies into wars, use chemical sprays to alarm and confuse enemies, capture slaves. The families of weaver ants engage in child labor, holding their larvae like shuttles to spin out the thread that sews the leaves together for their fungus gardens. They exchange information ceaselessly. They do everything but watch television.
>
> — Lewis Thomas, "On Societies as Organisms"

Cause and effect

When causes and effects are a matter of argument, they are too complex to be reduced to a simple pattern. However, if a writer wishes merely to describe a cause-and-effect relationship that has already been demonstrated, then the effect may be stated in the topic sentence, with the causes listed in the body of the paragraph:

> The fantastic water clarity of the Mount Gamier sinkholes results from several factors. The holes are fed from aquifiers holding rainwater that fell decades — even centuries — ago, and that has been filtered through miles of limestone. The high level of calcium that limestone adds causes the silty detritus from dead plants and animals to cling together and settle quickly to the bottom. Abundant bottom vegetation in the shallow sinkholes also helps bind the silt. And the rapid turnover prohibits stagnation.
>
> — Hillary Hauser, "Exploring a Sunken Realm in Australia"

Or the paragraph may move from cause to effects, as in this paragraph from a student's essay on the effects of her family's formal manners on her friends.

My family's formality often made visitors uncomfortable. Before coming to my house for dinner, my friends used to beg me to teach them to say grace the way we did, because they worried about not fitting in. During the meal they would watch anxiously to see which fork I used, and sometimes they could only stammer when my father asked them questions about world events. It wasn't long before I came to wonder if the purpose of good table manners was really to give guests indigestion. Friends who came to my house for dinner often didn't come again; more often, I went to their houses.

— Jane Betz, a student

Classification

Classification is the grouping of items into categories according to some consistent principle. Philosopher Francis Bacon was using classification when he wrote that "some books are to be tasted, others to be swallowed, and some few to be chewed and digested." Bacon's principle for classifying books is the degree to which they are worthy of our attention, but books of course can be classified according to other principles. For example, an elementary school teacher might classify children's books according to the level of difficulty, or a librarian might group them by subject matter. The principle of classification that a writer chooses ultimately depends on the purpose of the classification.

Writers frequently classify people or things for fairly whimsical purposes, as in the following paragraph by humorist Russell Baker.

Considering the millions and millions of antiques that one sees in London, it is surprising how little variety there is. A fairly careful survey of several London antique markets suggests that there are only eight basic items for sale. These are (1) the broken clock; (2) the old map, usually of a place unlisted in the geographies, called Novum Cloacum; (3) the incomplete set of dining-room chairs (commonly five or seven), one of which has a broken rung; (4) the set of three silver spoons; (5) the cracked demi-tasse with saucer; (6) the dining-room table with (Variation A) no leaves or (Variation B) a dangerous split in one leg; (7) the oil portrait of someone who, though unidentified, might very well be the Electress Sophia of Hanover or King Umberto the First; and (8) the first edition volume of a history of animal husbandry during the year 1703 in the environs of Dumfries.

— Russell Baker, *Poor Russell's Almanac*

Definition

A definition puts a word or concept into a general class and then provides enough details to distinguish it from others in the same class. For example, in one of its senses the term *grit* applies to the class of things that birds eat, but it is restricted to those items — such as small pebbles, eggshell, and ashes — that help the bird grind food.

Many definitions may be presented in a sentence or two, but abstract or difficult concepts may require a paragraph or even a full essay of definition. Extended definitions frequently make use of other patterns of development, such as examples or comparison and contrast. In the following paragraph, a student writer uses a number of illustrations to define the typical teenage victim in a "slasher" film.

Since teenagers are the target audience for slasher films, the victims in the films are almost always independent, fun-loving, just-out-of-high school partygoers. The girls all love to take late-night strolls alone through the woods or to skinny-dip at midnight in a murky lake. The boys, eager to impress the girls, prove their manhood by descending alone into musty cellars to restart broken generators or by chasing psychotic killers into haylofts and attics. Entering dark and gloomy houses, young men and women alike decide suddenly that now's a good time to save a few bucks on the family's electric bill — so they leave the lights off. After hearing a noise within the house, they always foolishly decide to investigate, thinking it's one of their many missing friends or pets. Disregarding the "safety in numbers" theory, they branch off in separate directions, never to see each other again. Or the teenagers fall into the common slasher-movie habit of walking backward, which naturally leads them right into you-know-who. Confronted by the ax-wielding maniac, the senseless youths lose their will to survive, close their eyes, and scream.

— Matthew J. Holicek, a student

EXERCISE 6 – 1

Write a paragraph modeled on one of the patterns discussed in this section. Some possible topics are listed below.

Examples: sexism in a comic strip, ways to include protein in a vegetarian diet, the benefits of a particular summer job, community services provided by your college, violence on the six o'clock news, educational software for children

Illustrations (extended examples): the active lifestyle of a grandparent, life with an alcoholic, working in an emergency room, the benefits (or problems) of intercultural dating, growing up in a large family, the rewards of working in a nursing home

Process: how to repair something, how to develop a successful job interview style, how to meet someone of the opposite sex, how to practice safe scuba diving, how to build a set for a play, how to survive in the wilderness, how to train a dog, how to quit smoking

Comparison and contrast: two neighborhoods, teachers, political candidates, colleges, products; country living versus city living; the stereotype of a job versus the reality; a change in attitude toward your family's religion or ethnic background

Analogy: between a family reunion and a circus, between training for a rigorous sport and boot camp, between settling an argument and being a courtroom judge, between a dogfight and a boxing match, between raising a child and tending a garden

Cause and effect: the effects of water pollution on a particular area, the effects of divorce on a child, the effects of an illegal drug, why a particular film or television show is popular, why an area of the country has high unemployment, why early training is essential for success as a ballet dancer, violinist, or athlete

Classification: types of clothing worn on your college campus, types of people who go to college mixers, types of dieters, types of television weather reports, types of rock bands, types of teachers

Definition: a computer addict, an ideal parent or teacher, an authoritarian personality, an intellectual, a sexist, anorexia nervosa, a typical heroine in a Harlequin romance, a typical blind date

7

Link sentences to sentences, paragraphs to paragraphs.

When sentences and paragraphs flow from one to another without discernible bumps, gaps, or shifts, they are said to be coherent. Coherence can be improved by strengthening the various ties between old information and new. A number of techniques for strengthening those ties are detailed in this section.

7a Repeat key words.

If too much information seems new, a paragraph will be hard to read. Unless we are already familiar with the soap opera summarized in the following paragraph, for example, we will find the paragraph nearly impenetrable:

> In the house Gunther hears intruders and hides Jamie in a closet. During a scuffle Donny falls to his death while Vic manages to escape. Standing Elk decides to drop the lawsuit

but Marty does not and plans to find out his true Indian name. Marty remembers that his uncle, Proud Bear, was stationed in Monticello before being shipped out to combat and later being listed as missing in action. On the farm Chris is beginning to realize that she doesn't have a deep physical love for Miles, and Miles realizes the same. Chris fears that her attacker will show up at the farm.

Notice how few repetitions tie these sentences together. We hear about Gunther and Jamie in the first sentence, Donny and Vic in the second, Standing Elk and Marty in the third. Only Marty gets picked up again, at which point we are introduced to yet another key player: Proud Bear.

Repeating key words is an important technique for improving coherence. If Gunther is mentioned in the first sentence, pick him up again in the second. To prevent such repetitions from becoming dull, you can use variations of the key word (*hike, hiker, hiking*), pronouns referring to the word (*gamblers . . . they*), and synonyms (*run, sprint, race, dash*). In the following paragraph describing plots among indentured servants in the seventeenth century, historian Richard Hofstadter binds sentences together by repeating the key word *plots* and echoing it with a variety of synonyms (which are italicized).

Plots hatched by several servants to run away together occurred mostly in the plantation colonies, and the few recorded servant *uprisings* were entirely limited to those colonies. Virginia had been forced from its very earliest years to take stringent steps against *mutinous plots,* and severe punishments for *such behavior* were recorded. Most servant *plots* occurred in the seventeenth century: a contemplated *uprising* was nipped in the bud in York County in 1661; apparently led by some left-wing offshoots of the *Great Rebellion,* servants *plotted* an *insurrection* in Gloucester County in 1663, and four leaders were condemned and executed; some discontented servants apparently joined *Bacon's Rebellion* in the 1670's. In the 1680's the planters became newly apprehensive of discontent among the servants "owing to their great necessities and want of clothes," and it was feared that they would *rise up* and *plunder* the storehouses and ships; in 1682 there were plant-cutting *riots* in which servants and laborers, as well as some planters, took part. [Italics added]

—Richard Hofstadter, *America at 1750*

7b Use parallel structures for parallel ideas.

Parallel grammatical structures are frequently used within sentences to underscore the similarity of ideas (see 9). They may also be used to bind together a series of sentences expressing similar information. In the following passage describing folk beliefs, anthropologist Margaret Mead presents similar information in parallel grammatical form.

Actually, almost every day, even in the most sophisticated home, something is likely to happen that evokes the memory of some old folk belief. The salt spills. A knife falls to the floor. Your nose tickles. Then perhaps, with a slightly embarrassed smile, the person who spilled the salt tosses a pinch over his left shoulder. Or someone recites the old rhyme, "Knife falls, gentleman calls." Or as you rub your nose you think, That means a letter. I wonder who's writing?

—Margaret Mead, "New Superstitions for Old"

A less skilled writer might have varied the structure, perhaps like this: *The salt spills. Mother drops a knife on the floor. Someone's nose is tickling.* But these sentences are less effective; the parallel structures help tie the paragraph together.

7c Provide transitions.

Certain words and phrases signal connections between ideas, connections that might otherwise be missed. Included in the following list are coordinating conjunctions, such as *and, but,* and *or;* subordinating conjunctions, such as *although* and *if;* conjunctive adverbs, such as *however* and *therefore;* and transitional expressions, such as *in addition* and *for example.*

TO SHOW ADDITION
and, also, besides, further, furthermore, in addition, moreover, next, too, first, second

TO GIVE EXAMPLES
for example, for instance, to illustrate, in fact, specifically

TO COMPARE
also, in the same manner, similarly, likewise

TO CONTRAST
but, however, on the other hand, in contrast, nevertheless, still, even though, on the contrary, yet, although

TO SUMMARIZE OR CONCLUDE
in other words, in short, in summary, in conclusion, to sum up, that is, therefore

TO SHOW TIME
after, as, before, next, during, later, finally, meanwhile, then, when, while, immediately

TO SHOW PLACE OR DIRECTION
above, below, beyond, farther on, nearby, opposite, close, to the left

TO INDICATE LOGICAL RELATIONSHIP
if, so, therefore, consequently, thus, as a result, for this reason, since

Skilled writers use transitional expressions with care, making sure, for example, not to use a *consequently* when an *also* would be more precise. They are also careful to select transitions with an appropriate tone, perhaps preferring *so* to *thus* in an informal piece, *in summary* to *in short* for a scholarly essay.

In the following paragraph, taken from an argument that dinosaurs had the " 'right-sized' brains for reptiles of their body size," biologist Stephen Jay Gould uses transitions (italicized) with skill:

> I don't wish to deny that the flattened, minuscule head of the large bodied "Stegosaurus" houses little brain from our subjective, top-heavy perspective, *but* I do wish to assert that we should not expect more of the beast. *First of all*, large animals have relatively smaller brains than related, small animals. The correlation of brain size with body size among kindred animals (all reptiles, all mammals, *for example*) is remarkably regular. *As* we move from small to large animals, from mice to elephants *or* small lizards to Komodo dragons, brain size increases, *but* not so fast as body size. *In other words*, bodies grow faster than brains, *and* large animals have low ratios of brain weight to body weight. *In fact*, brains grow only about two-thirds as fast as bodies. *Since* we have no reason to believe that large animals are consistently stupider than their smaller relatives, we must conclude that large animals require relatively less brain to do as well as smaller animals. *If* we do not recognize this relationship, we are likely to underestimate the mental power of very large animals, dinosaurs in particular. [Italics added]
>
> — Stephen Jay Gould, "Were Dinosaurs Dumb?"

EXERCISE 7–1

Identify the techniques of coherence — repetition of key words, parallel structures, and transitions — in the following paragraph.

> Once children have learned to read, they go beyond their textbooks and explore the popular books written just for them. In order to see how these books portray men and women, I decided to visit the St. Peter Public Library. One book I found, *The Very Worst Thing*, tells of the adventures of a little boy on his first day in a new school. He arrives at school wearing the new sweater his mother has knit for him and is greeted by his

teacher, Miss Pruce, and his male principal. At recess, the girls jump rope and toss a ball back and forth while the boys choose football teams and establish a tree house club. For show-and-tell that day, Henry, his new friend, brings a snake and some mice; Alice shows her foreign dolls, and Elizabeth demonstrates how to make fudge with Rice Krispies. In another book, *Come Back, Amelia Bedelia,* Amelia is fired from her job of baking for Mrs. Rogers, so she tries to find work as a beautician, a seamstress, a file clerk, and an office girl for a doctor. After trying all of these jobs unsuccessfully, she goes back to Mrs. Rogers and gets back her old job by making cream puffs. The rest of the books I looked at contained similar sex stereotypes — boys wear jeans and T-shirts, set up lemonade stands, and play broomball, while girls wear dresses, play dress-up, and jump rope. Men are businessmen, soldiers, veterinarians, and truck drivers. Women are housewives, teachers, and witches who make love potions for girls wanting husbands.

—Patricia Klein, a student

PART III

Revising Sentences

8

Coordinate equal ideas; subordinate minor ideas.

When combining ideas in one sentence, use coordination to create equal emphasis and use subordination to create unequal emphasis.

Coordination

Coordination draws attention equally to two or more ideas. To coordinate single words or phrases, join them with a coordinating conjunction or with a pair of correlative conjunctions (see 47g). To coordinate independent clauses, join them with a comma and a coordinating conjunction or with a semicolon:

, and	, but	, or	, nor
, for	, so	, yet	;

The semicolon is often accompanied by a conjunctive adverb such as *moreover, furthermore, therefore,* or *however* or with a transitional expression such as *for example* or *as a matter of fact.*

Assume, for example, that your intention is to draw equal attention to the following two ideas.

Grandmother lost her sight. Her hearing sharpened.

To coordinate these ideas, you can join them with a comma and the coordinating conjunction *but* or with a semicolon and the conjunctive adverb *however.*

Grandmother lost her sight, but her hearing sharpened.

Grandmother lost her sight; however, her hearing sharpened.

It is important to choose a coordinating conjunction or conjunctive adverb appropriate to your meaning. In the preceding example, the two ideas contrast with one another, calling for *but* or *however.*

Subordination

To give unequal emphasis to two or more ideas, express the major idea in an independent clause and place any minor ideas in phrases or subordinate clauses (see 49). Subordinate clauses, which cannot stand alone, typically begin with one of the following words.

after	before	unless	whether	whom
although	if	until	which	whose
as	since	when	while	
because	that	where	who	

Deciding which idea to emphasize is not simply a matter of right and wrong. Consider the two ideas mentioned earlier.

Grandmother lost her sight. Her hearing sharpened.

If your purpose were to stress your grandmother's acute hearing rather than her blindness, you would subordinate the idea concerning her blindness.

As she lost her sight, Grandmother's hearing sharpened.

To focus on her growing blindness, you would subordinate the idea concerning her hearing.

Though her hearing sharpened, Grandmother gradually lost her sight.

8a   Combine choppy sentences.

Short sentences demand attention, so they should be used primarily for emphasis. Too many short sentences, one after the other, make for a choppy style.

If an idea is not important enough to deserve its own sentence, try combining it with a sentence close by. Put any minor ideas in subordinate structures such as phrases or subordinate clauses.

> **CHOPPY**   The huts vary in height. They measure from ten to fifteen feet in diameter. They contain no modern conveniences.

> **IMPROVED**   The huts, which vary in height and measure from ten to fifteen feet in diameter, contain no modern conveniences.

Three sentences have become one, with minor ideas expressed in an adjective clause beginning with *which*.

▶ Agnes, ~~was~~ another student I worked with/, ~~She~~ was a hyperactive child.

The revision emphasizes that Agnes was a hyperactive child and de-emphasizes the rest of the information, which appears in an appositive phrase.

▶ *Although the* ~~The~~ Market Inn ~~is~~ located at 2nd and E Streets/, ~~It~~ doesn't look very impressive from the outside/, ~~The~~ food ~~however,~~ is excellent.

Three sentences have become one, with minor ideas expressed in a subordinate clause (*Although . . . outside*), which in turn contains a participial phrase (*located . . . Streets*) modifying *Market Inn*.

Although subordination is ordinarily the most effective technique for combining short, choppy sentences, coordination is appropriate when the ideas are equal in importance.

▶ The hospital decides when patients will sleep and wake./~~It~~

dictates what and when they will eat/~~,It~~ *and* tells them when they

may be with family and friends.

Three sentences have become one, with equivalent ideas expressed in a coordinate series.

8b Avoid ineffective coordination.

Coordinate structures are appropriate only when you intend to draw the reader's attention equally to two or more ideas: *Schwegler praises loudly, and he criticizes softly.* If one idea is more important than another — or if a coordinating conjunction does not clearly signal the relation between the ideas — the lesser idea should be subordinated.

INEFFECTIVE	Closets were taxed as rooms, and most colonists stored their clothes in chests or clothes presses.
IMPROVED	Because closets were taxed as rooms, most colonists stored their clothes in chests or clothes presses.

The revision subordinates the less important idea by putting it in a subordinate clause. Notice that the subordinating conjunction *because* signals the relation between the ideas more clearly than the coordinating conjunction *and*.

▶ *On Death and Dying,*~~was written~~ by Dr. Elisabeth Kübler-
   ^
Ross, ~~and it~~ describes the experiences of terminally ill

patients.

The minor idea has become a prepositional phrase.

     noticing
▶ My uncle,~~noticed~~ the frightened look on my face ~~and~~ told me
      ^   ^

that Grandma had to feel my face because she was blind.

The less important idea has become a participial phrase modifying the noun *uncle.*

After four hours,
▶ ~~Four hours went by, and~~ a rescue truck finally arrived, but
   ^

by that time we had been evacuated in a helicopter.

Three independent clauses were excessive. The least important
idea has become a prepositional phrase.

EXERCISE 8 – 1

Combine or restructure the following sentences by subordinating minor ideas or by coordinating ideas of equal importance. You must
decide which ideas are minor because the sentences are given out of
context. Revisions of lettered sentences appear in the back of the
book. Example:

> The team rowed until their strength nearly gave out and
>   *where they*   *to*
> finally returned to shore,~~and~~ had a party on the beach ~~and~~
> *celebrate*   ^   ^
> ~~celebrated~~ the start of the season.

a. A couple of minutes went by, and the teacher walked in smiling.
b. Mary will graduate from high school in June. She has not yet
   decided on a college.

c. Some major companies dictate where their employees must live. They determine where their children should go to school. They exert an overwhelming influence on their employees.

d. The aides help the younger children with reading and math. These are the children's weakest subjects.

e. My first sky dive was from an altitude of 12,500 feet, and it was the most frightening experience of my life.

1. The American crocodile could once be found in abundance in southern Florida. It is now being threatened with extinction.

2. We bought nothing but snacks. The total cost for food was twenty-five dollars.

3. Shore houses were flooded up to the first floor. Beaches were washed away. Brandt's Lighthouse was swallowed by the sea.

4. We arrived at the Capital Center, and to my dismay we had to pay five dollars for parking.

5. We met every Monday morning in the home of one of the members. These meetings would last about three hours.

6. Marta was her father's favorite. She felt free to do whatever she wanted.

7. He walked up to the pitcher's mound. He dug his toe into the ground. He swung his arm around backward and forward. Then he threw the ball and struck the batter out.

8. Alan walked over to his car, and he noticed a few unusual dark spots on the hood.

9. The menu is large and varied and includes everything from enchiladas, which are tortillas stuffed with meat or cheese, to sizzling strips of steak sautéed with vegetables and served over a flame at the table.

10. Karate is a discipline based on the philosophy of nonviolence. It teaches the art of self-defense.

8c Do not subordinate major ideas.

If a sentence buries its major idea in a subordinate construction, readers are not likely to give it enough attention. Express the major idea in an independent clause and subordinate any minor ideas.

▶ Lanie, who now walks with the help of braces/.had polio as a ~~child.~~

had polio as a child,

The writer had wanted to focus on Lanie's ability to walk, but the original sentence buried this information in an adjective clause. The revision puts the major idea in an independent clause and tucks the less important idea into an adjective clause (*who had polio as a child*).

As

▶ I was driving home from my new job, heading down New

York Avenue, ~~when~~ my car suddenly overheated.

The writer wanted to emphasize that the car was overheating, not the fact of driving home. The revision expresses the major idea in an independent clause, the less important idea in an adverb clause (*As I was driving home from my new job*).

8d Do not subordinate excessively.

In attempting to avoid short, choppy sentences, writers sometimes move to the opposite extreme, putting more subordinate ideas into a sentence than its structure can bear. If a sentence collapses of its own weight, occasionally it can be restructured. More often, however, such sentences must be divided.

▶ Our job is to stay between the stacker and the tie machine

If they do,

watching to see if the newspapers jam/.~~in which case~~ we pull

the bundles off and stack them on a skid, because otherwise

they would back up in the stacker and the press would have

to be turned off.

EXERCISE 8 – 2

In each of the following sentences, the idea that the writer wished to emphasize is buried in a subordinate construction. Restructure each sentence so that the independent clause expresses the major idea and lesser ideas are subordinated. Revisions of lettered sentences appear in the back of the book. Example:

Though
∧Catherine has weathered many hardships, ~~though~~ she has

rarely become discouraged. [*Emphasize that Catherine has*

rarely become discouraged.]

a. This highly specialized medical training is called a "residency," which usually takes four years to complete. [*Emphasize the length of time.*]
b. His starting salary is roughly $15,000, which will increase by 10 to 15 percent yearly until it reaches $25,000. [*Emphasize the increase.*]
c. I presented the idea of job sharing to my supervisors, who to my surprise were delighted with the idea. [*Emphasize the supervisors' response to the idea.*]
d. Although the Hawaiians try to preserve their ancestors' sacred customs, outsiders have forced changes on them. [*Emphasize the Hawaiians' attempt to preserve their customs.*]
e. Sharon's country kitchen, which overlooks a field where horses and cattle graze among old tombstones, was formerly a lean-to porch. [*Emphasize that the kitchen overlooks the field.*]

1. Manuel worked at many odd jobs before finally securing a position in a restaurant, where he was paid twelve pesos a month. [*Emphasize that Manuel secured a position.*]
2. The building housed a school, a grocery store, an auto repair shop, and three families when it burned to the ground last week. [*Emphasize that the building burned down.*]
3. The principal lived on Latches Lane, where parents and teachers met to discuss the suspension of several students for misconduct. [*Emphasize the discussion.*]

4. We were traveling down I-96 when we were hit in the rear by a speeding Oldsmobile. [*Emphasize the accident.*]
5. Cecilia, who graduated first in her class, stood last in line. [*Emphasize Cecilia's graduating first in her class.*]

9

Balance parallel ideas.

If two or more ideas are parallel, they should be expressed in parallel grammatical form. Single words should be balanced with single words, phrases with phrases, clauses with clauses.

A kiss can be a comma, a question mark, or an exclamation point. —Mistinguett

This novel is not to be tossed lightly aside, but to be hurled with great force. —Dorothy Parker

In matters of principle, stand like a rock; in matters of taste, swim with the current. —Thomas Jefferson

9a Balance parallel ideas linked with coordinating conjunctions.

Coordinating conjunctions (*and, but, or, nor, for, so, yet*) are used to connect a pair or a series of items. When those items are closely parallel in content, they should be expressed in parallel grammatical form.

NOT PARALLEL	Theft, vandalism, and cheating can result in *suspension* or even *being expelled* from school.
PARALLEL	Theft, vandalism, and cheating can result in *suspension* or even *expulsion* from school.

The coordinating conjunction *or* links two parallel ideas. Expressing one of those ideas as a noun (*suspension*) and the other as a gerund phrase (*being expelled*) is awkward. The revision balances the noun *expulsion* with the noun *suspension*.

▶ As the judge reviewed her case, Mary told him that she had been pulled out of a line of fast-moving traffic and ~~of her~~ *that she had a* ∧ perfect driving record.

A *that* clause is now paired with a *that* clause, not with an *of* phrase. The writer might also restructure the sentence by balancing the verb *told* with another verb such as *mentioned: As the judge reviewed her case, Mary told him that she had been pulled out of a line of fast-moving traffic and mentioned her perfect driving record.*

▶ David is responsible for stocking merchandise, ~~all in-store~~ *repairing* *items in the store,* ~~repairs,~~ writing orders for delivery, and ~~sales of~~ *selling* ∧ computers. ∧

The items in the series must be made parallel: *stocking, repairing, writing,* and *selling.*

NOTE: Clauses beginning with *and who* or *and which* should be balanced with an earlier *who* or *which*, or the conjunction *and* should be dropped.

▶ Austin is a young man of many talents ~~and~~ who promises to be a successful artist.

Deleting *and* is the best way to revise this sentence, for repeating *who* leads to unnecessary words: *Austin is a young man who has many talents and who promises to be a successful artist.*

9b   Balance parallel ideas linked with correlative conjunctions.

Correlative conjunctions come in pairs: *either . . . or, neither . . . nor, not only . . . but also, both . . . and, whether . . . or.* Make sure that the grammatical structure following the first half of the pair is the same as that following the second half.

▶ The shutters were not only too long but also ~~were~~ too wide.

The words *too long* follow *not only*, so *too wide* should follow *but also.* Repeating *were* creates an unbalanced effect.

▶ I was advised either to change my flight or ⁀to take the train.

To change my flight, which follows *either*, should be balanced with *to take the train*, which follows *or.*

9c   Balance comparisons linked with *than* or *as.*

In comparisons linked with *than* or *as,* the elements being compared should appear in parallel grammatical structure.

▶ It is easier to speak in abstractions than ~~grounding~~ *to ground* one's thoughts in reality.

▶ Bill finds it harder to be fair to himself than ~~being fair~~ to others.

▶ Mother could not persuade me that giving is as much a joy
as <del>to receive.</del> *receiving.*

NOTE: Comparisons should also be logical and complete. See 10c.

9d Repeat function words to clarify parallels.

Function words such as prepositions (*by, to*) and subordinating conjunctions (*that, because*) signal the grammatical nature of the word groups to follow. Although they can sometimes be omitted, include them whenever they signal parallel structures that might otherwise be missed by readers.

▶ Many smokers try switching to a brand they find distasteful
or *to* a low tar and nicotine cigarette.

In the original sentence the prepositional phrase was too complex for easy reading. The repetition of the preposition *to* prevents readers from losing their way.

▶ The ophthalmologist told me that Julie was extremely
farsighted but *that* corrective lenses would help considerably.

A second subordinating conjunction helps readers sort out the two parallel ideas: *that* Julie was extremely farsighted and *that* corrective lenses would help.

NOTE: If it is possible to streamline the sentence, repetition of the function word may not be necessary.

▶ The board reported that their investments had done well in
the first quarter but <del>that they</del> had since dropped in value.

With the deletion of *they,* a second *that* is unnecessary. The revision balances the two verb phrases *had done well in the first quarter* and *had since dropped in value.*

EXERCISE 9 – 1

Edit the following sentences to correct faulty parallelism. Revisions of lettered sentences appear in the back of the book. Example:

> We began the search by calling the Department of Social
> *requesting*
> Services and ~~requested~~ a list of licensed day care centers in
> ^
> our area.

a. Karen was a friend of many years and who helped us through some rough times.
b. The personnel officer told me that I would answer the phone, welcome visitors, distribute mail, and some typing.
c. This summer I want a job more than to go to Disney World.
d. I quit Weight Watchers not because I didn't want to continue but my friend stopped going with me.
e. Nancy not only called the post office but she checked with the neighbors to see if the package had come.

1. Many states are reducing property taxes for homeowners as well as extend financial aid in the form of tax credits to renters.
2. Arch-ups are done on the floor face down, with arms extended over the head, toes pointed, and knees stay straight.
3. The boys decided that either Carla had hidden the money or had never had it in the first place.
4. During basic training, I was not only told what to do but also what to think.
5. The Food and Drug Administration has admitted that sodium nitrite can deform the fetuses of pregnant women and it can cause serious harm to anemic persons.
6. The car dealer claimed that the price was good only that night and the car would cost more the next day.
7. More plants fail from improper watering than any other cause.

8. Your adviser familiarizes you with the school and how to select classes appropriate for your curriculum.
9. Yoga requires you to stretch muscles slowly with regular breathing and you hold each position.
10. After assuring us that he was sober, Sam drove down the middle of the road, ran one red light, and two stop signs.

10

Add needed words.

Do not omit words necessary for grammatical or logical completeness. Readers need to see at a glance how the parts of a sentence are connected.

10a Add words needed to complete compound structures.

In compound structures, words are often omitted for economy: *The first half of our life is ruined by our parents,* [*and*] *the second half* [*is ruined*] *by our children.* Such omissions are perfectly acceptable as long as the omitted words are common to both parts of the compound structure.

If the shorter version defies grammar or idiom because an omitted word is not common to both parts of the compound structure, the word must be put back in.

▶ Some of the regulars are acquaintances whom we see at
   who
   work or‸live in our community.

The word *who* must be included because *whom live in our community* is not grammatically correct.

accepted
▶ I never have and never will accept a bribe.
　　　　　Λ

Have . . . accept is not grammatically correct, so *accepted* must be inserted to complete *have*.

in
▶ Many of these tribes still believe and live by ancient laws.
　　　　　　　　　　　　　Λ

Believe . . . by is not idiomatic in English, so the appropriate preposition must be inserted: *believe in*.

NOTE: Even when the omitted word is common to both parts of the compound structure, occasionally it must be inserted to avoid ambiguity. The sentence *My favorite English professor and mentor influenced my choice of a career* suggests that the professor and mentor are the same person. If they are not, *my* must be repeated: *My favorite English professor and my mentor influenced my choice of a career.*

10b　Add the word *that* if there is any danger of misreading without it.

If there is no danger of misreading, the subordinating conjunction *that* may be omitted: *The value of a principle is the number of things [that] it will explain.* Occasionally, however, a sentence might be misread without *that*.

that
▶ As Joe began to prepare dinner, he discovered the oven
　　　　　　　　　　　　　　　　　　Λ
wasn't working properly.

Joe didn't discover the oven; he discovered that the oven wasn't working properly.

that
▶ Many civilians believe the Air Force has a vigorous exercise
　　　　　　　　　　Λ
program.

The subordinating conjunction tells readers to expect a clause, not just *the Air Force*, as the direct object of *believe*.

10c Add words needed to make comparisons logical and complete.

Comparisons should be made between like items. To compare unlike items is illogical and distracting.

▶ Agnes had an attention span longer than *that of* most of her

classmates.

It is illogical to compare an attention span and classmates. Since repeating the words *attention span* would be awkward, inserting *that of* corrects the problem.

▶ Henry preferred the hotels in Pittsburgh to *those in* Philadelphia.

Hotels must be compared with hotels.

Sometimes the word *other* must be inserted to make a comparison logical.

▶ Chicago is larger than any *other* city in Illinois.

Since Chicago is not larger than itself, the original comparison was not logical. The word *other* corrects the problem.

Sometimes the word *as* must be inserted to make a comparison grammatically complete.

▶ Geoffrey is as talented *as*, if not more talented than, the other

actors.

The construction *as talented . . . than* is not grammatical. Adding *as* corrects the problem: *as talented as . . . the other actors.*

Finally, comparisons should be complete enough to ensure clarity. The reader should understand what is being compared.

INCOMPLETE	Brand X is a lighter beer.
COMPLETE	Brand X is a lighter beer than Brand Y.

Also, there should be no ambiguity. In the following sentence, two interpretations are possible.

AMBIGUOUS	Mr. Kelly helped me more than my roommate.
CLEAR	Mr. Kelly helped me more than he helped my roommate.
CLEAR	Mr. Kelly helped me more than my roommate did.

10d Add the articles *a*, *an*, and *the* where necessary for grammatical completeness.

Articles are sometimes omitted in recipes and other instructions that are meant to be followed while they are being read. Such omissions are inappropriate, however, in nearly all other forms of writing, whether formal or informal.

▶ Blood can be drawn from ⌃*a* patient's femoral bone only by ⌃*a* doctor or by ⌃*an* authorized person who has been trained in ⌃*the* procedure.

NOTE: For a fuller discussion of articles, see 30.

EXERCISE 10–1

Add any words needed for grammatical or logical completeness in the following sentences. Revisions of lettered sentences appear in the back of the book. Example:

The officer at the desk feared ^*that* the prisoner in the

interrogation room would escape.

a. Dip paint brush into paint remover and spread thick coat on small section of door.
b. Some say that Ella Fitzgerald's renditions of Cole Porter's songs are better than any singer.
c. SETI (the Search for Extraterrestrial Intelligence) has and will continue to excite interest among space buffs.
d. The study showed that tenth graders are more polite to strangers than ninth graders.
e. Gunther Gebel-Williams, whom we watched today and is a star of the Ringling Brothers and Barnum & Bailey Circus, is well known for his training of circus animals.

1. We were glad to see the State House in Springfield was being restored.
2. For many years Americans had trust and affection for Walter Cronkite.
3. Mother says that she never has and never will vote for a Republican.
4. Our nursing graduates are as skilled, if not more skilled than, those of any other state college.
5. My current life is not as exciting as some of my friends.
6. If statistics are accidentally removed from patient's chart, inspectors will note error and Medical Records Department will receive reprimand.
7. My story isn't much different from thousands of other young people who decided to join the navy and see the world.
8. Thomas finally decided to join the army and been in it ever since.
9. Many citizens do not believe the leaders of this administration are serious about reducing the deficit.
10. It was obvious that the students liked the new teacher better than the principal.

11

Untangle mixed constructions.

A mixed construction contains parts that do not sensibly fit together. The mismatch may be a matter of grammar or of logic.

11a Untangle the grammatical structure.

Once you head into a sentence, your choices are limited by the range of grammatical patterns in English. (See 48 and 49.) You cannot begin with one grammatical plan and switch without warning to another.

> **MIXED** For most drivers who have a blood alcohol content of .05 percent double their risk of causing an accident.

> **REVISED** For most drivers who have a blood alcohol content of .05 percent, the risk of causing an accident is doubled.

> **REVISED** Most drivers who have a blood alcohol content of .05 percent double their risk of causing an accident.

The writer began with a long prepositional phrase that was destined to be a modifier but then tried to press it into service as the subject of the sentence. This cannot be done. If the sentence is to begin with the prepositional phrase, the writer must finish the sentence with a subject and verb (*risk . . . is doubled*). The writer who wishes to stay with the original verb (*double*) must head into the sentence another way: *Most drivers. . . .*

▶ ~~When one is~~ *Being* promoted without warning can be alarming.

The adverb clause *When one is promoted* cannot serve as the subject of the sentence. The revision replaces the adverb clause with a gerund phrase, a word group that can function as the subject.

▶ Although I feel that Mr. Dawe is an excellent calculus

instructor, ~~but~~ a few minor changes in his method would

benefit both him and the class.

The *although* clause is subordinate, so it cannot be linked to an independent clause with the coordinating conjunction *but.*

Occasionally a mixed construction is so tangled that it defies grammatical analysis. When this happens, back away from the sentence, rethink what you want to say, and then say it again as clearly as you can.

MIXED   In the whole-word method children learn to recognize entire words rather than by the phonics method in which they learn to sound out letters and groups of letters.

REVISED   The whole-word method teaches children to recognize entire words; the phonics method teaches them to sound out letters and groups of letters.

11b   Straighten out the logical connections.

The subject and the predicate should make sense together; when they don't, the error is known as *faulty predication.*

▶ The ~~growth in the~~ number of applications is increasing ,

rapidly.

It is not the growth that is increasing but the number of applications.

▶ Under the revised plan, the elderly, ~~who now receive a~~ *double exemption for the*

~~double personal exemption.~~ will be abolished.

The exemption, not the elderly, will be abolished.

An appositive and the noun to which it refers should be logically equivalent. When they are not, the error is known as *faulty apposition.*

▶ ~~The tax accountant,~~ a very lucrative field, requires *Tax accounting,*

intelligence, patience, and attention to detail.

The tax accountant is a person, not a field.

11c Avoid *is . . . when, is . . . where,* and *reason is . . . because* constructions.

In formal English many readers object to *is . . . when, is . . . where,* and *reason is . . . because* constructions on both grammatical and logical grounds. Grammatically, the verb *is* (as well as *are, was,* and *were*) should be followed by a noun that renames the subject or by an adjective that describes it, not by an adverb clause beginning with *when, where,* or *because.* (See 48b, 48c, and 49b.) Logically, the words *when, where,* and *because* suggest relations of time, place, and cause—relations that do not always make sense with *is, was,* or *were.*

▶ Anorexia nervosa is ~~where people,~~ believing they are too fat, *a disorder suffered by people who,*

diet to the point of starvation.

Anorexia nervosa is a disorder, not a place.

▶ ~~The reason~~ I missed the exam ~~is~~ because my motorcycle

broke down.

The writer might have changed *because* to *that* (*The reason I missed the exam is that my motorcycle broke down*), but the revision above is more concise.

EXERCISE 11–1

Edit the following sentences to untangle mixed constructions. Revisions of lettered sentences appear in the back of the book. Example:

L
~~By~~ /loosening the soil around your jade plant will help the air

and nutrients penetrate to the roots.

a. My instant reaction was filled with anger and disappointment.
b. I brought a problem into the house that my mother wasn't sure how to handle it.
c. It is through the misery of others that has made old Harvey rich.
d. One controversial application of the polygraph is when employers use it to screen job applicants.
e. By encouraging the players to excel may help them learn to overcome obstacles later in life.

1. By winning all the primaries in the western states helped the senator from Wyoming claim the final victory.
2. Depending on the number and strength of drinks, the amount of time that has passed since the last drink, and one's body weight determines the concentration of alcohol in the blood.
3. The change in the quality of students has worsened each year.
4. For people who are incapacitated or bedridden they may have their meals delivered by a service known as "meals on wheels."
5. The reason I must cancel the party is because I have been called out of town on business.
6. To look at rolling hills of virgin snow or snow-capped evergreens is far more beautiful than the brown slush on city streets.

7. Pat had to train herself on a mainframe computer that was designed for data entry but it was not intended for word processing.
8. One service available to military personnel living on base, the Special Services Building, provides half-price tickets to local movie theaters.
9. The section of the perimeter for which my unit was responsible for came under fire.
10. The little time we have together we try to use it wisely.

12

Repair misplaced and dangling modifiers.

Modifiers, whether they are single words, phrases, or clauses, should point clearly to the words they modify.

12a Put limiting modifiers in front of the words they modify.

Limiting modifiers such as *only, even, almost, nearly,* and *just* should appear in front of a verb only if they modify the verb: *At first, I couldn't even touch my toes.* If they limit the meaning of some other word in the sentence, they should be placed in front of that word.

▶ You will ~~only~~ need to plant *only* one package of seeds.

Our team didn't ~~even~~ score *even* once.

Bob ~~almost~~ *almost* ate the whole chicken.

Only limits the meaning of *one,* not *need. Even* modifies *once,* not *score; almost* modifies *the whole chicken,* not *ate.*

12b Position phrases and clauses so that readers can see at a glance what they modify.

When whole phrases or clauses have been positioned oddly, absurd misreadings can result.

> **MISPLACED** The king returned to the clinic where he underwent heart surgery in 1972 in a limousine sent by the White House.

> **REVISED** Traveling in a limousine sent by the White House, the king returned to the clinic where he underwent heart surgery in 1972.

The king did not undergo heart surgery in a limousine. The revision corrects this false impression.

> *on the walls*
> ▶ ~~There~~ are many pictures of comedians ~~on the walls~~ who have
>   ^
> performed at Gavin's.

The walls didn't perform at Gavin's; the comedians did. The writer at first revised the sentence like this: *There are many pictures of comedians who have performed at Gavin's on the walls.* But this creates another absurd effect. The comedians weren't performing on the walls.

> *150-pound,*
> ▶ The robber was described as a six-foot-tall man with a heavy
>   ^
> mustache.~~weighing 150 pounds.~~
>   ^

The robber, not the mustache, weighed 150 pounds. The revision makes this clear.

Occasionally the placement of a modifier leads to an ambiguity, in which case two revisions will be possible, depending on the writer's intended meaning.

AMBIGUOUS	We promised when the play was over that we would take Charles to an ice cream parlor.
CLEAR	When the play was over, we promised Charles that we would take him to an ice cream parlor.
CLEAR	We promised Charles that we would take him to an ice cream parlor when the play was over.

The first revision suggests that the promising occurred when the play was over, the second that the taking would occur when the play was over.

EXERCISE 12–1

Edit the following sentences to correct misplaced modifiers. Revisions of lettered sentences appear in the back of the book. Example:

in a telephone survey
Answering questions can be annoying, ~~in a telephone survey~~.
Λ   Λ

a. This form is only required when the traveler is receiving an advance.

b. Within the next few years, orthodontists will be using the technique Kurtz developed as standard practice.

c. Celia received a flier about a workshop on making a kimono from a Japanese nun.

d. Maria almost played the whole game, but she was taken out in the last ten minutes.

e. Each state would set a program into motion of recycling all reusable products.

1. We will inherit the library of a professor of exceptional quality.

2. Sarah said she could handle the diet because she only had to stay on it for a week.

3. Eric took a course at the university that represents a new low in education.

4. Jeff's guitar was made for a seven-year-old, which was much too small for him.

5. He promised never to remarry at her deathbed.

6. Chuck met a girl named Paula when he was nineteen, who soon moved in with him.

7. Though he is seventy-three, my uncle can lift a load of bricks without a thought that would have had most twenty-five-year-olds straining.

8. It just took experience with two clients to convince my mother to avoid interior design.

9. The Secret Service was falsely accused of mishandling the attempted assassination by the media.

10. I told the children when the movie was over to go to bed.

12c Repair dangling modifiers.

A dangling modifier fails to refer logically to any word in the sentence. Dangling modifiers are usually introductory word groups (such as verbal phrases) that suggest but do not name an actor. When a sentence opens with such a modifier, readers expect the subject of the following clause to name the actor. If it doesn't, the modifier dangles.

DANGLING Deciding to join the navy, the recruiter enthusiastically pumped Joe's hand. [*participial phrase*]

DANGLING While waiting in line for gas, the attendant washed my windshield and checked under the hood. [*preposition followed by a gerund phrase*]

DANGLING To please the children, some fireworks were set off a day early. [*infinitive phrase*]

DANGLING Though only sixteen, UCLA accepted Martha's application. [*elliptical clause with an understood subject and verb*]

These dangling modifiers falsely suggest that the recruiter decided to join the navy, that the attendant waited in line for gas, that the fireworks intended to please the children, and that UCLA is only sixteen years old.

To repair a dangling modifier, you must restructure the sentence in one of two ways: (1) change the subject of the sentence so that it names the actor implied by the introductory modifier or (2) turn the modifier into a word group that includes the actor.

DANGLING   When watching a classic film such as *Gone With the Wind,* commercials are especially irritating.

REPAIRED   When watching a classic film such as *Gone With the Wind,* I find commercials especially irritating.

REPAIRED   When I am watching a classic film such as *Gone With the Wind,* commercials are especially irritating.

A dangling modifier cannot be repaired simply by moving it: *Commercials are especially irritating when watching. . . .* Readers still don't know who is doing the watching.

▶ ~~Opening~~ *When the driver opened* the window to let out a huge bumblebee, the car
       ∧

   accidentally swerved into the lane of oncoming cars.

   The car didn't open the window; the driver did. The writer corrected the problem by turning the opening participial phrase into an adverb clause, a word group naming the actor.

▶ After completing seminary training, ~~women's~~ *women have often been denied* access to the
       ∧

   pulpit ∧ ~~has often been denied.~~

   The modifier dangled because the subject of the sentence, *access,* did not name those who had completed seminary training. (The word *women's* simply modifies *access.*) The writer corrected the problem by making *women* the subject of the sentence.

EXERCISE 12–2

Edit the following sentences to correct dangling modifiers. Most sentences can be revised in more than one way. Revisions of lettered sentences appear in the back of the book. Example:

<u>a student must complete</u>

To acquire a degree in almost any field, two science courses,
∧   ∧

~~must be completed.~~

a. To protest the arms buildup, bonfires were set throughout the park.
b. Nestled in the cockpit, the pounding of the engine was muffled only slightly by my helmet.
c. Feeling unprepared for the exam, the questions were as hard as June's instructor had suggested they would be.
d. While still a beginner at tennis, the coaches recruited my sister to train for the Olympics.
e. To get the most from walking, Dr. Curtis recommends striding rather than strolling.

1. Thinking that justice had finally prevailed, Lydia's troubles were just beginning.
2. Excited about winning the championship, a raucous celebration was held in the locker room.
3. While looking at the map, a police officer approached and asked if he could help.
4. As president of the missionary circle, one of Grandmother's duties is to raise money for the church.
5. Shortly after being seated, a waiter approached our table with a smile.
6. Spending four hours on the operating table, a tumor as large as a golf ball was successfully removed from the patient's stomach.
7. To become an attorney, two degrees must be earned and a bar examination must be passed.
8. At the age of twelve, my mother entered me in a public speaking contest.
9. Although too expensive for her budget, Joan bought the lavender skirt.
10. Carrying a twenty-pound pack, the trail seemed very difficult.

13

Pull related words together.

13a Make the sentence flow from subject to verb to object, without lengthy detours along the way.

Readers can hold fairly long word groups in mind, but they can do so more easily if related words are kept together.

▶ ~~Kilmer,~~ A ~~a~~fter doctors told him that he would never walk again, ^Kilmer initiated on his own an intensive program of rehabilitation.

There is no reason to separate the subject *Kilmer* from the verb *initiated* with a long adverb clause.

13b Put helping verbs close to their main verbs.

It is perfectly acceptable to put one or two words between a helping verb and its main verb: *The jury has not yet reached a decision.* However, when longer word groups intervene between the two parts of a verb, the result can be awkward.

▶ ^By ~~Many students have, by~~ the time they reach their senior year, ^many students have completed all the requirements for their major.

The helping verb *have* should be closer to its main verb *completed.*

13c Do not split infinitives needlessly.

An infinitive consists of *to* plus a verb: *to think, to breathe, to dance.* When words appear between its two parts, an infinitive is said to be "split": *to carefully balance.* If a split infinitive is obviously awkward, it should be revised.

▶ ~~The~~ patient should try to, ~~if possible,~~ avoid going up and down stairs.

If possible, the

Usage varies when a split infinitive is less awkward than the preceding one. To be on the safe side, however, you should not split such infinitives, especially in formal writing.

▶ The candidate decided to ~~formally~~ launch her campaign.

formally

When a split infinitive is more natural and less awkward than alternative phrasing, most readers find it acceptable: *We decided to actually enforce the law* is a perfectly natural construction in English. *We decided actually to enforce the law* is not.

EXERCISE 13–1

Edit the following sentences to pull together sentence parts that have been awkwardly separated. Revisions of lettered sentences appear in the back of the book. Example:

~~Nancy,~~ After she won the big jackpot in the lottery, went completely crazy.

A *Nancy*

a. I want to on behalf of the team thank you for this award.

b. The prospectors found, despite horrid weather, poor equipment, and long odds, gold.

c. Some of these friends have, since being employed, received degrees, but their degrees have not led to advancement.

d. Jurors are encouraged to carefully and thoroughly sift through the evidence.

e. To even tie her shoes was difficult for the girl with the sprained wrist.

1. The candidate promised to once and for all lower taxes and raise the standard of living.

2. The way to most conveniently purchase the ticket is to give your credit card number over the phone.

3. The firefighters finally, after running up the stairs, barging through the door, and shouting to one another from room to room, found a charred and smoking piece of toast in the kitchen sink.

4. Eventually John discovered how to more effectively supervise his employees.

5. The journal has a circulation, not including copies sent to libraries and schools, of 30,000.

14

Eliminate distracting shifts.

14a Make the point of view consistent in person and number.

The point of view of an essay is the perspective from which it is written: first-person singular (*I*), first-person plural (*we*), second-person singular or plural (*you*), third-person singular (*he, she, it, one*), or third-person plural (*they*). Writers who are having difficulty settling on an appropriate point of view sometimes shift confusingly from one to another. The solution is to choose a suitable perspective and then stay with it. (See 3b).

▶ One week our class met in a junkyard to practice rescuing a

victim trapped in a wrecked car. We learned to dismantle the

car with the essential tools. ~~You~~ *We* were graded on ~~your~~ *our* speed

and ~~your~~ *our* skill in extricating the victim.

The writer should have stayed with the *we* point of view. *You* is inappropriate because the writer is not addressing the reader directly. *You* should not be used in a vague sense meaning *anyone.* See 23c.

▶ ~~Everyone~~ *You* should purchase a lift ticket unless you plan to

spend most of your time walking or crawling up a steep hill.

Here *you* is an appropriate choice, since the writer is giving advice directly to readers.

▶ ~~A police officer is~~ *Police officers are* often criticized for always being there when

they aren't needed and never being there when they are.

The writer shifted from the third-person singular (*police officer*) to the third-person plural (*they*), probably in an effort to avoid the wordy *he or she* construction: *A police officer is often criticized for always being there when he or she is not needed and never being there when he or she is.* The most effective revision, this writer decided, was to draft the sentence in the plural. See 22 and 17f.

14b   Maintain consistent verb tenses.

Consistent verb tenses clearly establish the time of the actions being described. When a passage begins in one tense and then shifts without warning and for no reason to another, readers are distracted and confused.

▶ My hopes ~~rise~~ *rose* and ~~fall~~ *fell* as Joseph's heart started and

stopped. The doctors ~~insert~~ *inserted* a large tube into his chest, and

blood ~~flows~~ *flowed* from the incision onto the floor. The tube

drained some blood from his lung, but it was all in vain. At

8:35 P.M. Joseph was declared dead.

The writer had tried to make his narrative vivid by casting it in the present tense, but he found this choice too difficult to sustain. A better approach, he decided, was to draft the whole narrative in the past tense.

Writers often encounter difficulty with verb tenses when writing about literature. Because fictional events occur outside the time frames of real life, the past and the present tenses may seem equally appropriate. The literary convention, however, is to describe those events consistently in the present tense. See 27c.

▶ The scarlet letter is a punishment sternly placed upon

Hester's breast by the community, and yet it ~~was~~ *is* an

extremely fanciful and imaginative product of Hester's own

needlework.

14c Make verbs consistent in mood and voice.

Unnecessary shifts in the mood of a verb can be as distracting as needless shifts in tense. There are three moods in English:

the indicative, used for facts, opinions, and questions; the imperative, used for orders or advice; and the subjunctive, used for wishes or conditions contrary to fact (see 27d).

The following passage shifts confusingly from the indicative to the imperative mood.

▶ The officers advised against allowing access to our homes
without proper identification. ~~Also,~~ *They also suggested that we* alert neighbors to

vacation schedules.

Since the writer's purpose was to report the officers' advice, the revision puts both sentences in the indicative.

The voice of a verb may be either active (with the subject doing the action) or passive (with the subject receiving the action). If a writer shifts without warning from one to the other, readers may be left wondering why.

▶ When the tickets are ready, the travel agent notifies the
client, ~~Each ticket is then listed~~ *lists each ticket* on a daily register form, and
a copy of the itinerary. ~~is filled.~~ *files*

The passage began in the active voice (*agent notifies*) and then switched to the passive (*ticket is listed*). Because the active voice is clearer and more direct, the revision puts the verbs consistently in the active voice.

14d Avoid sudden shifts from indirect to direct questions or quotations.

An indirect question reports a question without asking it: *We asked whether we could take a swim.* A direct question asks directly: *Can we take a swim?* Sudden shifts from indirect to direct questions are awkward. In addition, sentences containing such shifts are impossible to punctuate because indirect questions must end with a period and direct questions must end with a question mark (see 38b).

▶ I wonder whether the sister knew of murder and, if so, ~~did~~ *whether she reported*

~~she report~~ it to the police.

The revision poses both questions indirectly. The writer could also ask both questions directly: *Did the sister know of the murder and, if so, did she report it to the police?*

An indirect quotation reports someone's words without quoting word for word: *Ann said that she was a Virgo.* A direct quotation presents the exact words of a speaker or writer, set off with quotation marks: *Ann said, "I am a Virgo."* Unannounced shifts from indirect to direct quotations are distracting and confusing, especially when the writer fails to insert the necessary quotation marks, as in the following example.

▶ Mother said that she would be late for dinner and ~~please do~~ *asked me not to*

~~not~~ leave for choir practice until Dad ~~comes~~ home from *came*

work.

The revision reports the mother's words. The writer could also quote directly: *Mother said, "I will be late for dinner. Please do not leave for choir practice until Dad comes home from work."*

EXERCISE 14–1

Edit the following sentences to eliminate distracting shifts. Revisions of lettered sentences appear in the back of the book. Example:

For most people it is not easy to quit smoking once ~~you~~ *they* are

hooked.

a. We waited in the emergency room for about an hour. Finally, the nurse comes in and tells us that we are in the wrong place.

b. Newspapers put the lurid details of an armed robbery on page 1, and the warm, human-interest stories are relegated to page G-10.

c. A minister often has a hard time because they have to please so many different people.

d. We drove for eight hours until we reached the South Dakota Badlands. You could hardly believe the eeriness of the landscape at dusk.

e. The interviewer asked if we had brought our proof of birth and citizenship and did we bring our passports.

1. Next we measure the heart rate by placing the index and middle fingers over the arteries on either side of the neck. Count six seconds and then determine the pulse rate.

2. For a minimal fee one may join the class. Once you arrive for class, a medical form is filled out by each person and submitted to the instructor.

3. According to Dr. Winfield, a person who wants to become a doctor must first earn a B.S. degree. After this they must take a medical aptitude test called the MCAT.

4. The principal asked whether I had seen the fight and, if so, why didn't you report it.

5. The highlight of my weekends at home was riding up and down Main Street and seeing how much beer you could drink.

6. When the director travels, you will make the hotel and airline reservations and you will arrange for a rental car. A detailed itinerary must be prepared.

7. To get the most from your practice time, a group should practice together, as a band, instead of individually.

8. Rescue workers put water on her face and lifted her head gently onto a pillow. Finally, she opens her eyes.

9. With a little self-discipline and a desire to improve oneself, you too can enjoy the benefits of running.
10. One man collects the tickets and another will search the concert patrons for drugs.

15

Provide some variety.

When a rough draft is filled with too many same-sounding sentences, try injecting some variety—as long as you can do so without sacrificing clarity or ease of reading.

15a Use a variety of sentence openings.

Most sentences in English begin with the subject, move to the verb, and continue along to the object, with modifiers tucked in along the way or put at the end. For the most part, such sentences are fine. Put too many of them in a row, however, and they become monotonous.

Adverbial modifiers, being easily movable, can often be inserted ahead of the subject. Such modifiers might be single words, phrases, or clauses.

▶ *Eventually a*
  ~~A~~ few drops of sap ~~eventually~~ began to trickle into the pail.
  ∧

Like most adverbs, *eventually* does not need to appear close to the verb it modifies (*began*).

▶ *Just as the sun was coming up, a*
  ~~A~~ pair of black ducks flew over the blind. ~~just as the sun was~~
  ∧   ∧
  ~~coming up.~~

The adverb clause, which modifies the verb *flew*, is as clear at the beginning of the sentence as it is at the end.

Adjectives and participial phrases can frequently be moved to the beginning of a sentence, as long as the subject of the sentence names the person or thing being described in the introductory phrase.

▶ *Dejected and withdrawn,*
Edward, ~~dejected and withdrawn,~~ nearly gave up his search for a job.

The single-word adjectives *dejected* and *withdrawn* can be moved ahead of the subject, *Edward*, which they modify.

▶ ~~John and I,~~ ^*A* anticipating a peaceful evening, *John and I* sat down at the campfire to brew a cup of coffee.

Many participial phrases can be moved without mishap. *Anticipating a peaceful evening* can open the sentence as long as the subject of the sentence names the persons doing the anticipating. If the words *John and I* were not the subject of the sentence, the modifier would dangle. (See 12c.)

15b Use a variety of sentence structures.

A writer should not rely too heavily on simple sentences and compound sentences, for the effect tends to be both monotonous and choppy. (See 8a and 8b.) Too many complex or compound-complex sentences, however, can be equally monotonous. If your style tends to one or the other extreme, try to achieve a better mix of sentence types.

The major sentence types are illustrated in the following sentences, all taken from Flannery O'Connor's "The King of the Birds," an essay describing the author's pet peafowl.

SIMPLE	Frequently the cock combines the lifting of his tail with the raising of his voice.
COMPOUND	Any chicken's dusting hole is out of place in a flower bed, but the peafowl's hole, being the size of a small crater, is more so.
COMPLEX	The peacock does most of his serious strutting in the spring and summer when he has a full tail to do it with.
COMPOUND-COMPLEX	The cock's plumage requires two years to attain its pattern, and for the rest of his life, this chicken will act as though he designed it himself.

For a fuller discussion of sentence types, see 50.

15c Try inverting sentences occasionally.

A sentence is inverted if it does not follow the normal subject-verb-object pattern. Many inversions sound artificial and should be avoided except in the most formal contexts. But if an inversion sounds natural, it can provide a welcome touch of variety.

▶ *Opposite the produce section is a* ~~A~~ refrigerated case of mouth-watering cheeses ~~is opposite~~ ;

~~the produce section;~~ a friendly attendant will cut off just the

amount you want.

The revision inverts the normal subject-verb order by moving the verb, *is*, ahead of its subject, *case*.

▶ *Set at the top two corners of the stage were huge* ~~Huge~~ lavender hearts outlined in bright white lights ~~were set~~

~~at the top two corners of the stage.~~

In the revision the subject, *hearts,* appears after the verb, *were set.* Notice that the two parts of the verb are also inverted — and separated from one another — without any awkwardness or loss of meaning.

EXERCISE 15 – 1

Edit the following paragraph to increase variety in sentence structure.

I have spent thirty years of my life on a tobacco farm, and I cannot understand why people smoke. The whole process of raising tobacco involves deadly chemicals. The ground is treated for mold and chemically fertilized before the tobacco seed is ever planted. The seed is planted and begins to grow, and then the bed is treated with weed killer. The plant is then transferred to the field. It is sprayed with poison to kill worms about two months later. Then the time for harvest approaches, and the plant is sprayed once more with a chemical to retard the growth of suckers. The tobacco is harvested and hung in a barn to dry. These barns are havens for birds. The birds defecate all over the leaves. After drying, these leaves are divided by color, and no feces are removed. They are then sold to the tobacco companies. I do not know what the tobacco companies do after they receive the tobacco. I do not need to know. They cannot remove what I know is in the leaf and on the leaf. I don't want any of it to pass through my mouth.

Changing Words

16

Tighten wordy sentences.

In a rough draft we are rarely economical: We repeat our-selves, we belabor the obvious, we cushion our thoughts in verbiage. As a general rule, advises writer Sidney Smith, "run a pen through every other word you have written; you have no idea what vigor it will give your style."

Long sentences are not necessarily wordy, nor are short sentences always concise. A sentence is wordy if it can be tightened without loss of meaning.

16a　Eliminate redundancies.

Writers often repeat themselves unnecessarily. Afraid, per-haps, that they won't be heard the first time, they insist that a teacup is small *in size* or yellow *in color,* that married people should cooperate *together,* that a fact is not just a fact but a *true* fact. Such redundancies may seem at first to add em-phasis. In reality they do just the opposite, for they divide the reader's attention.

▶ Mr. Barker still hasn't paid last month's rent ⌃ yet.

▶ Black slaves were ~~called or~~ stereotyped as lazy even though they were the main labor force of the South.

Though modifiers ordinarily add meaning to the words they modify, occasionally they are redundant.

▶ Sylvia ~~very hurriedly~~ scribbled her name, address, and phone number on the back of a greasy napkin.

Joel was determined ~~in his mind~~ to lose weight.

The words *scribbled* and *determined* already contain the notions suggested by the modifiers *very hurriedly* and *in his mind.*

16b   Avoid unnecessary repetition of words.

Though words may be repeated deliberately, for effect, repetitions will seem awkward if they are clearly unnecessary. When a more concise version is possible, choose it.

▶ Our fifth patient, in room six, is ~~a~~ mentally ill.~~patient.~~
                                                        ∧

▶ The best teachers help each student to ~~become a better~~
                                        grow
                                        ∧
~~student~~ both academically and emotionally.

16c   Cut empty or inflated phrases.

An empty phrase can be cut with little or no loss of meaning. Common examples are introductory word groups that apologize or hedge: *in my opinion, I think that, it seems that, one must admit that,* and so on.

▶ ~~In my opinion, our~~ current policy in Central America is
      Our
      ∧
misguided on several counts.

~~It seems that~~ *Lonesome Dove* is one of Larry McMurtry's

most ambitious novels.

Readers understand without being told that they are hearing the writer's opinion or educated guess.

Inflated phrases can be reduced to a word or two without loss of meaning.

INFLATED	CONCISE
along the lines of	like
at this point in time	now
by means of	by
due to the fact that	because
for the purpose of	for
for the reason that	because
in order to	to
in spite of the fact that	although (though)
in the event that	if
in the final analysis	finally
in the neighborhood of	about
until such time as	until

▶ We will file the appropriate papers ~~in the event that~~ *if* we are

unable to meet the deadline.

▶ ~~Due to the fact that~~ *Because* the guest of honor is ill, the party is

being postponed until next Saturday.

16d Simplify the structure.

If the structure of a sentence is needlessly indirect, try simplifying it. Look for opportunities to strengthen the verb.

▶ The financial analyst claimed that because of volatile market

conditions she could not ~~make an~~ estimate ~~of~~ the company's

future profits.

The verb *estimate* is more vigorous and more concise than *make an estimate of*.

The colorless verbs *is, are, was,* and *were* frequently generate excess words.

▶ The administrative secretary ~~is responsible for monitoring~~ *monitors and balances* ^

~~and balancing~~ the budgets for travel, contract services, and

personnel.

The revision is more direct and concise. Actions originally appearing in subordinate structures have become verbs replacing *is*.

The constructions *there is* and *there are* (or *there was* and *there were*) also generate excess words.

▶ ~~There is~~ ^A ~~a~~nother module ~~that~~ tells the story of Charles

Darwin and introduces the theory of evolution.

16e Reduce clauses to phrases, phrases to single words.

Word groups functioning as modifiers can often be made more compact. Look for any opportunities to reduce clauses to phrases or phrases to single words.

▶ Thermography, ~~which is~~ a new method of detecting breast
cancer, records heat patterns on black and white or color-
coded film.

A subordinate clause has been reduced to an appositive phrase.

leather
▶ Susan's stylish jeans, ~~made of leather,~~ were too warm for
our climate.

A verbal phrase has become a single word.

EXERCISE 16 – 1

Edit the following sentences for wordiness. Revisions of lettered sentences appear in the back of the book. Example:

even though
The Wilsons moved into the house ~~in spite of the fact that~~
the back door was only ten yards from the train tracks.

a. When visitors come to visit her, Grandmother just stares at the
   wall.
b. The colors of the reproductions were precisely exact.
c. In my opinion, Bloom's race for the governorship is a futile
   exercise.
d. Even the placement of ten terry cloth towels stuffed under the
   door did nothing to stop the flow.
e. In Biology 10A you will be assigned a faculty tutor who will be
   available to assign you eight taped modules and help you clarify
   any information on the tapes.

1. Seeing the barrels, the driver immediately slammed on his brakes.
2. The thing data sets are used for is communicating with other
   computers.
3. The town of New Harmony, located in Indiana, was founded as
   a utopian community.

4. Though orange in color, the letters were still too dim to be seen and read clearly at night.
5. You will be the contact person for arranging interviews between the institute and the office of personnel.
6. Martin Luther King, Jr., was a man who set a high standard for future leaders to meet.
7. The institute was established to develop and provide training for highway agency employees.
8. A typical autocross course consists of at least two straightaways, and the rest of the course is made up of numerous slaloms and sharp turns.
9. The program is called the Weight Control Program, and it has been remarkably successful in helping airmen and airwomen lose weight.
10. The price of driving while drunk or while intoxicated can be extremely high.

EXERCISE 16–2

Edit the following paragraph for wordiness.

We examined the old house from top to bottom. In fact, we started in the attic, which was hot and dusty, and made our way down two flights of stairs, and down one more descent, which was a spiral staircase, into the basement. On our way back up, we thought we heard the eerie noise, the one that had startled us from our sound sleep in the first place. This time the noise was at the top of the staircase that led to the second-floor hallway. We froze and stood quietly at exactly the same moment, listening very intently. Finally, after a few moments, someone said, "Why don't we all go in together and see what it is?" Cautiously, with great care, we stepped over the threshold into the dark hallway, which disappeared into darkness in front of us. There was an unearthly emanating light shining from underneath the door that led into the kitchen. All at once we jumped when we heard a loud crashing sound from behind that door. Before we could rush into the kitchen at high speed, the light went out suddenly, and instantly we were in total pitch black darkness. I thought I heard someone's teeth chattering; then I realized with a shock that it was my own teeth I heard chattering. Without saying a word, we backed silently away from the kitchen door — no one wanted to go in now. Then it was as if someone had shot off a gun, because before we realized what we were doing, we tore up the stairs as fast as we could, and each of us dove into our beds and pulled the covers up and over us to shut out any more frightening sounds and thoughts.

17

Choose appropriate language.

Language is appropriate when it suits your subject, conforms to the needs of your audience, and blends naturally with your own voice.

17a Stay away from jargon.

Jargon is specialized language used among members of a trade, profession, or group. Use jargon only when readers will be familiar with it; even then, use it only when plain English will not do as well.

Sentences filled with jargon are likely to be long and lumpy. To revise such sentences, you must rewrite them, usually in fewer words.

> **JARGON** The indigenous body politic of South Africa has attempted to negotiate legal enfranchisement without result.

> **REVISED** The native population of South Africa has negotiated in vain for the right to vote.

Though a political scientist might feel comfortable with the original version, jargon such as *indigenous body politic* and *legal enfranchisement* is needlessly complicated for ordinary readers.

Broadly defined, jargon includes puffed-up language designed more to impress readers than to inform them. Common examples in business, government, higher education, and the military are listed below, with plain English translations in parentheses.

ameliorate (improve)	indicator (sign)
commence (begin)	optimal (best, most favorable)
components (parts)	parameters (boundaries, limits)
endeavor (try)	peruse (read, look over)
exit (leave)	prior to (before)
facilitate (help)	utilize (use)
factor (consideration, cause)	viable (workable)
impact on (affect)	

▶ ~~In order that I may increase my expertise in the area of~~

~~delivery of services to clients, I feel that participation in this~~
This   *train me to serve our clients better.*
conference will ~~be beneficial~~.

At first the writer tinkered with this sentence — changing *in order that I may* to *to, the area of delivery of* to *delivering,* and so on. The sentence was improved, but it still sounded unnatural. A better solution, this writer discovered, was to rethink what he wanted to say and then rewrite the sentence. Notice that only three words of the original have been preserved.

17b Avoid pretentious language and most euphemisms.

Hoping to sound profound or poetic, some writers embroider their thoughts with large words and flowery phrases, language that in fact sounds pretentious. Pretentious language is so ornate and often so wordy that it obscures the thought that lies beneath.

> When our ~~progenitors reach their silver-haired and golden~~
> *parents become old,*
> ~~years,~~ we frequently ~~ensepulcher~~ them in ~~homes for senes-~~
> *entomb* *old-age homes*
> ~~cent beings~~ as if they were already among the ~~deceased.~~
> *dead.*

The writer of the original sentence had turned to a thesaurus (a dictionary of synonyms and antonyms) in an attempt to sound educated. When such a writer gains enough confidence to speak in his or her own voice, pretentious language disappears.

Related to pretentious language are euphemisms, nice-sounding words or phrases substituted for words thought to sound harsh or ugly. Like pretentious language, euphemisms are wordy and indirect. Unlike pretentious language, they are sometimes appropriate. It is our social custom, for example, to use euphemisms when speaking or writing about death (*Her sister passed on*), excretion (*I have to go to the bathroom*), sexual intercourse (*They did not sleep together until they were married*), and the like. We may also use euphemisms out of concern for someone's feelings. Telling parents, for example, that their daughter is "unmotivated" is more sensitive than saying she's lazy. Tact or politeness, then, can justify an occasional euphemism.

Most euphemisms, however, are needlessly evasive or even deceitful. Like pretentious language, they obscure the intended meaning.

EUPHEMISM	PLAIN ENGLISH
adult entertainment	pornography
preowned automobile	used car
economically deprived	poor
selected out	fired
negative savings	debts
strategic withdrawal	retreat or defeat
revenue enhancers	taxes
chemical dependency	drug addiction

EXERCISE 17–1

Edit the following sentences to eliminate jargon, pretentious or flowery language, and euphemisms. You may need to make substantial changes in some sentences. Revisions of lettered sentences appear in the back of the book. Example:

After two weeks in the legal department, Sue has ~~worked~~ *mastered*
~~into~~ the routine, ~~of the office,~~ and her ~~functional and self-~~
office   *performance has*
~~management skills have~~ exceeded all expectations.

a. It is a widespread but unproven hypothesis that the parameters of significant personal change for persons in midlife are extremely narrow.
b. All employees functioning in the capacity of work-study students will be required to give evidence of current enrollment.
c. Dan's early work hours leave him free to utilize afternoons for errands and for helping the children with their homework.
d. When our father was selected out from his high-paying factory job, we learned what it was like to be economically depressed.
e. It is your responsibility to impose the regulation standards on the preparation of correspondence. It is also your responsibility to prepare the agenda for each staff meeting with an emphasis on clarification of questions aired during the time lapsed since the last meeting.

1. Sam's arguments failed to impact positively on his parents or his male siblings.
2. As I approached the edifice of confinement where my brother was incarcerated, several inmates loudly vocalized a number of lewd remarks.
3. The publicity office believes that the college, through any one of its component members, will be participating in activities that are pregnant with publicity potential. We feel certain that there will be guests and visitors and activities on campus that will be newsworthy. In these instances, we would appreciate any assistance that would alert us to such occurrences.

4. When we returned from our evening perambulation, we shrank back in horror as we surmised that our domestic dwelling was being swallowed up in hellish flames.
5. The bottom line is that the company is experiencing a negative cash flow.

17c Avoid obsolete, archaic, or invented words.

Obsolete words are words found in the writing of the past that have dropped out of use entirely. Archaic words are old words that are still used, but only in special contexts such as literature or advertising. Although dictionaries list obsolete words such as *recomfort* and *reechy* and archaic words such as *anon* and *betwixt*, these words are not appropriate for current use.

Invented words (also called *neologisms*) are words too recently created to be part of standard English. Many invented words fade out of use without becoming standard. *Build-down, throughput,* and *palimony* are neologisms that may not last. *Scuba, disco, sexist, software,* and *spinoff* are no longer neologisms; they have become standard English. Avoid using invented words in your writing unless they are given in the dictionary as standard.

17d In most contexts, avoid slang, regional expressions, and nonstandard English.

Slang is an informal and sometimes private vocabulary that expresses the solidarity of a group such as teenagers, rock musicians, or football fans; it is subject to more rapid change than standard English. For example, the slang teenagers use to express approval changes every few years; *cool, groovy, neat, wicked,* and *awesome* have replaced one another within the last three decades. Sometimes slang becomes so widespread that it is accepted as standard vocabulary. *Jazz,* for example, started out as slang but is now generally accepted to describe a style of music.

Although slang has a certain vitality, it is a code that not everyone understands, and it is very informal. Therefore, it is inappropriate in most written work.

▶ If we don't begin studying for the final, a whole semester's
   will be wasted.
   work ~~is going down the tubes,~~
    ∧

                                   disgust you.
▶ The government's "filth" guidelines for food will ~~gross your~~
                                         ∧
   ~~out.~~

Regional expressions are common to a group in a geographical area. *Let's talk with the bark off* (for *Let's speak frankly*) is an expression in the southern United States, for example. Regional expressions have the same limitations as slang and are therefore inappropriate in most writing.

▶ John was four blocks from the house before he remembered
   turn on
   to ~~cut~~ the headlights. ~~on.~~
    ∧   ∧

▶ I'm not ~~for~~ sure, but I think the dance has been postponed.

Standard English is the language used by educated people in all academic, business, and professional fields. Nonstandard English is spoken by people with a common regional or social heritage. Dropping -s endings from verbs (*Sylvia enjoy working as a lifeguard*), omitting necessary verbs (*I been to Texas*), and using double negatives (*They don't live there no more*) are all nonstandard. Nonstandard English may be appropriate when spoken within a close group, but it is out of place in both formal and informal writing. See Part VI, Editing for Standard English, for practical advice.

17e Choose an appropriate level of formality.

In deciding on a level of formality, consider both your subject and your audience. Does the subject demand a dignified treatment, or is a relaxed tone more suitable? Will the audience be put off if you assume too close a relationship with them, or might you alienate them by seeming too distant?

Formal writing emphasizes the importance of its subject and the exactness of its information. Its tone is dignified, and it maintains a certain distance between writer and audience. A sophisticated vocabulary and complex sentence structures are compatible with a formal writing style, although simple words and short sentences do not necessarily destroy it. Contractions (*don't, he'll*) and colloquial words (*kids, buddy*) are out of place.

For most college and professional writing, some degree of formality is appropriate. In a letter applying for a job, for example, it is a mistake to sound too breezy and informal.

> **TOO INFORMAL** I'd like to get that receptionist's job you've got in the paper.
>
> **MORE FORMAL** I would like to apply for the receptionist's position listed in the *Peoria Journal Star*.

Informal writing is appropriate for private letters, articles in popular magazines, and business correspondence between close associates. Like spoken conversation, it allows contractions and colloquial words. Vocabulary and sentence structure are rarely complex.

In choosing a level of formality, above all be consistent. When a writer's voice shifts from one level of formality to another, readers receive mixed messages.

▶ Once a pitcher for the Cincinnati Reds, Bob shared with me

the secrets of his trade. His lesson commenced with his
began
∧

famous curve ball, ~~implemented~~ *done* by tucking the little finger

behind the ball instead of holding it straight out. Next he

~~elucidated~~ *revealed* the mysteries of the sucker pitch, a slow ball

coming behind a fast windup.

Words such as *commenced* and *elucidated* are inappropriate for the subject matter, and they clash with informal terms such as *sucker pitch* and *fast windup.*

EXERCISE 17–2

Edit the following paragraph to eliminate slang and maintain a consistent level of formality.

> The graduation speaker really blew it. He should have discussed the options and challenges facing the graduating class. Instead, he shot his mouth off at us and trashed us for being lazy and pampered. He did make some good points, however. Our profs have certainly babied us by not holding fast to deadlines, by dismissing assignments that the class ragged them about, by ignoring our tardiness, and by handing out easy C's like hotcakes. Still, we resented this speech as the final word from the college establishment. It should have been the orientation speech for us when we entered as freshmen.

17f Avoid sexist language.

The pronouns *he, him,* and *his* were traditionally used to refer indefinitely to persons of either sex.

TRADITIONAL   A journalist is stimulated by *his* deadline.

Today, however, such usage is widely viewed as sexist because it excludes women and encourages sex-role stereotyping—the view that men are somehow more suited than women to be journalists, doctors, and so on.

One option, of course, is to substitute *his or her* for *his*: *A journalist is stimulated by his or her deadline.* This strategy is fine in small doses, but it generates needless words that become awkward when repeated throughout an essay. A better strategy, many writers have discovered, is simply to write in the plural.

> **REVISED** *Journalists* are stimulated by *their* deadlines.

Yet another strategy is to recast the sentence so that the problem does not arise:

> **REVISED** A journalist is stimulated by *a* deadline.

When sexist language occurs throughout an essay, it is sometimes possible to adjust the essay's point of view. If the essay might be appropriately rewritten from the *I,* the *we,* or the *you* point of view, the problem of sexist English will not arise. See 3b.

Like the pronouns *he, him,* and *his,* the nouns *man* and *men* were once used indefinitely to refer to persons of either sex. Current usage demands gender-neutral terms instead.

INAPPROPRIATE	APPROPRIATE
chairman	chairperson, moderator, chair
clergyman	member of the clergy
congressman	member of Congress, representative, legislator
fireman	firefighter
foreman	supervisor
mailman	mail carrier, postal worker
mankind	people, humans
manpower	personnel
policeman	police officer
salesman	salesperson, sales associate
to man	to operate, to staff
weatherman	weather forecaster, meteorologist
workman	worker, laborer

18

Find the exact words.

Whatever you want to say, claimed French writer Gustave Flaubert, "there is but one word to express it, one verb to give it movement, one adjective to qualify it; you must seek until you find this noun, this verb, this adjective." Even if you are not reaching for such perfection in your writing, you will sometimes find yourself wishing for better words. The dictionary is the obvious first place to turn, a thesaurus the second.

A good desk dictionary—such as *The American Heritage Dictionary, The Random House College Dictionary,* or *Webster's New Collegiate* or *New World Dictionary of the American Language* — lists synonyms and antonyms for many words, with helpful comments on various shades of meaning. Under *fertile,* for example, *Webster's New World Dictionary* carefully distinguishes the meanings of *fertile, fecund, fruitful,* and *prolific:*

> SYN. —*fertile* implies a producing, or power of producing, fruit or offspring, and may be used figuratively of the mind; *fecund* implies the abundant production of offspring or fruit, or, figuratively, of creations of the mind; *fruitful* specifically suggests the bearing of much fruit, but it is also used to imply fertility (of soil), favorable results, profitableness, etc.; *prolific,* a close synonym for *fecund,* more often carries derogatory connotations of overly rapid production or reproduction — ANT. *sterile, barren*

If the dictionary doesn't yield the word you need, try a sourcebook of synonyms and antonyms such as *Roget's International Thesaurus.* In the back of *Roget's* is an index to the groups of synonyms that make up the bulk of the book. Look up the adjective *still,* for example, and you will find references to lists containing the words *dead, motionless, silent,* and *tranquil.* If *tranquil* is close to the word you have in mind, turn to its section in the front of the book. There you will find a long list of synonyms, including such words as *quiet, quiescent, reposeful, calm, pacific, halcyon, placid,* and *unruffled.* Unless your vocabulary is better than average, the list will contain words you've never heard or with which you are only vaguely familiar. Whenever you are tempted to use one of these words, look it up in the dictionary first to avoid misusing it.

On discovering the thesaurus, many writers use it for the wrong reasons, so a word of caution is in order. Do not turn to a thesaurus in search of exotic, fancy words — such as *halcyon* — with which to embellish your essays. Look instead for words that exactly express your meaning. Most of the time these words will be familiar to both you and your readers. *Tranquil* was probably the word you were looking for all along.

18a Select words with appropriate connotations.

In addition to their strict dictionary meanings (or *denotations*), words have *connotations,* emotional colorings that affect how readers respond to them. The word *steely* denotes "made of or resembling commercial iron that contains carbon," but it also calls up a cluster of images associated with steel, such as the sensation of touching it. These associations give the word its connotations — cold, smooth, unbending.

If the connotation of a word does not seem appropriate for your purpose, your audience, or your subject matter, the word should be changed. When a more appropriate synonym does not come quickly to mind, consult a dictionary or a thesaurus.

▶ The model was ~~skinny~~ *slender* and fashionable.

The connotation of the word *skinny* was too negative.

▶ As I covered the boats with marsh grass, the ~~perspiration~~ I *sweat* had worked up evaporated in the wind, making the cold

morning air seem even colder.

The term *perspiration* was too dainty for the context, which suggested vigorous exercise.

EXERCISE 18–1

Use a dictionary or thesaurus to find at least four synonyms for each of the following words. Be prepared to explain any slight differences in meaning.

1. decay (verb)
2. difficult (adjective)
3. hurry (verb)
4. pleasure (noun)
5. secret (adjective)
6. talent (noun)

18b Prefer specific, concrete nouns and active verbs.

Unlike general nouns, which refer to broad classes of things, specific nouns point to definite and particular items. *Film,* for example, names a general class, *horror film* names a narrower class, and *Carrie* is more specific still. Other examples: *team, football team, New York Jets; music, symphony, Beethoven's Ninth; work, carpentry, cabinetmaking.*

Unlike abstract nouns, which refer to qualities and ideas (*justice, beauty, realism, dignity*), concrete nouns point to immediate, often sensuous experience and to physical objects (*steeple, asphalt, lilac, stone, garlic*).

Specific, concrete nouns express meaning more vividly than general or abstract ones. Although general and abstract language is sometimes necessary to convey your meaning, ordinarily prefer specific, concrete alternatives.

▶ The senator spoke about the challenges of the future: ~~problems concerning the environment and world peace.~~ *of famine, pollution, dwindling resources, and arms control.*

Nouns such as *thing, area, aspect, factor,* and *individual* are especially dull and imprecise.

▶ A career in transportation management offers many ~~things.~~ *rewards.*

▶ Try pairing a trainee with an ~~individual with technical experience.~~ *experienced technician.*

Like specific, concrete nouns, active verbs express meaning more vividly than their duller counterparts — linking verbs or verbs in the passive voice. The linking verbs *be, am, is, are, was, were, being,* and *been* lack color because they convey no action (see 48b). Verbs in the passive voice lack vigor because their subjects receive the action instead of doing it (see 27g and 48b). Linking and passive verbs have legitimate uses, but if an active verb can carry your meaning, prefer it.

LINKING   A surge of power *was* responsible for the destruction of the coolant pumps.

PASSIVE   The coolant pumps *were destroyed* by a surge of power.

ACTIVE   A surge of power *destroyed* the coolant pumps.

▶ The moods of a manic-depressive ~~are unpredictable.~~ *fluctuate without warning.*

Although the original version (with the linking verb *are*) is correct, the active verb *fluctuate* makes the point more powerfully.

▶ ~~The transformer was struck by a bolt of lightning,~~ plunging

A bolt of lightning struck the transformer,

us into darkness.

The active voice (*struck*) makes the point more forcefully than the passive (*was struck*). See 27g.

Even among active verbs, some are more active — and therefore more vigorous and colorful — than others. Carefully selected verbs can energize a piece of writing.

▶ The goalie crouched low, ~~reached~~ *swept* out his stick, and ~~sent~~ *hooked* the

puck away from the mouth of the goal.

EXERCISE 18–2

The verbs in the following sentences are italicized. Revise passive or linking verbs with active alternatives; do not change active verbs. If a sentence's verbs are all active, write the word "active" after the sentence. Revisions of lettered sentences appear in the back of the book. Example:

~~The campfire was doused by the ranger before we were~~

The ranger doused the campfire before giving us

~~given~~ a ticket for unauthorized use of a campsite.

a. The developing, fixing, washing, and drying of the film *is* automatically *performed* by the processor.
b. The entire operation *is overlooked* by the producer.
c. Finally the chute *caught* air and *popped* open with a jolt at around 2,000 feet.
d. Escaping into the world of drugs, I *was* rebellious about anything and everything laid down by the establishment.
e. There *were* fighting players on both sides of the rink.

1. The maintaining of an accurate and orderly log by the radiologist *is required* according to hospital protocol.
2. Sam *was* unsuccessful in his attempt to pass the first performance test.
3. A respirator *pushes* oxygen into his lungs through a tube inserted through his neck.
4. C.B.'s *are used* to find parts, equipment, food, lodging, and anything else a trucker might need.
5. At the crack of rocket and mortar blasts, I *jumped* from the top bunk and *landed* on my buddy below, who *was crawling* on the floor looking for his boots.

18c Do not misuse words.

If a word is not in your active vocabulary, you may find yourself misusing it, sometimes with embarrassing consequences. Imagine the chagrin of the young woman who wrote that the "aroma of pumpkin pie and sage stuffing acted as an *aphrodisiac*" when she learned that aphrodisiacs are drugs or foods stimulating sexual desire. Such blunders are easily prevented: When in doubt, check the dictionary.

▶ The fans were ~~migrating~~ climbing up the bleachers in search of good seats.

▶ Mrs. Johnson tried to fight but to no ~~prevail~~ avail.

▶ Drugs have so ~~diffused~~ permeated our culture that they touch all segments of our society.

EXERCISE 18–3

Edit the following sentences to correct misused words. Revisions of lettered sentences appear in the back of the book. Example:

The training required for a ballet dancer is ~~all-absorbent~~ all-absorbing.

a. Many of us are not persistence enough to make a change for the better.
b. Hours of long practice often determine an excellent musician from a sloppy one.
c. Sam Brown began his career as a lawyer, but now he is a real estate mongrel.
d. When Robert Frost died at age eighty-eight, he left a legacy of poems that will make him immortal for years to come.
e. This patient is kept in isolation to prevent her from obtaining our germs.

1. Ada's plan is to require education and experience to prepare herself for a position as property manager.
2. Trifle, a popular English dessert, contains a ménage of ingredients that do not always appeal to American tastes.
3. Washington's National Airport is surrounded on three sides by water.
4. Many family relationships have been absolved because of a drug-related incident.
5. Tom Jones is an illegal child who grows up under the care of Squire Western.

18d Use standard idioms.

Idioms are speech forms that follow no easily specified rules. The English say "Maria went *to hospital*," an idiom strange to American ears, which are accustomed to hearing *the* in front of *hospital*. Native speakers of a language seldom have problems with idioms, but prepositions sometimes cause trouble, especially when they follow certain verbs and adjectives. When in doubt, consult a good desk dictionary: Look up the word preceding the troublesome preposition.

UNIDIOMATIC	IDIOMATIC
according with	according to
abide with (a decision)	abide by (a decision)

UNIDIOMATIC	IDIOMATIC
agree to (an idea)	agree with (an idea)
angry at (a person)	angry with (a person)
capable to	capable of
comply to	comply with
desirous to	desirous of
different than	different from
intend on doing	intend to do
off of	off
plan on doing	plan to do
preferable than	preferable to
prior than	prior to
superior than	superior to
sure and	sure to
try and	try to
type of a	type of

EXERCISE 18–4

Edit the following sentences to eliminate errors in the use of idiomatic expressions. If a sentence is correct, write "correct" after it. Answers to lettered sentences appear in the back of the book. Example:

by
We agreed to abide ~~with~~ the decision of the judge.

a. I was so angry at the salesperson that I took her bag of samples and emptied it on the floor in front of her.
b. Prior to the Russians' launching of *Sputnik, nik* was not an English suffix.
c. Try and come up with the rough outline, and we will find someone who can fill in the details.
d. "Your prejudice is no different than mine," she shouted.
e. The parade moved off of the street and onto the beach.

1. Be sure and report on the danger of releasing genetically engineered bacteria into the atmosphere.
2. Our painkiller is far superior than any other medicine on the market.

3. The American public regards arms control as one of the most important issues facing us in the late twentieth century.
4. If we want a license, we have to comply to federal regulations.
5. I intend on writing letters to my representatives in Congress demanding that they do something about homelessness in this state.

18e   Avoid worn-out expressions.

The frontiersman who first announced that he had "slept like a log" no doubt amused his companions with a fresh and unlikely comparison. Today, however, that comparison is a cliché, a saying that has lost its dazzle from overuse. No longer can it surprise.

To see just how dully predictable clichés are, put your hand over the right-hand column below and then finish the phrases on the left.

cool as a	cucumber
beat around	the bush
blind as a	bat
busy as a	bee
crystal	clear
dead as a	doornail
from the frying pan	into the fire
light as a	feather
like a bull	in a china shop
playing with	fire
nutty as a	fruitcake
selling like	hotcakes
starting out at the bottom	of the ladder
water over the	dam
white as a	sheet, ghost
avoid clichés like the	plague

The cure for clichés is frequently simple: Just delete them. When this won't work, try adding some element of surprise.

One student, for example, who had written that she had butterflies in her stomach, revised her cliché like this:

> If all of the action in my stomach is caused by butterflies, there must be a horde of them, with horseshoes on.

The image of butterflies wearing horseshoes is fresh and unlikely, not dully predictable like the original cliché.

18f Use figures of speech with care.

A figure of speech is an expression that uses words imaginatively (rather than literally) to invigorate an idea or make abstract ideas concrete. Most often, figures of speech compare two seemingly unlike things to reveal surprising similarities. For example, Richard Selzer compares an aging surgeon who has lost his touch to an old lion whose claws have become blunted. Readers enjoy such fresh comparisons, and you will find that creating them is one of the greatest pleasures in writing.

In a *simile,* the writer makes the comparison explicitly, usually by introducing it with *like* or *as.* One student, for instance, writes of his grandfather, "By the time cotton had to be picked, his neck was as red as the clay he plowed." In one of his short stories, William Faulkner describes the eyes of a plump old woman who had locked herself in her house for years as "like two small pieces of coal pressed into a lump of dough." J. D. Salinger's troubled adolescent Holden Caulfield in *The Catcher in the Rye* finds one of his fellow students "as sensitive as a goddam toilet seat," and actress Mae West tells us that men are "like streetcars. There's always another one around the corner."

In a *metaphor,* the *like* or *as* is omitted, and the comparison is implied. For example, Mark Twain's Huck Finn describes his drunken father's face as "fish-belly white." In the Old Testament's Song of Solomon, a young woman compares the man she loves to a fruit tree: "With great delight I sat in his shadow, and his fruit was sweet to my taste." And a student poet describes a fierce summer storm like this: "It growls and barks at me, / jumping at its leash, / as if it guards the gates of heaven."

Writers sometimes use figures of speech without thinking through the images they evoke. This can result in a *mixed metaphor,* the combination of two or more images that don't make sense together.

▶ Crossing Utah's salt flats in his new Corvette, my father flew
  at jet speed.
  ~~under a full head of steam.~~
  ∧

Flew suggests an airplane, while *under a full head of steam* suggests a train. To clarify the image, the writer should stick with one comparison or the other.

▶ Our office had decided to put all controversial issues on a

back burner.~~in a holding pattern.~~
         ∧
Here the writer is mixing stoves and airplanes. Simply deleting one of the images corrects the problem.

EXERCISE 18–5

Edit the following sentences to replace worn-out expressions and clarify mixed figures of speech. Revisions of lettered sentences appear in the back of the book. Example:

                         the color drained from his face.
When he heard about the accident, ~~he turned white as a~~
                                    ∧
~~sheet.~~

a. John stormed into the room like a bull in a china shop.
b. The president thought that the scientists were using science as a sledgehammer to grind their political axes.

c. I told Al that he was playing with fire when I learned that he intended to spy on the trustees' meeting.
d. We ironed out the sticky spots in our relationship.
e. Mel told us that he wasn't willing to put his neck out on a limb.

1. I could read him like a book; he had egg all over his face.
2. At the first staff meeting, we realized that we had been saddled with a ship of fools.
3. My roommate was great fun, but she was as nutty as a fruitcake.
4. When I graduated from high school and started college, I realized that I was leaping from the frying pan into the fire.
5. Once she had sunk her teeth into it, Helen burned through the assignment.

Editing for Grammar

19

Repair sentence fragments.

A sentence fragment is a word group that pretends to be a sentence. To be a sentence, a word group must consist of at least one full independent clause. An independent clause has a subject and a verb, and it either stands alone or could stand alone. See 50.

Some sentence fragments are clauses that contain a subject and a verb but begin with a subordinating word. Others are phrases that lack a subject, a verb, or both.

You can repair most fragments in two ways. Either pull the fragment into a nearby sentence, making sure to punctuate the new sentence correctly, or turn the fragment itself into a sentence.

19a Attach fragmented subordinate clauses or turn them into sentences.

Subordinate clauses are patterned like sentences, with subjects and verbs, but they begin with a word or words that mark them as subordinate — words such as *although, because, if, so that, unless, when, who, which,* and *that.* Subordinate clauses function within sentences as adjectives, as adverbs, or as nouns. It is a mistake, therefore, to separate them from the sentences in which they function. (See subordinate clauses, 49b.)

Most fragmented clauses beg to be pulled into a sentence nearby.

▶ Jane promises to address the problem of limited on-campus
parking/~~If~~ she is elected special student adviser.
if
∧

If introduces a subordinate clause that modifies the verb *promises*.

▶ **When we approached the entrance, the security officer**

informed us that visitors would be searched/ And that the

(with inserted *a* above and strikethrough on "And")

women's purses would be thoroughly inspected.

That visitors would be searched and *that the women's purses would be thoroughly inspected* both function as the direct object of the verb *informed*.

If a fragmented clause cannot be attached to a nearby sentence or if you feel that attaching it would be awkward, try rewriting it. The simplest way to turn a subordinate clause into a sentence is to delete the opening word or words that mark it as subordinate.

▶ **Violence has produced a great deal of apprehension among**

Self-preservation

students and teachers. ~~So that self-preservation~~ has become

their primary concern.

For clarity the writer might consider adding a transitional expression: *In fact, self-preservation has become their primary concern.*

19b Attach fragmented phrases or turn them into sentences.

Fragmented phrases are usually prepositional or verbal phrases; occasionally they are appositives, words or word groups that rename nouns or pronouns. (See 49a, 49c, and 49d.)

Many fragmented phrases may simply be pulled into nearby sentences.

▶ On Sundays James read the newspaper's employment
sections scrupulously, ~~Scrutinizing~~ *scrutinizing* every position that held
even the remotest possibility.

Scrutinizing every position that held even the remotest possibility is a verbal phrase modifying *James.*

▶ Wednesday morning Phil allowed himself half a grapefruit, ~~The~~ *t*he only food he had eaten in two days.

The only food he had eaten in two days is an appositive renaming the noun *grapefruit.*

If a fragmented phrase cannot be pulled into a nearby sentence effectively, turn it into a sentence. You may need to add a subject, a verb, or both.

▶ If Eric doesn't get his way, he goes into a fit of rage. For
example, ~~lying~~ *he lies* on the floor screaming or ~~opening~~ *opens* the cabinet
doors and then ~~slamming~~ *slams* them shut.

The writer corrected this fragment by adding a subject — *he* — and substituting verbs for the participles *lying, opening,* and *slamming.*

19c Attach other fragmented word groups or turn them into sentences.

Other word groups that are commonly fragmented are parts of compound predicates and lists.

A predicate consists of a verb and its objects, complements, and modifiers (see 48). A compound predicate includes two or more predicates joined by a coordinating conjunction, usually *and, but,* or *or.* Because the parts of a compound predicate share the same subject, they should appear in the same sentence.

▶ Aspiring bodybuilders must first ascertain their strengths

and weaknesses/ And then develop a clear picture of what

they want to achieve.

The writer might also correct the fragment by turning the second predicate into a sentence: *They must then develop a clear picture of what they want to achieve.*

When a list is mistakenly fragmented, it can often be attached to a nearby sentence with a colon or a dash. (See 35 and 39a.)

▶ The side effects of lithium are many/ Nausea, stomach

cramps, thirst, muscle weakness, vomiting, diarrhea,

confusion, and tremors.

19d Exception: Occasionally a fragment may be used deliberately, for effect.

Skilled writers occasionally use sentence fragments for emphasis. In the following passage, Richard Rodriguez uses a fragment (italicized) to draw attention to his mother.

Following the dramatic Americanization of their children, even my parents grew more publicly confident. *Especially my mother.* She learned the names of all the people on our block.
— *Hunger of Memory*

Fragments are occasionally used to save words. For example, a fragment may be a concise way to mark a transition (*And now the opposing arguments*) or to answer a question (*Are these new drug tests 100% reliable? Not in the opinion of most experts*). Unless you are an experienced writer, however, you will find it safer to write in complete sentences.

EXERCISE 19–1

Repair any fragment by attaching it to a nearby sentence or by rewriting it as a complete sentence. If a word group is correct, write "correct" after it. Revisions of lettered sentences appear in the back of the book. Example:

I was exhausted/, Having studied for forty-eight hours

straight.

a. Sam told us that he would soon be getting out on work release. And that he might be able to come home for a visit on certain weekends.

b. It has been said that there are only three indigenous American art forms. Jazz, musical comedy, and soap opera.

c. College students can supplement their income by house-sitting and pet-sitting for families who are away. Furthermore, the money they earn is seldom taxed.

d. Myra did not tell us about her new job for six weeks. Although she saw one or the other of us every day.

e. While on a tour of Italy, Maria and Kathleen sneaked away from their group to spend some quiet minutes with Leonardo da Vinci's *Last Supper*. A stunning fresco painted in the fifteenth century in a Milan monastery.

1. There are four breeds of dog known in the Arctic. All probably having the same ancestry.

2. The effects of poverty and illness were all about us. Malnourished children, dead animals, vermin, an overwhelming stench. There were even bloated bodies lying in the streets.

3. Underneath all his brashness, Henry is really a thoughtful person. Few of his colleagues realize how sensitive he is.
4. I had pushed these fears into one of those quiet places in my mind. Hoping they would stay there asleep.
5. To give my family a comfortable, secure home life. That is the most important goal to me.
6. If a woman from the desert tribe showed anger toward her husband, she was whipped in front of the whole village. And shunned by the rest of the women.
7. A tornado is a violent whirling wind. One that produces a funnel-shaped cloud and moves over land in a narrow path of destruction.
8. With machetes, the explorers cut their way through the tall grasses to the edge of the canyon. Where they began to lay out their tapes for the survey.
9. My brothers are both working for the government in permanent positions. Bill is employed at the Space Center and Alan is with a military agency.
10. Theodosia had hated her name for as long as she could remember. Because it sounded so old-fashioned.

EXERCISE 19–2

Repair each fragment in this paragraph by attaching it to a sentence nearby or by rewriting it as a complete sentence.

One trip through the pound unnerves me. It's not that I want to adopt all those animals. I don't even like most of them. Especially little dogs and big cats. I'm actually afraid of animals like gerbils and hamsters. Because they remind me of rats. What bothers me is the attitude of society that an institution such as a pound reflects. The attitude that we have no obligations toward our pets. Knowing what's going to happen to most of the animals. That bothers me too. I tried to beg off when my aunt asked me to go help pick out a dog. A pet for my seven-year-old cousin, Jerry. But I went. It was painful to see all the abandoned animals. Puppies chasing their tails, kittens cocking their heads to watch us, snakes coiling and uncoiling in their cages. I hated the whole experience. The only good thing about it was the look on Jerry's face when we left the pound with a small, full-grown sheltie walking at the end of the leash he proudly held.

20

Revise comma splices and fused sentences.

Comma splices and fused sentences contain independent clauses that have been too weakly separated. (An independent clause has at least a subject and a verb and can stand alone as a separate sentence. See 50.) When a writer puts no mark of punctuation between independent clauses, the result is a fused sentence (also called a *run-on sentence*).

> ┌─INDEPENDENT CLAUSE─┐┌─INDEPENDENT CLAUSE─┐
> **FUSED** Power tends to corrupt absolute power corrupts
> ────────────
> absolutely.

A far more common error is the comma splice, which consists of independent clauses separated by only a comma.

> **COMMA** Power tends to corrupt, absolute power corrupts
> **SPLICE** absolutely.

If two independent clauses are to appear in one sentence, they must be firmly separated, either by a comma and a coordinating conjunction (*and, but, or, nor, for, so, yet*) or by a semicolon.

REVISED   Power tends to corrupt, and absolute power corrupts absolutely.

REVISED   Power tends to corrupt; absolute power corrupts absolutely.

Even if the clauses are joined by a comma and a conjunctive adverb such as *however, moreover,* or *therefore* or by a comma and a transitional expression such as *in fact* or *for example,* the separation is still not firm enough. When a conjunctive adverb or transitional expression is used to join independent clauses, the independent clauses must be separated by a semicolon.

COMMA   Power tends to corrupt, moreover, absolute power
SPLICE   corrupts absolutely.

REVISED   Power tends to corrupt; moreover, absolute power corrupts absolutely.

Unlike coordinating conjunctions, conjunctive adverbs and transitional expressions are frequently movable: *Power tends to corrupt; absolute power, moreover, corrupts absolutely.* Notice that the semicolon goes between the independent clauses. (See 34b.)

To correct a comma splice or a fused sentence, you have four choices:

1. Use a comma and a coordinating conjunction.
2. Use a semicolon (or, if appropriate, a colon).
3. Make the clauses into separate sentences.
4. Restructure the sentence, perhaps by subordinating one of the clauses.

One of these revision techniques will usually work better than the others for a particular sentence. The fourth technique, the one requiring the most extensive revision, is frequently the most effective.

20a Consider separating the clauses with a comma and a coordinating conjunction.

There are seven coordinating conjunctions in English: *and, but, or, nor, for, so,* and *yet.* When a coordinating conjunction joins independent clauses, it must be preceded by a comma. (See 32a.)

▶ Theo and Fanny had hoped to spend their final days in the

old homestead, *but* they had to change their plans and move

together to a retirement home.

▶ Many government officials privately admit that the polygraph

is unreliable, ~~however,~~ *yet* they continue to use it as a security

measure.

However is a conjunctive adverb, not a coordinating conjunction. See 20b.

20b Consider separating the clauses with a semicolon (or, if appropriate, with a colon).

When the independent clauses are closely related and their relation is clear without a coordinating conjunction, a semicolon is an acceptable method of revision. (See 34a.)

▶ The kitchen was ordinarily the hub of activity/; in the

summer, though, it was nearly always empty.

A semicolon is required between independent clauses that have been linked with a conjunctive adverb such as *however, therefore,* or *moreover* or with a transitional expression such as *in fact, for example,* or *as a matter of fact.* (See 34b.)

▶ The timber wolf looks much like a large German shepherd/**;** however, the wolf has longer legs, larger feet, a wider head, and a long, bushy tail.

▶ Everyone in my outfit had a specific job/**;** as a matter of fact, most of the officers had three or four duties.

If the first independent clause formally introduces the second, a colon may be an appropriate method of revision. (See 35.)

▶ As I walked into the assembly, a special report flashed onto the screen/**:** Martin Luther King, Jr., had been shot.

20c Consider making the clauses into separate sentences.

▶ In one episode viewers saw two people smashed by a boat, one choked, and another shot to death./*What* ~~what~~ purpose does this violence serve?

Since one independent clause is a statement and the other is a question, they should be separate sentences.

▶ I gave the necessary papers to the police officer. ~~then~~ *Then* he said

I would have to accompany him to the police station, where

a counselor would talk with me and call my parents.

Because the second independent clause is quite long, a sensible revision is to use separate sentences.

20d Consider restructuring the sentence, perhaps by subordinating one of the clauses.

If one of the independent clauses is less important than the other, turn it into a subordinate clause or phrase. That way, ideas that are logically subordinate will be expressed in grammatically subordinate structures. (For more about subordination, see 8 and 49.)

▶ Lindsey is a top competitor ~~she~~ *who* has been riding since the

age of seven.

When the
~~The~~ new health plan was explained to the employees in my

division, everyone agreed to give it a try.

Saturday afternoon Julie came running into the house / ~~she~~

~~wanted~~ to get permission to go to the park.

Minor ideas in these sentences are now expressed in subordinate clauses or phrases.

EXERCISE 20–1

Revise any comma splices or fused sentences using the method of revision suggested in brackets. Revisions of lettered sentences appear in the back of the book. Example:

> *Because*
> ∧Orville was obsessed with his weight, he rarely ate anything
>
> sweet and delicious. [*Restructure the sentence.*]

a. The city had one public swimming pool, it stayed packed with children all summer long. [*Restructure the sentence.*]

b. Most babies come down with a high temperature at some point mine was no exception. [*Use a comma and a coordinating conjunction.*]

c. Why should we pay taxes to support public transportation, we prefer to save energy dollars by carpooling. [*Make two sentences.*]

d. Charles was like any of us he resisted having an idea pulled from under him. [*Use a semicolon.*]

e. The experience taught Marianne a lesson, she could not always rely on her parents to bail her out of trouble. [*Restructure the sentence.*]

1. For the first time in her adult life, Lisa had time to waste, she could spend a whole day curled up with a good book. [*Use a semicolon.*]

2. It is impossible for parents to monitor all the television their children see, therefore, many parents just give up and offer no supervision at all. [*Restructure the sentence.*]

3. My sister Elaine was awarded the Medal of Honor, however, she was not able to attend the awards ceremony. [*Use a comma and a coordinating conjunction.*]

4. While we were walking down Grover Avenue, Gary told us about his Aunt Elsinia, she was an extraordinary woman. [*Restructure the sentence.*]

5. The president of Algeria was standing next to the podium he was waiting to be introduced. [*Restructure the sentence.*]

6. On most days I had only enough money for bus fare, lunch was a luxury I could not afford. [*Use a semicolon.*]

7. There was one major reason for John's wealth, his grandfather had been a multimillionaire. [*Use a colon.*]

8. Why shouldn't divorced wives receive half of their husbands' pensions and other retirement benefits, they were partners for many years. [*Make two sentences.*]

9. We usually think of children as innocent and guileless, however, they are often cruel and unjust. [*Use a comma and a coordinating conjunction.*]

10. Our house is still in good shape, it needs only a paint job and some gutter repair. [*Restructure the sentence.*]

EXERCISE 20–2

Revise any comma splices or fused sentences using a technique that you find effective. If a sentence is correct, write "correct" after it. Revisions of lettered sentences appear in the back of the book. Example:

> I ran the three blocks as fast as I could, ~~however~~ I still
> ^*but*
>
> missed the bus.

a. The trail up Mount Finegold was declared impassable, therefore, we decided to return to our hotel a day early.

b. The duck hunter set out his decoys in the shallow bay and then settled in to wait for the first real bird to alight.

c. Residents have a variety of complaints about the windmills, for instance, the noise keeps people awake at night, the vibrations have been known to break windows, television reception is affected, and the windmills themselves are just plain ugly.

d. Researchers were studying the fertility of Texas land tortoises they X-rayed all the female tortoises to see how many eggs they had.

e. The Chevy Chase swimmers were determined to win this medley relay for one reason, it was their last chance to beat their archrivals from Kensington.

1. Are you able to endure boredom, isolation, and potential violence, then the army may well be the adventure for you.
2. Maria gave her mother half of her weekly pay then she used the rest as a down payment on a stereo system at Brown's Sounds.
3. My business is very competitive, therefore I need to continue my education.
4. The volunteers worked hard to clean up and restore calm after the tornado, as a matter of fact, many of them did not sleep for the first three days of the emergency.
5. Taking drugs to keep alert on the job or in school can actually cause a decline in work performance and can lead to severe depression as well.
6. Pablo had not prepared well for his first overseas assignment, but luck was with him, he performed better than most of the more experienced members of his unit.
7. It was obvious that Susan had already been out walking in the woods, her boots were covered with mud and leaves.
8. Josie had all the equipment necessary for her first parachute jump, however, she forgot the required checklist and had to remain on the ground.
9. Last year's tomatoes were the best we had ever grown, they were plump, firm, and extraordinarily sweet.
10. If you want to lose weight and keep it off, consider this advice, don't try to take it off faster than you put it on.

21

Make subjects and verbs agree.

In the present tense, verbs agree with their subjects in number (singular or plural) and in person (first, second, or third). The present-tense ending *-s* is used on a verb if its subject is third-person singular; otherwise the verb takes no ending.

Consider, for example, the present-tense forms of the verb *give:*

	SINGULAR	PLURAL
FIRST PERSON	I give	we give
SECOND PERSON	you give	you give
THIRD PERSON	he/she/it gives	they give
	Alison gives	parents give

The verb *be* varies from this pattern, and unlike any other verb it has special forms in *both* the present and the past tense.

PRESENT TENSE FORMS OF BE		PAST TENSE FORMS OF BE	
I am	we are	I was	we were
you are	you are	you were	you were
he/she/it is	they are	he/she/it was	they were

Speakers of standard English know by ear that *he talks, she has,* and *it doesn't* (not *he talk, she have,* and *it don't*) are the correct forms. For such speakers, problems with subject-verb agreement arise only in certain tricky situations, which are detailed in this section.

If you don't trust your ear, consult 28, which contrasts the present-tense verb systems of standard and nonstandard English. Also see 48a and 48b on subjects and verbs.

21a Make the verb agree with its subject, not with a word that comes between.

Word groups often come between the subject and the verb. Such word groups, usually modifying the subject, may contain a noun that at first appears to be the subject. By mentally stripping away such modifiers, you can isolate the noun that is in fact the subject.

The *tulips* in the pot on the balcony *need* watering.

► High levels of air pollution ~~causes~~ *cause* damage to the respiratory

tract.

A good set of golf clubs ~~cost~~ *costs* about three hundred dollars.

The nouns *pollution* and *clubs,* which the writers at first treated as subjects, appear in prepositional phrases. When the writers mentally stripped away these phrases, they heard the correct verbs: *levels cause, set costs.*

NOTE: Phrases beginning with the prepositions *as well as, in addition to, accompanied by, together with,* and *along with* do not make a singular subject plural.

► The president, as well as his press secretary, ~~were~~ *was* shot.

The writer at first thought the subject was plural because two people were shot. Grammatically, however, *president* alone is the subject, because *as well as his press secretary* is a prepositional phrase. To emphasize the fact that two people were shot, the writer can use *and* instead: *The president and his press secretary were shot.*

21b Treat most compound subjects connected by *and* as plural.

A subject with two or more parts is said to be compound. If the parts are connected by *and,* the subject is nearly always plural.

Leon and *Jan* often *jog* together.

► Remember that your safety and welfare ~~is~~ *are* in your own

hands.

The compound subject *safety and welfare* is plural, requiring the verb *are*.

▶ Jill's natural ability and her desire to help others ~~has~~ *have* led to

a career in the ministry.

Ability and desire is a plural subject, so its verb should be *have*.

EXCEPTIONS: When the parts of the subject form a single unit or when they refer to the same person or thing, treat the subject as singular.

Strawberries and cream was a last-minute addition to the menu.

Sue's friend and adviser was surprised by her decision.

When a compound subject is preceded by *each* or *every*, treat it as singular.

Each tree, shrub, and vine needs to be sprayed.

Every car, truck, and van is required to pass inspection.

This exception does not apply when a compound subject is followed by *each: Alan and Marcia each have different ideas.*

21c With compound subjects connected by *or* or *nor*, make the verb agree with the part of the subject nearer to the verb.

A driver's *license* or credit *card is* required.

A driver's *license* or two credit *cards are* required.

▶ If a relative or neighbor ~~are~~ *is* abusing a child, notify the police.

Neither the instructor nor her students ~~was~~ *were* able to find the
^

classroom.

Neither the students nor the instructor ~~were~~ *was* able to find the
^

classroom.

The verb must be matched with the part of the subject closer to
it: *neighbor is* in the first sentence, *students were* in the second,
instructor was in the third.

21d Treat most indefinite pronouns as singular.

Indefinite pronouns are pronouns that do not refer to specific
persons or things. *Any, anyone, anybody, each, either,
everyone, everybody, everything, neither, none, no one,
someone,* and *something* are common examples. Many of these
words appear to have plural meanings, and they are treated
as such in casual speech. In formal, written English, however,
they are nearly always considered singular.

Everyone on the team *supports* the coach.

▶ Each of the furrows ~~have~~ *has* been seeded.
^

Everybody who signed up for the ski trip ~~were~~ *was* taking
^

lessons.

The subjects are *each* and *everybody.* These indefinite pronouns are singular, so the verbs must be *has* and *was.*

The indefinite pronouns *none* and *neither* are considered
singular when used alone.

None is immune from this disease.

Neither is able to attend.

When these pronouns are followed by prepositional phrases with a plural meaning, however, usage varies. Some experts insist on treating the pronouns as singular, but many writers disagree. It is safer to treat them as singular.

None of these trades *requires* a college education.

Neither of those pejoratives *fits* Warren Burger.

A few indefinite pronouns (*all, any, some*) may be singular or plural depending on the noun or pronoun they refer to.

Some of the *lemonade has* disappeared.

Some of the *rocks were* slippery.

21e Treat collective nouns as singular unless the meaning is clearly plural.

Collective nouns such as *jury, committee, audience, crowd, class, troop, family,* and *couple* name a class or a group. In American English collective nouns are nearly always treated as singular: They emphasize the group as a unit. Occasionally, when there is some reason to draw attention to the individual members of the group, a collective noun may be treated as plural.

SINGULAR The *class respects* the teacher.

PLURAL The *class are* debating among themselves.

To underscore the notion of individuality in the second sentence, many writers would add a clearly plural noun such as *members:*

PLURAL   The class *members are* debating among themselves.

▶ The scout troop ~~meet~~ *meets* in our basement on Tuesdays.

The meaning is singular because there is no reason to draw attention to the individual members of the troop. The troop as a whole meets in the basement.

▶ A young couple ~~was~~ *were* arguing about politics while holding hands.

The meaning is clearly plural. A collective unit doesn't argue and hold hands. Only individuals can engage in such activities.

NOTE: The phrase *the number* is treated as singular, *a number* as plural.

SINGULAR   *The number* of school-age children *is* declining.

PLURAL   *A number* of children *are* attending the wedding.

NOTE: When units of measurement are used collectively, treat them as singular.

Twenty-five miles is the greatest distance I have bicycled.

Three-fourths of the pie has been eaten.

Sixty-five dollars was more than we were willing to spend.

When units of measurement refer to individual persons or things, treat them as plural.

Nearly two-thirds of those who die in single-car accidents are drunk.

A majority of the board members plan to vote no.

21f Make the verb agree with its subject even when the subject follows the verb.

Verbs ordinarily follow subjects. When this normal order is reversed, it is easy to become confused. Sentences beginning with *there is* or *there are* (or *there was* or *there were*) are inverted; the subject follows the verb.

There *is* an *apple* on the counter.

are
▶ There ~~is~~ surprisingly few children in our neighborhood.

The subject is *children;* therefore the verb should be *are: children are.*

were
▶ There ~~was~~ a social worker and a crew of twenty volunteers.

The subject is compound and therefore plural: *worker and crew were.*

NOTE: Occasionally a writer may invert sentences for variety or effect.

are
▶ Behind the fence ~~is~~ a fierce dog and an even fiercer cat.

The compound subject *dog and cat* is plural, so the verb must be *are.*

21g Make the verb agree with its subject, not with a subject complement.

One basic sentence pattern in English consists of a subject, a linking verb, and a subject complement: *Jack is an attor-*

ney. Because the subject complement (*an attorney*) names or describes the subject (*Jack*), it is sometimes mistaken for the subject. (See 48c on subject complements.)

These *problems are* a way to test your skill.

▶ A tent and a sleeping bag ~~is~~ the required equipment.
    are

Tent and bag is the subject, not *equipment.*

▶ A major force in today's economy ~~are~~ women — as earners,
    is

consumers, and investors.

Force is the subject, not *women.* If the corrected version seems awkward, make *women* the subject: *Women are a major force in today's economy — as earners, consumers, and investors.*

21h Who, which, and that take verbs that agree with their antecedents.

Like most pronouns, the relative pronouns *who, which,* and *that* have antecedents, nouns or pronouns to which they refer. Relative pronouns used as subjects of subordinate clauses take verbs that agree with their antecedents.

Take a *suit that travels* well.

▶ Our ability to use language is one of the things that ~~sets~~ us
    set

apart from animals.

The relative pronoun *that* appears to have two possible antecedents, *one* and *things.* Only by considering the meaning of the sentence can the writer decide which word is in fact the antecedent. The sentence speaks of language ability as one of a group of things *all of which* set us apart from animals. Therefore the antecedent is *things,* and the verb should be *set: things that set.*

▶ The man decided that Frank was the only one of his four
        was
  sons who ~~were~~ responsible enough to handle the estate.
       ^

The antecedent of *who* is *one,* not *sons,* since the meaning is clearly singular: Only *one was* responsible enough.

21i Words such as *athletics, economics, mathematics, physics, statistics, measles, mumps,* and *news* are usually singular, despite their plural form.

       is
▶ Statistics ~~are~~ among the most difficult courses in our
       ^

program.

EXCEPTION: When the meaning is clearly plural, words ending in *-ics* are treated as plural: *The statistics are impressive.*

21j Titles of works and words mentioned as words are singular.

       describes
▶ *Lost Cities* ~~describe~~ the discoveries of many ancient
       ^

civilizations.

                  is
▶ *Controlled substances* ~~are~~ a euphemism for illegal drugs.
                 ^

EXERCISE 21 – 1

Underline the subject (or compound subject) and then select the verb that agrees with it. (If you have difficulty identifying the subject, consult 48a.) Answers to lettered sentences appear in the back of the book. Example:

Someone in the audience (has/have) volunteered to

participate in the experiment.

a. Your friendship over the years and your support on a wide variety of national issues (has/have) meant a great deal to us.
b. Two-week-old onion rings in the ashtray (is/are) not a pretty sight.
c. Neither of the police officers (was/were) called to testify.
d. The main source of income for Trinidad (is/are) oil and pitch.
e. There (is/are) several street people living by the tracks behind the mall.

1. Neither my cousin nor his rowdy friends (was/were) accused of the prank.
2. Quilts made by the Amish (commands/command) high prices.
3. Seized in the raid (was/were) $400 in cash, two color televisions, and a set of stereo speakers.
4. A tall glass of club soda with a twist of lime (suits/suit) me just fine at the end of a hard tennis match.
5. The old iron gate and the brick wall (makes/make) our courthouse appear older than its fifty years.
6. The dangers of smoking (is/are) well documented.
7. There (was/were) a Peanuts cartoon and a few Mother Goose rhymes pinned to the bulletin board.
8. When food supplies (was/were) scarce, the slaves had to make do with the less desirable parts of the animals.
9. The slaughter of pandas for their much-sought-after pelts (has/have) caused the panda population to decline dramatically.
10. Neither of the two new supervisors (has/have) earned the respect of the staff.

EXERCISE 21–2

Edit the following sentences for problems with subject-verb agreement. If a sentence is correct, write "correct" after it. Answers to lettered sentences appear in the back of the book. Example:

were
Jack's first days in the infantry ~~was~~ grueling.
∧

a. High concentrations of carbon monoxide result in headaches, dizziness, unconsciousness, and even death.
b. At the back of the room is an aquarium and a terrarium.
c. After hearing the evidence and the closing arguments, the jury was sequestered.
d. Crystal chandeliers, polished floors, and a new oil painting has transformed Sandra's apartment.
e. Either Alice or Jan usually work the midnight shift.

1. The board of directors, ignoring the wishes of the neighborhood, has voted to allow further development.
2. Of particular concern are penicillin and tetracyclinne, antibiotics used to make animals more resistant to disease.
3. I am one of those who does not believe that a national debt is a national blessing.
4. Nearly everyone on the panel favor the arms control agreement.
5. The federal government have established a meals-on-wheels program for senior citizens.
6. Until recently, economics was not considered a major academic field.
7. All of the witnesses claimed that neither Tom nor his partner was at the scene of the crime.
8. Steve Winwood, as well as Paul Simon, were attending the Grammy Award ceremony.
9. Sheila is the only one of the many applicants who has the ability to step into this position.
10. The key program of Alcoholics Anonymous are the twelve steps to recovery.

22

Make pronouns and antecedents agree.

The antecedent of a pronoun is the word the pronoun refers to. A pronoun and its antecedent agree when they are both singular or both plural.

SINGULAR   The *doctor* finished *her* rounds.

PLURAL   The *doctors* finished *their* rounds.

22a Do not use plural pronouns to refer to singular antecedents.

Occasionally a writer is tempted to use a plural pronoun even though its antecedent is singular, as in this sentence:

FAULTY   Every runner must train rigorously if they want to excel.

Notice that the plural pronoun *they* does not agree with its singular antecedent, *runner.* Some years ago it was acceptable to write *if he wants to excel,* trusting readers to understand that *he* really meant "he or she." Today, however, many readers find this use of *he* offensive because it excludes women. (See 17f.) One option is to write *he or she;* another is to use the plural.

SINGULAR   Every runner must train rigorously if he or she wants to excel.

PLURAL   Runners must train rigorously if they want to excel.

A third option is to restructure the sentence so that no problem of agreement arises.

RESTRUCTURED   To excel, a runner must train rigorously.

Depending on the sentence and the context, one of these options is likely to be more effective than the others, so it is best to experiment before settling on a revision. Try to be sparing in your use of *he or she* and *his or her.* These wordy constructions can be awkward when they echo throughout a paragraph or essay.

▶ The amount of annual leave a federal worker may accrue
  his or her
depends on ~~their~~ length of service.
            ∧

The singular antecedent *worker* demands the singular construction *his or her.* The writer could have changed the antecedent to the plural instead: *The amount of annual leave federal workers may accrue depends on their length of service.*

                              men and women   *know*
▶ The navy has much to offer ~~any man or woman~~ who ~~knows~~
                              ∧   ∧
what they want.

Here the writer decided to make the antecedent plural to match the plural pronoun *they.* Notice that the verb *knows* must be changed to *know: men and women who know.*

22b Treat most indefinite pronouns as singular.

Indefinite pronouns are pronouns that do not refer to specific persons or things. *Any, anyone, anybody, each, either, everyone, everybody, everything, neither, none, no one, someone,* and *something* are examples. Many of these words appear to have plural meanings and are treated as such in casual speech. But in formal English they are nearly always considered singular.

Someone has left *her* purse under the desk.

                                    his or her
▶ At some time in life everyone has had ~~their~~ rights violated.
                                        ∧

The writer treated *everyone* as singular when selecting the verb *has* but as plural when choosing the pronoun *their.* This is inconsistent, but it is fairly common when a writer is trying to avoid *his* or the wordy *his or her* construction. One way to skirt the problem is to change *everyone* to *we*: *At some time in life we have all had our rights violated.*

▶ I was taught that no one ⋀ could escape the fires of purgatory ⋅

~~if they wanted to reach heaven.~~

who wanted to reach heaven

Here the writer, not wanting to change *they* to *he or she*, re-structured the sentence. The pronoun *who* applies to persons of either sex, so no problem of agreement arises.

▶ A year later somebody finally admitted ~~that they were~~ ⋀

involved in the kidnapping.

having been

With the word *they* eliminated, no problem of agreement arises.

22c Treat collective nouns as singular unless the meaning is clearly plural.

Collective nouns such as *jury, committee, audience, crowd, class, troop, family, team,* and *couple* name a class or a group. Ordinarily the group functions as a unit, so the noun should be treated as singular; if the members of the group function as individuals, however, the noun should be treated as plural.

AS A UNIT	The *committee* granted *its* permission to build.
AS INDIVIDUALS	The *committee* put *their* signatures on the document.

▶ The jury has reached ~~their~~ decision.

its

There is no reason to draw attention to the individual members of the jury, so *jury* should be treated as singular. Notice also that the writer treated the noun as singular when choosing the verb *has*, so for consistency the pronoun must be *its*.

their
▶ The audience shouted "Bravo" and stamped ~~its~~ feet.

It is difficult to see how the audience as a unit can stamp *its* feet. The meaning here is clearly plural, requiring *their*.

22d Treat most compound antecedents connected by *and* as plural.

Joanne and John moved to the mountains, where *they* built a log cabin.

22e With compound antecedents connected by *or* or *nor*, make the pronoun agree with the nearer antecedent.

Either *Bruce* or *James* should receive first prize for *his* sculpture.

Neither the *lawyer* nor the *accountants* could trace *their* mistake.

NOTE: If one of the antecedents is singular and the other plural, as in the second example, put the plural one last to avoid awkwardness.

EXERCISE 22 – 1

Edit the following sentences to eliminate problems with pronoun-antecedent agreement. Most of the sentences can be revised in more than one way, so experiment before choosing a solution. If a sentence is correct, write "correct" after it. Revisions of lettered sentences appear in the back of the book. Example:

his or her
In this class everyone performs at ~~their~~ own fitness level.
    ∧

a. An employee on extended leave may continue their life insurance.
b. The freshman class elects its president tomorrow.
c. When I looked out the window of our tenement during these periods of insomnia, I sometimes saw a priest or a brother entering the side door of the church, their faces silhouetted briefly in the moonlight.
d. When a person has been drinking or using drugs, they are more likely to abuse their children.
e. If you have anyone attending class who is still not on your roster, please send them to the registration office.

1. If a driver refuses to take a blood or breath test, he or she will have their licenses suspended for six months.
2. An adult panda must consume ninety pounds of bamboo if they are to remain healthy.
3. No one should be forced to sacrifice their prized possession — life — for someone else.
4. Everyone who wants to see the movie must give Joyce the money for their ticket today.
5. The recruiter may tell the truth, but there is much that they choose not to tell.
6. The committee plans to distribute copies of their proposal on Monday.
7. Every applicant wants to know how much they will make.
8. By the final curtain, ninety percent of the audience had voted with their feet.
9. A mountain climber must shift his or her emphasis from self-preservation to group survival. They must learn to rely completely on others.
10. The Old and New Testaments are alike in their insistence on the primacy of love, mercy, and justice.

23

Make pronoun references clear.

Pronouns substitute for nouns; they are a kind of shorthand. In a sentence like *After Andrew intercepted the ball, he kicked it as hard as he could,* the pronouns *he* and *it* substitute for the nouns *Andrew* and *ball.* The word a pronoun refers to is called its *antecedent.*

23a   Avoid ambiguous or remote pronoun reference.

Ambiguous pronoun reference occurs when the pronoun could refer to two possible antecedents.

▶ ~~When Gloria set the pitcher~~ on the glass-topped table,~~.~~it
  The pitcher broke when Gloria set it
  ~~broke.~~

Tom told James ,~~that he had~~ won the lottery.~~"~~
  "You have

What broke — the table or the pitcher? Who won the lottery — Tom or James? The revisions eliminate the ambiguity.

Remote pronoun reference occurs when a pronoun is too far away from its antecedent for easy reading.

▶ After the court ordered my ex-husband to pay child support,

he refused. Approximately eight months later, we were back

in court. This time the court ordered him to make payments

directly to the Support and Collections Unit, which would in

turn pay me. For the first six months I received regular

payments, but then they stopped. Again ~~he~~ was summoned
my ex-husband
                 ∧

to appear in court; he did not respond.

The pronoun *he* was too distant from its antecedent, *ex-husband,* which appeared several sentences earlier.

23b Avoid the vague use of *this, that,* and *which.*

The pronouns *this, that,* and *which* should not refer vaguely to earlier word groups or ideas. These pronouns should refer to specific antecedents. When a pronoun's reference is too vague, either replace the pronoun with a noun or supply an antecedent to which the pronoun clearly refers.

▶ More and more often, especially in large cities, we are

finding ourselves victims of serious crimes. We learn to
our fate
accept ~~this~~ with minor gripes and groans.
       ∧

For clarity the writer substituted a noun (*fate*) for the pronoun *this,* which referred loosely to the idea expressed in the preceding sentence.

▶ Romeo and Juliet were both too young to have acquired
a fact
much wisdom, which accounts for their rash actions.
        ∧

The writer added an antecedent (*fact*) that the pronoun *which* clearly refers to.

23c **Do not use a pronoun to refer to an implied antecedent.**

A pronoun must refer to a specific antecedent, not to a word that is implied but not present in the sentence.

the braids

▶ After braiding Ann's hair, Sue decorated ~~them~~ with ribbons.
  ∧

The pronoun *them* referred to Ann's braids (implied by the term *braiding*), but the word *braids* did not appear in the sentence.

Modifiers, such as possessives, cannot serve as antecedents. A modifier may strongly imply the noun that the pronoun might logically refer to, but it is not itself that noun.

Euripides

▶ In ~~Euripides'~~ *Medea,* ~~he~~ describes the plight of a woman
  ∧

rejected by her husband.

The pronoun *he* cannot refer logically to the possessive modifier *Euripides'*. The revision substitutes the noun *Euripides* for the pronoun *he,* thereby eliminating the problem.

23d **Avoid the indefinite use of *they, it,* and *you.***

Do not use the pronoun *they* to refer indefinitely to persons who have not been specifically mentioned. *They* should always refer to a specific antecedent.

▶ Sometimes a list of ways to save energy is included with the
    the gas company suggests
  gas bill. For example, ~~they suggest~~ setting a moderate
                          ∧

temperature for the hot water heater.

The word *it* should not be used indefinitely in constructions such as "In the article it says that. . . ."

▶ ~~In the~~ *The* report ~~it~~ points out that lifting the ban on Compound

1080, a long-lifed pesticide, would prove detrimental to the

bald eagle.

The pronoun *you* is appropriate when the writer is addressing the reader directly: *Once you have kneaded the dough, let it rise in a warm place.* (See 3b.) Except in very informal contexts, however, the indefinite *you* (meaning "anyone in general") is inappropriate.

▶ In Ethiopia ~~you don't~~ *one doesn't* need much property to be considered

well off.

If the pronoun *one* seems too stilted, the writer might recast the sentence: *Ethiopians don't need much property to be considered well off.*

23e To refer to persons, use *who, whom,* or *whose,* not *that* or *which.*

In most contexts, use *who, whom,* or *whose* to refer to persons, *that* or *which* to refer to animals or things. Although *that* is occasionally used to refer to persons, it is more polite to use a form of *who. Which* is reserved only for animals or things, so it is impolite to use it to refer to persons.

▶ When he heard about my seven children, four of ~~which~~ *whom* lived

at home, Gill smiled and said, "I love children."

ref

▶ Fans wondered how an out-of-shape old man ~~that~~ walked *who*

with a limp could play football.

NOTE: Occasionally *whose* may be used to refer to animals and things to avoid the awkward *of which* construction.

▶ It is a tree ~~the~~ name ~~of which~~ I have forgotten. *whose*

EXERCISE 23 – 1

Edit the following sentences to correct errors in pronoun reference. In some cases you will need to decide on an antecedent that the pronoun might logically refer to. Revisions of lettered sentences appear in the back of the book. Example:

Following the breakup of AT&T, many other companies began to offer long-distance phone service. ~~This~~ has led to *The competition*

lower long-distance rates.

a. The detective removed the blood-stained shawl from the body and then photographed it.
b. In Professor Johnson's class, you are lucky to earn a C.
c. I am proud of all my children, three of which have become legislators.
d. The Comanche braves' lifestyle was particularly violent; they gained respect for their skill as warriors.
e. All students can secure parking permits from the campus police office; they are open from 8 A.M. until 8 P.M.

1. The racetrack is well equipped for emergencies. They even have an ambulance at the track on racing days.

2. Many people believe that the polygraph test is highly reliable if you employ a licensed examiner.

3. We expected the concert to last for at least two hours. Since the average ticket sells for twenty dollars, this was not being unrealistic.

4. In my hometown, you "wait on" the bus and "fix" dinner and go to the store for "light bread."

5. In the encyclopedia it states that male moths can smell female moths from several miles away.

6. Marianne told Jenny that she was worried about her mother's illness.

7. Employees are beginning to take advantage of the company's athletic facilities. They offer squash and tennis courts, a small track, and several trampolines.

8. Uncle John still felt uneasy about taking Mary Jane with him on house calls, which was offset by her cheerful chatter and delight in the scenery.

9. The transportation specialist reviews the airlines' tariffs to determine if they have added any new fares applicable to government travelers.

10. My favorite newcasters are those which reveal their point of view.

24

Use personal pronouns and nouns in the proper case.

The personal pronouns in the following chart change what is known as case form according to their grammatical function in a sentence. Pronouns functioning as subjects (or subject complements) appear in the *subjective* case; those functioning as objects appear in the *objective* case; and those functioning as possessives appear in the *possessive* case.

	SUBJECTIVE CASE	OBJECTIVE CASE	POSSESSIVE CASE
SINGULAR	I	me	my
	you	you	your
	he/she/it	him/her/it	her/his/its
PLURAL	we	us	our
	you	you	your
	they	them	their

Pronouns in the subjective and objective cases are frequently confused. Most of the rules in this section specify when to use one or the other of these cases (*I* or *me, he* or *him,* and so on). Rule 24g details a special use of pronouns and nouns in the possessive case.

24a Use the subjective case (*I, you, he, she, we, they*) for subjects and subject complements.

When personal pronouns are used as subjects, ordinarily your ear will tell you the correct pronoun. Problems sometimes arise, however, with compound word groups containing a pronoun, so it is not always safe to trust your ear.

▶ Joel ran away from home because his stepfather and ~~him~~ *he*

had quarreled.

His stepfather and he is the subject of the verb *had quarreled.* If we strip away the words *his stepfather and,* the correct pronoun becomes clear: *he had quarreled* (not *him had quarreled*).

When a pronoun is used as a subject complement (a word following a linking verb), your ear may mislead you, since the correct form is infrequently heard in casual speech. (See subject complement, 48c.)

▶ Sandra confessed that the artist was ~~her.~~ *she*

The pronoun *she* functions as a subject complement with the linking verb *was*. In formal, written English, subject complements must be in the subjective case. If your ear rejects *artist was she* as too stilted, try rewriting the sentence: *Sandra confessed that she was the artist.*

24b Use the objective case (*me, you, him, her, us, them*) for all objects.

When a personal pronoun is used as a direct object, an indirect object, or the object of a preposition, ordinarily your ear will lead you to the correct pronoun. When an object is compound, however, you may occasionally become confused.

▶ Janice was indignant when she realized that the salesclerk

was insulting her mother and ~~she.~~ *her.*

Her mother and her is the direct object of the verb *was insulting.* Strip away the words *her mother and* to hear the correct pronoun: *was insulting her* (not *was insulting she*).

▶ Father Minnorra gave Dorrie and ~~she~~ *her* each a white flower.

Dorrie and her is the indirect object of the verb *gave.* We would not say *gave she a white flower.*

▶ Geoffrey went with my family and ~~I~~ *me* to King's Dominion.

Me is the object of the preposition *with.* We would not say *Geoffrey went with I.*

When in doubt about the correct pronoun, some writers try to evade making the choice by using a reflexive pronoun such as *myself.* Such evasions are nonstandard, even though they are used by some educated persons.

▶ The Egyptian cab driver gave my husband and ~~myself~~ *me* some

good tips on traveling in North Africa.

My husband and me is the indirect object of the verb *gave*. For correct uses of *myself*, see the Glossary of Usage at the back of the book.

24c Put an appositive and the word it refers to in the same case.

Appositives are noun phrases that rename nouns or pronouns. Any pronouns that appear in an appositive are assumed to have the same function (usually subject or object) as the word(s) the appositive renames.

▶ At the drama festival, two actors, Christina and ~~me~~ *I*, were

selected to do the last scene of *King Lear*.

The appositive *Christina and I* renames the subject (*actors*).

▶ The college interviewed only two applicants for the job,

Professor Stevens and ~~I~~ *me*.

The appositve *Professor Stevens and me* renames the direct object (*applicants*).

24d In elliptical constructions, choose the pronoun that would be appropriate if the construction were completed.

Elliptical constructions are those in which words are understood or omitted. Sentence parts, usually verbs, are often omitted in comparisons beginning with *than* or *as*. In such cases, finish the sentence mentally and your ear will tell you the correct pronoun.

▶ My husband is six years older than ~~me~~.
(I)

I is the subject of the verb *am*, which is understood: *My husband is six years older than I (am)*. If the correct English seems too formal, you can always add the verb.

▶ We respected no other candidate as much as ~~she~~.
(her)

This sentence means that we respected no other candidate as much as (*we respected*) *her*. *Her* is the direct object of an understood verb.

24e When deciding whether *we* or *us* should precede a noun, choose the pronoun that would be appropriate if the noun were omitted.

▶ ~~Us~~ tenants would rather fight than move.
(We)

Management is short-changing ~~we~~ tenants.
(us)

No one would say *Us would rather fight than move* or *Management is short-changing we*.

24f Use the objective case for subjects of infinitives.

Subjects of infinitives are an exception to the general rule that subjects must be in the subjective case. Whenever an infinitive has a subject, it must be in the objective case.

▶ We expected Chris and ~~he~~ to win the doubles championship.
(him)

Chris and him is the subject of the infinitive *to win*.

24g Use the possessive case to modify a gerund.

A gerund is a verb form ending in *-ing* that functions as a noun. Gerunds frequently appear in phrases, in which case the whole gerund phrase functions as a noun. (See 49c.) If a pronoun or a noun modifies a gerund or a gerund phrase, it should appear in the possessive case: *her leaving, the girl's leaving.*

▶ John Lennon's involvement with Yoko Ono gradually led to *his* ~~him~~ losing interest in the Beatles.

The possessive pronoun *his* modifies the gerund phrase *losing interest in the Beatles.*

▶ We had to pay a fifty-dollar fine for ~~Brenda~~ *Brenda's* driving without a permit.

The possessive noun *Brenda's* modifies the gerund phrase *driving without a permit.*

Gerund phrases should not be confused with participial phrases, which function as adjectives, not as nouns: *We saw Brenda driving a yellow convertible.* Here *driving a yellow convertible* is a participial phrase modifying the noun *Brenda.* (See 49c.)

NOTE: Do not use the possessive if it creates an awkward effect. Try to reword the sentence instead.

AWKWARD	The president agreed to the applications' being reviewed by a faculty committee.
REVISED	The president agreed that the applications could be reviewed by a faculty committee.

EXERCISE 24 – 1

Edit the following sentences to eliminate errors in case. If a sentence is correct, write "correct" after it. Answers to lettered sentences appear in the back of the book. Example:

> *We*
> ~~Us~~ women really have come a long way.
> ∧

a. The most traumatic experience for her father and I occurred long after her operation.

b. Andrea whispered, "Who's there?" and Alfred replied softly that it was he.

c. The supervisor claimed that she was much more experienced than I.

d. The winners, Julie and him, were unable to attend the awards ceremony.

e. My father always tolerated us whispering after the lights were out.

1. Doctors should take more seriously what us patients say about our treatment.

2. Grandfather said he would give anything to live nearer to Paulette and me.

3. Even though he is constantly being ridiculed by the other boys, Norman is much better off than them.

4. In February 1970, several other Americans and myself were stalking an unseen enemy through the stifling jungles of South Vietnam.

5. Because of last night's fire, we are fed up with him drinking and smoking.

6. While diving for pearls, Ikiko and she found a treasure chest full of gold bars.

7. The swirling cyclone caused he and his horse to race for shelter.

8. The four candidates — Paul, Erica, Tracy, and I — will participate in tonight's televised debate.

9. During the testimony the witness pointed directly at the defendant and announced that the thief was him.

10. When in Aruba, Marlena bought several shell paintings for Donelle and I.

25

Use *who* and *whom* in the proper case.

Who and *whom* are relative pronouns used to introduce subordinate clauses. They are also interrogative pronouns used to open questions.

   Who, a subjective-case pronoun, can be used only for subjects and subject complements. *Whom*, an objective-case pronoun, can be used only for objects. (For more about pronoun case, see 24.)

25a Use the relative pronouns *who* and *whom* in the proper case.

When *who* and *whom* (or *whoever* and *whomever*) appear in subordinate clauses, their case is determined by their function *within the clause they introduce*. To choose the correct pronoun, you must isolate the subordinate clause and then look at its internal structure. (See subordinate clauses, 49b.) In the following examples, the relative pronouns function as subjects in the subordinate clauses.

▶ The prize goes to the runner ~~whom~~ *who* collects the most points.

The subordinate clause is *who collects the most points.* The verb of the clause is *collects,* and its subject is *who.*

▶ He tells that story to ~~whomever~~ *whoever* will listen.

The writer selected the pronoun *whomever* thinking that it was the object of the preposition *to.* However, the object of the preposition is the entire noun clause *whoever will listen.* The verb of the clause is *will listen,* and its subject is *whoever.*

When it functions as an object in a subordinate clause, *whom* appears out of order, before both the subject and the verb. To choose the correct pronoun, you must mentally restructure the clause.

▶ You will work with our senior industrial engineers, ~~who~~ *whom* you

    will meet later.

The subordinate clause is *whom you will meet later*. The subject of the clause is *you*, the verb is *will meet*, and *whom* is the direct object of the verb. This becomes clear if we mentally restructure the clause: *you will meet whom*.

▶ The tutor ~~who~~ *whom* I was assigned to was very supportive.

Whom is the object of the preposition *to*. That preposition can be moved in front of its object to make smoother reading: *The tutor to whom I was assigned was very supportive.*

NOTE: Inserted expressions such as *they know*, *I think*, and *she says* should be ignored in determining the case of a relative pronoun.

▶ All of the show-offs, bullies, and tough guys in school want

    to take on a big guy ~~whom~~ *who* they know won't hurt them.

Who is the subject of *won't hurt*, not the object of *know*.

25b Use the interrogative pronouns *who* and *whom* in the proper case.

When *who* and *whom* are used to open questions, their case is determined by their function within the question. For example, *who* functions as the subject of this question:

▶ ~~Whom~~ *Who* is responsible for this dastardly deed?

Who is the subject of the verb *is*. Most writers will use the correct form in this sentence without even thinking about grammar. The writer who selected *whom* was probably overcorrecting, using the form that seemed to be "more correct."

When *whom* appears as an object in a question, it appears out of order, before both the subject and the verb. To choose the correct pronoun, you must mentally restructure the question.

> *Whom*
> ► ~~Who~~ did the committee select?
> ⋀

Whom is the direct object of the verb *did select*. To choose the correct pronoun, restructure the question: *The committee did select whom?*

> *Whom*
> ► ~~Who~~ did you enter into the contract with?
> ⋀

Whom is the object of the preposition *with*, as is clear once the question has been restructured: *You did enter into the contract with whom?*

USAGE NOTE: In spoken English *who* is frequently used to open a question even when it functions as an object: *Who did Joe replace?* Although some readers will accept such constructions in informal written English, it is safer to use the correct form *whom: Whom did Joe replace?*

EXERCISE 25 – 1

Edit the following sentences to eliminate errors in the use of *who* and *whom* (or *whoever* and *whomever*). If a sentence is correct, write "correct" after it. Answers to lettered sentences appear in the back of the book. Example:

> *whom*
> What is the name of the person ~~who~~ you are sponsoring for
> ⋀
> membership in the club?

a. In his first production of *Hamlet*, who did Laurence Olivier replace?
b. Who was Martin Luther King's mentor?
c. Datacall allows you to talk to whoever needs you no matter where you are in the building.
d. Some group leaders cannot handle the pressure; they give whomever makes the most noise most of their attention.
e. The shift supervisor will ask you to relieve whoever you think needs a break.

1. One of the women whom Johnson hired became the most successful lawyer in the agency.
2. Samuels hoped to become the business partner of whomever found the treasure.
3. Now that you have seen both fighters in action, who in your opinion will win the championship?
4. Mr. Barnes is the elementary school teacher who I recall most fondly.
5. Who conferred with Roosevelt and Stalin at Yalta in 1945?
6. They will become business partners with whoever is willing to contribute to the company's coffers.
7. When a horse clattered by, carrying a lone body with a jack-o'-lantern head, even those of us who knew about the trick were startled.
8. The elderly woman who I was asked to take care of was a clever, delightful companion.
9. Ada always seemed to be bestowing a favor on whomever she worked for.
10. Who did the president nominate to be our next secretary of state?

26

Choose adjectives and adverbs with care.

Adjectives ordinarily modify nouns or pronouns; occasionally they function as subject complements following linking verbs. Adverbs modify verbs, adjectives, or other adverbs. (See 47d and 47e.)

Many adverbs are formed by adding *-ly* to adjectives (*formal, formally; smooth, smoothly*). But don't assume that all words ending in *-ly* are adverbs or that all adverbs end in *-ly*. Some adjectives end in *-ly* (*lovely, friendly*) and some adverbs don't (*always, here, there*). When in doubt, consult a dictionary.

26a Use adverbs, not adjectives, to modify verbs, adjectives, and adverbs.

When adverbs modify verbs (or verbal phrases), they nearly always answer the question When? Where? How? Why? Under what conditions? How often? or To what degree? When adverbs modify adjectives or other adverbs, they usually qualify or intensify the meaning of the word they modify. (See adverbs, 47e.)

The incorrect use of adjectives in place of adverbs to modify verbs occurs primarily in casual or nonstandard speech.

▶ The arrangement worked out ~~perfect~~ *perfectly* for everyone.

We discovered that the patients hadn't been bathed ~~regular.~~ *regularly*

Perfect and *regular* are adjectives, so they should not be used to modify the verbs *worked* and *had been bathed*.

The incorrect use of the adjective *good* in place of the adverb *well* is especially common in casual and nonstandard speech.

▶ We were surprised to hear that Louise had done so ~~good~~ *well* on the CPA exam.

The adverb *well* (not the adjective *good*) should be used to modify the verb *had done*.

Adjectives are sometimes used incorrectly to modify adjectives or adverbs.

▶ For a man eighty years old, Joe plays golf ~~real~~ well.
really

We were ~~awful~~ sorry to hear about your uncle's death.
awfully

Only adverbs can be used to modify adjectives or other adverbs. *Really* intensifies the meaning of the adverb *well*, and *awfully* intensifies the meaning of the adjective *sorry*. The writers could of course substitute other intensifiers: *very well*, for example, or *terribly sorry*.

26b Use adjectives, not adverbs, as subject complements.

Adjectives ordinarily precede nouns, but they can also function as subject complements following linking verbs (see 48c). When an adjective functions as a subject complement, it describes the subject:

Justice is *blind*.

Problems can arise with verbs such as *smell, taste, look,* and *feel*, which may or may not be linking. If the word following one of these verbs describes the subject, use an adjective; if it modifies the verb, use an adverb.

ADJECTIVE   The detective looked *cautious*.

ADVERB   The detective looked *cautiously* for fingerprints.

The adjective *cautious* describes the detective; the adverb *cautiously* modifies the verb *looked*.

Linking verbs suggest states of being, not actions. Notice, for example, the different meanings of *looked* in the preceding examples. To look cautious suggests the state of being cautious; to look cautiously is to perform an action in a cautious way.

▶ The lilacs in our backyard smell especially ~~sweetly~~ *sweet* this year.

Lori looked ~~well~~ *good* in her new raincoat.

The verbs *smell* and *looked* suggest states of being, not actions. Therefore, they should be followed by adjectives, not adverbs. (Contrast with action verbs: *We smelled the flowers. Lori looked for her raincoat.*)

26c Use adjectives, not adverbs, as object complements.

Although adjectives ordinarily precede nouns, occasionally they function as object complements following direct objects. (See 48c). When an adjective functions as an object complement, it describes the direct object.

Sorrow makes us *wise*.

Object complements occur with verbs such as *call, consider, create, find, keep,* and *make.* When a modifier follows the direct object of one of these verbs, check to see whether it functions as an adjective describing the direct object or as an adverb modifying the verb.

ADJECTIVE   The referee called the plays *perfect.*

ADVERB   The referee called the plays *perfectly.*

The first sentence means that the referee considered the plays to be perfect; the second means that the referee did an excellent job of calling the plays.

▶ God created all men and women ~~equally.~~ *equal.*

The adjective *equal* is an object complement describing the direct object *men and women*.

26d Use the comparative to compare two things, the superlative to compare three or more things.

Most adjectives and adverbs have three forms: the positive, the comparative, and the superlative.

POSITIVE	COMPARATIVE	SUPERLATIVE
soft	softer	softest
fast	faster	fastest
careful	more careful	most careful
bad	worse	worst
good	better	best

Writers occasionally confuse the comparative and superlative forms.

▶ Which of these two brands of toothpaste is ~~best~~? *better*

Though Shaw and Jackson are impressive, Hobbs is the ~~more~~ *most* qualified of the three candidates running for mayor.

Since two brands are being compared in the first sentence, the comparative form *better* is appropriate; because three candidates are being compared in the second sentence, the superlative form *most* is appropriate.

26e Form comparatives and superlatives according to convention.

To form comparatives and superlatives of most one- and two-syllable adjectives, use the endings *-er* and *-est: smooth, smoother, smoothest; easy, easier, easiest.* With longer adjectives, use *more* and *most* (or *less* and *least* for downward comparisons): *exciting, more exciting, most exciting; helpful, less helpful, least helpful.*

Some one-syllable adverbs take the endings *-er* and *-est* (*fast, faster, fastest*), but longer adverbs and all of those ending in *-ly* form the comparative and superlative with *more* and *most* (or *less* and *least*).

The comparative and superlative forms of the following adjectives and adverbs are irregular: *good, better, best; bad, worse, worst; badly, worse, worst.*

▶ The Kirov was the ~~superbest~~ ballet company we had ever
                    most superb
seen.

▶ Lloyd's luck couldn't have been ~~worser~~ than David's.
                                  worse

26f Do not use double comparatives or superlatives.

If you have added *-er* or *-est* to an adjective or an adverb, do not also use *more* or *most* (or *less* or *least*).

▶ Of all her family, Julia is ~~most~~ happiest about the move.

▶ That is the most ~~vilest~~ joke I have ever heard.
                    vile

26g Do not use comparatives or superlatives with absolute concepts such as *unique* or *perfect.*

Avoid expressions such as *more straight, less perfect, very round,* and *most unique.* Either something is *unique* or it isn't. It is illogical to suggest that absolute concepts come in degrees.

▶ That is the most ~~unique~~ *unusual* wedding gown I have ever seen.

▶ The painting would have been even more ~~priceless~~ *valuable* had it

been signed.

EXERCISE 26 – 1

Edit the following sentences to eliminate errors in the use of adjectives and adverbs. If a sentence is correct, write "correct" after it. Answers to lettered sentences appear in the back of the book. Example:

> When I watched Carl run the 440 on Saturday, I was amazed
> *well*
> at how ~~good~~ he paced himself.

a. My mechanic showed me exactly where to wrap the wire firm around the muffler.

b. Bill's apple fritters taste real good.

c. My mother thinks that Carmen is the most pleasant of the twins.

d. The vaulting box, commonly known as the horse, is the easiest of the four pieces of equipment to master.

e. Last Christmas was the most perfect day of my life.

1. Mr. Miller visits his doctor regularly for a complete physical.

2. Which restaurant do you think makes the better hamburger, McDonald's, Burger King, or Wendy's?

3. We wanted a hunting dog. We didn't care if he smelled badly, but we really did not want him to smell bad.

4. When I hear one of my children call me in the night, I jump out of bed real quick.

5. Phyllis dresses in the most unique style.

6. The manager must see that the office runs smooth and efficient.

7. Eammon wondered which of his two rivals was the smarter.

8. Of all my relatives, Uncle Robert is the most cleverest.

9. Please make my steak rare and my iced tea sweet.

10. Marcia performed very well at her Drama Club audition.

27

Choose verbs with care.

The verb is the heart of the sentence, so it is important to get it right. Section 21 dealt with the problem of subject-verb agreement. This section describes a number of other potential problems involving verbs.

VERB FORMS

Except for the verb *be*, all verbs in English have five forms. The following chart lists the five forms and provides a sample sentence in which each might appear.

INFINITIVE	Today I (*walk, ride*).
PAST TENSE	Yesterday I (*walked, rode*).
PAST PARTICIPLE	I have (*walked, ridden*) many times before.
PRESENT PARTICIPLE	I am (*walking, riding*) right now.
-S FORM	He/she/it (*walks, rides*) regularly.

Both the past-tense and past-participle forms of regular verbs end in *-ed* (*walked, walked*). Irregular verbs form the past tense and past participle in other ways (*rode, ridden*).

The verb *be* has eight forms instead of the usual five: *be, am, is, are, was, were, being, been.*

27a Use the correct forms of irregular verbs.

For all regular verbs, the past-tense and past-participle forms are the same (ending in *-ed* or *-d*), so there is no danger of confusion. This is not true, however, for irregular verbs, such as the following:

INFINITIVE	PAST TENSE	PAST PARTICIPLE
go	went	gone
fight	fought	fought
fly	flew	flown

You will find a list of irregular verbs beginning on page 196.

The past-tense form of a verb, used to express action that occurred entirely in the past, never has a helping verb.

Last week Chris *went* to Harbor Island.

The past-participle form is used with a helping verb, either with *has, have,* or *had* to form one of the perfect tenses (see tenses on p. 201) or with *be, am, is, are, was, were, being,* or *been* to form the passive voice (see 48b).

Betty *has fought* for equal rights for women.

Kate *was flown* to Bishop Hill to accept the award.

In nonstandard speech, the past-tense and past-participle forms may differ from those of standard English, as in the following sentences.

▶ Yesterday we ~~seen~~ *saw* an unidentified flying object.

The reality of the situation finally ~~sunk~~ *sank* in.

Because there are no helping verbs, the past-tense forms *saw* and *sank* are required.

▶ The driver had apparently ~~fell~~ *fallen* asleep at the wheel.

The teacher asked Dwain if he had ~~did~~ *done* his homework.

Because of the helping verbs, the past-participle forms are required: *had fallen, had done.*

When in doubt about the standard English forms of irregular verbs, consult the following list or look up the infinitive form of the verb in the dictionary, which also lists any irregular forms. (If no additional forms are listed, the verb is regular, not irregular.)

Common irregular verbs

INFINITIVE	PAST TENSE	PAST PARTICIPLE
arise	arose	arisen
awake	awoke	awaked
be	was, were	been
beat	beat	beaten, beat
become	became	become
begin	began	begun
bend	bent	bent
bite	bit	bitten, bit
blow	blew	blown
break	broke	broken
bring	brought	brought
build	built	built
burst	burst	burst
catch	caught	caught
choose	chose	chosen
cling	clung	clung
come	came	come
cost	cost	cost
deal	dealt	dealt
dig	dug	dug
dive	dived, dove	dived
do	did	done
drag	dragged	dragged
draw	drew	drawn
dream	dreamed, dreamt	dreamed, dreamt
drink	drank	drunk
drive	drove	driven

INFINITIVE	PAST TENSE	PAST PARTICIPLE
drown	drowned	drowned
eat	ate	eaten
fall	fell	fallen
fight	fought	fought
find	found	found
fly	flew	flown
forget	forgot	forgotten, forgot
freeze	froze	frozen
get	got	gotten, got
give	gave	given
go	went	gone
grow	grew	grown
hang (suspend)	hung	hung
hang (execute)	hanged	hanged
have	had	had
hear	heard	heard
hide	hid	hidden
hurt	hurt	hurt
keep	kept	kept
know	knew	known
lay (put)	laid	laid
lead	led	led
lend	lent	lent
let (allow)	let	let
lie (recline)	lay	lain
lose	lost	lost
make	made	made
prove	proved	proved, proven
read	read	read
ride	rode	ridden
ring	rang	rung
rise (get up)	rose	risen
run	ran	run
say	said	said
see	saw	seen
send	sent	sent
set (place)	set	set
shake	shook	shaken
shoot	shot	shot

INFINITIVE	PAST TENSE	PAST PARTICIPLE
shrink	shrank, shrunk	shrunk, shrunken
sing	sang, sung	sung
sink	sank, sunk	sunk
sit (be seated)	sat	sat
slay	slew	slain
sleep	slept	slept
speak	spoke	spoken
spin	spun	spun
spring	sprang, sprung	sprung
stand	stood	stood
steal	stole	stolen
sting	stung	stung
strike	struck	struck, stricken
swear	swore	sworn
swim	swam	swum
swing	swung	swung
take	took	taken
teach	taught	taught
throw	threw	thrown
wake	woke, waked	waked, woken
wear	wore	worn
wring	wrung	wrung
write	wrote	written

27b Distinguish among the forms of *lie* and *lay*.

Writers and speakers frequently confuse the various forms of *lie* (meaning to recline or rest on a surface) and *lay* (meaning to put or place something). *Lie* is an intransitive verb; it does not take a direct object: *The tax forms lie on the table.* The verb *lay* is transitive; it takes a direct object: *Please lay the tax forms on the coffee table.* (See 48b and 48c.)

In addition to confusing the meaning of *lie* and *lay*, writers and speakers are often unfamiliar with the standard English forms of these verbs.

INFINITIVE	PAST TENSE	PAST PARTICIPLE	PRESENT PARTICIPLE
lie	lay	lain	lying
lay	laid	laid	laying

▶ Sue was so exhausted that she ~~laid~~ *lay* down for a nap.

The past-tense form of *lie* (to recline) is *lay.*

▶ The patient had ~~laid~~ *lain* in an uncomfortable position all night.

The past-participle form of *lie* (to recline) is *lain.*

▶ Mary ~~lay~~ *laid* the baby on my lap.

The past-tense form of *lay* (to place) is *laid.*

▶ My grandmother's letters were ~~laying~~ *lying* in the corner of the chest.

The present participle of *lie* (to rest on a surface) is *lying.*

EXERCISE 27–1

Edit the following sentences for problems with irregular verbs. If a sentence is correct, write "correct" after it. Answers to lettered sentences appear in the back of the book. Example:

> Was it you I ~~seen~~ *saw* last night at the concert?

a. Last June my cousin Albert swum the length of the lake in forty minutes.
b. When I get the urge to exercise, I lay down until it passes.
c. On our way to the airport we realized that Bob had forgotten to pick up our passports from the hotel.

    d. The team of engineers watched in horror as the newly built dam bursted and flooded the small valley.

    e. The young girl looked soulfully into her mother's eyes as she laid the wheezing puppy on its mat.

1. How many times have you swore to yourself, "I'll diet tomorrow, after one more piece of cheesecake"?
2. The girl said that she had been having difficulty sleeping, laying awake, because she feared the dark.
3. How did the detective know that the suspect had went to the office on the night of the murder?
4. When Sarah saw Mr. Johnson coming home from the corner store, she ran over to him to see if he had brung her some candy.
5. All parents were asked to send a mat for their children to lay on.
6. The officer practically thrown Jim into the transport wagon.
7. Have you ever dreamed that you were falling from a cliff or flying through the air?
8. I locked my brakes, leaned the motorcycle to the left, and laid it down to keep from slamming into the fence.
9. In her junior year, Cindy run the 440-yard dash in 51.1 seconds.
10. We apologized for having broke the vase.

TENSE

Tenses indicate the time of an action in relation to the time of the speaking or writing about that action. Tenses are classified as present, past, and future, with simple, perfect, and progressive forms for each.

    The simple tenses indicate relatively simple time relations. The present tense is used primarily for actions occurring at the time of the speaking or for actions occurring regularly. The past tense is used for actions completed in the past. The future tense is used for actions that will occur in the future. In the following chart, the simple tenses are given for the regular verb *walk*, the irregular verb *ride*, and the highly irregular verb *be*.

PRESENT TENSE

SINGULAR		PLURAL	
I	walk, ride, am	we	walk, ride, are
you	walk, ride, are	you	walk, ride, are
he/she/it	walks, rides, is	they	walk, ride, are

PAST TENSE

SINGULAR		PLURAL	
I	walked, rode, was	we	walked, rode, were
you	walked, rode, were	you	walked, rode, were
he/she/it	walked, rode, was	they	walked, rode, were

FUTURE TENSE

I, you, he/she/it, we, they   will walk, ride, be

More complex time relations are indicated by the perfect and progressive tenses. A verb in one of the perfect tenses (a form of *have* plus the past participle) expresses an action that was or will be completed at the time of another action. A verb in a progressive tense (a form of *be* plus the present participle) expresses a continuing action.

PRESENT PERFECT

I, you, we, they   have walked, ridden, been
he/she/it   has walked, ridden, been

PAST PERFECT

I, you, he/she/it, we, they   had walked, ridden, been

FUTURE PERFECT

I, you, he/she/it, we, they   will have walked, ridden, been

PRESENT PROGRESSIVE

I	am walking, riding, being
he/she/it	is walking, riding, being
you, we, they	are walking, riding, being

PAST PROGRESSIVE

I, he/she/it   was walking, riding, being
you, we, they   were walking, riding, being

FUTURE PROGRESSIVE

I, you, he/she/it, we, they   will be walking, riding, being

27c Use the present tense when writing about literature and when expressing general truths.

When writing about a work of literature, you may be tempted to use the past tense. The convention, however, is to describe fictional events in the present tense (known in this use as the *historical present*). See 14b.

▶ In Masuji Ibuse's *Black Rain*, a child ~~reached~~ *reaches* for a

pomegranate in his mother's garden, and a moment later

he ~~was~~ *is* dead, killed by the blast of the atomic bomb.

Scientific principles or general truths should appear in the present tense, unless such principles have been disproved.

▶ Galileo taught that the earth ~~revolved~~ *revolves* around the sun.

Since Galileo's teaching has not been discredited, the verb should be in the present tense. The following sentence, however, is acceptable: *Ptolemy taught that the sun revolved around the earth.*

27d Use the past perfect tense for an action already completed by the time of another past action.

The past perfect tense consists of a past participle preceded by *had* (*had worked, had gone*).

▶ We built our cabin high on a pine knoll, forty feet above an
abandoned quarry that ~~was~~ *had been* flooded in 1920 to create a lake.

The building of the cabin and the flooding of the quarry both
occurred in the past, but the flooding was completed before the
building.

27e Use the appropriate sequence of tenses with infinitives and participles.

An infinitive is the dictionary form of a verb preceded by *to*.
Use the present infinitive to show action at the same time as
or later than the action of the verb in the sentence.

▶ The club had hoped to ~~have raised~~ *raise* a thousand dollars by

April 1.

The action expressed in the infinitive (*to raise*) occurred later
than the action of the sentence's verb (*had hoped*).

Use the perfect form of an infinitive (*to have* followed by
the past participle) for an action occurring earlier than that
of the verb in the sentence.

▶ David would like to ~~join~~ *have joined* the Green Berets, but he did not

pass the physical.

The liking occurs in the present; the joining would have occurred in the past.

The tense of a participle is also governed by the tense of
the sentence's verb. Use the present participle (ending in
-ing) for an action occurring at the same time as that of the
sentence's verb.

Hiking the Appalachian Trail in early spring, we spotted many wildflowers.

Use the past participle (such as *given* or *helped*) or the present perfect participle (*having* plus the past participle) for an action occurring before that of the verb.

Discovered off the coast of Florida, the *Atocha* yielded many treasures.

Having worked her way through college, Melanie graduated with honors.

MOOD

There are three moods in English: the indicative, used for facts, opinions, and questions; the imperative, used for orders or advice; and the subjunctive, used for wishes or conditions contrary to fact. Of these three moods, only the subjunctive causes problems for native speakers of English.

27f Use the subjunctive mood in *if* clauses expressing conditions contrary to fact and in *that* clauses following verbs such as *ask, insist, recommend, request,* and *wish.*

In the subjunctive mood, present-tense verbs do not change form to indicate the number and person of the subject (see 21). Instead, all subjects of present-tense verbs take the infinitive verb form (*be, drive, employ*). Also, in the subjunctive mood there is only one past-tense form of *be: were* (never *was*).

Use the subjunctive mood in *if* clauses expressing conditions contrary to fact.

> ▶ If I ~~was~~ a member of Congress, I would vote for that bill.
>   *were*

were
We could be less cautious if Jake ~~was~~ more trustworthy.
⋀

Ordinarily *I was* and *he was* are correct (see 21), but in the subjunctive mood *were* is the only past-tense form of *be*. The verbs express conditions that do not exist: The writer is not a member of Congress, and Jake is not trustworthy.

Use the subjunctive in *that* clauses following verbs such as *ask, insist, recommend, request,* and *wish.*

be
▶ Professor Moore insists that her students ~~are~~ on time.
⋀

file
We recommend that Lambert ~~files~~ form 1050 soon.
⋀

were
Don't you wish that Janet ~~was~~ here to help us celebrate?
⋀

Ordinarily *students are, Lambert files,* and *Janet was* are correct (see 21), but in the subjunctive mood verbs do not change form to indicate number and person. If the subjunctive seems too formal, the writers might recast their sentences. For example: *Professor Moore requires her students to be on time.*

EXERCISE 27–2

Edit the following sentences to eliminate errors in verb tense or mood. If a sentence is correct, write "correct" after it. Answers to lettered sentences appear in the back of the book. Example:

had been
The path ~~was~~ plowed, so we were able to walk through the
⋀

park.

a. The fire was thought to have been started around nine o'clock.
b. Watson and Crick discovered the mechanism that controlled inheritance in all life: the workings of the DNA molecule.
c. Marion would write more if she wasn't distracted by a house full of children.

d. Sharon told me that she went to the meeting the day before.
e. Ken recommended that John remain on the beginners' slope for at least a week.

1. By the time we arrived, the cake had been eaten.
2. They had planned to have gone to Canada last summer, but they were unable to coordinate their vacations.
3. If I were in better health, I would enjoy competing in the dance marathon.
4. As soon as my aunt applied for the position of assistant pastor, the post was filled by an inexperienced seminary graduate who had been so hastily snatched that his mortarboard was still in midair.
5. Sheila knew that Bruce would have preferred to have double-dated, but she really wanted to be alone with him.
6. Don Quixote, in Cervantes' novel, was an idealist ill suited for life in the real world.
7. On arrival at the police station, Cindy pulled Tom out of the car and he had fallen face down on the ground.
8. I would like to have been on the *Mayflower,* but not to have lived through that first winter.
9. This isn't the Waldorf; if it was, we wouldn't be here.
10. Hearing the screams and wondering whether Chuck had had an accident, I ran to the garage.

VOICE

27g Prefer the active voice.

Transitive verbs appear in either the active or the passive voice (see 48b). In the active voice, the subject of the sentence does the action; in the passive, the subject receives the action. Although both voices are grammatically correct, the active voice is usually more effective because it is simpler and more direct.

ACTIVE The committee *reached* a decision.

PASSIVE A decision *was reached* by the committee.

To transform a sentence from the passive to the active voice, make the actor the subject of the sentence.

▶ For the opening flag ceremony, ~~a dance was choreographed~~
choreographed a dance
~~by~~ Mr. Martins to the song "Two Hundred Years and Still a

Baby."

The original version of this sentence, with the subject, *dance,* receiving the action, was needlessly indirect. Notice that the actor — Mr. Martins — appeared in a prepositional phrase, where he received very little emphasis. The revision gives Mr. Martins the emphasis he deserves by making him the subject.

We did not take down the

▶ ~~The~~ Christmas decorations ~~were not taken down~~ until

Valentine's Day.

Very often the actor does not even appear in a passive-voice sentence. To turn such a sentence into the active voice, the writer must decide on an appropriate subject, in this case *we.*

The passive voice is appropriate if you wish to emphasize the receiver of the action or to minimize the importance of the doer.

APPROPRIATE PASSIVE	Many native Hawaiians *are forced* to leave their beautiful beaches to make room for hotels and condominiums.
APPROPRIATE PASSIVE	As the time for harvest approaches, the tobacco plants *are sprayed* with a chemical to retard the growth of suckers.

The writer of the first sentence wished to emphasize the receivers of the action, *Hawaiians.* The writer of the second sentence wished to focus on the tobacco plants, not on the people spraying them.

EXERCISE 27–3

Change the following sentences from the passive to the active voice. You may need to invent an actor. Revisions of lettered sentences appear in the back of the book. Example:

> We
>
> ~~It was~~ learned from the test that our son was reading on the
>   ^
>
> second-grade level.

a. The results were reported by the research assistant.

b. Not enough discretion is used by parents in deciding which television programs their children may watch.

c. As the patient undressed, scars were seen on his back, stomach, and thighs. Child abuse was what we suspected.

d. It was noted right away that the taxi driver had been exposed to Americans because he knew all the latest slang.

e. The buttons were replaced, the hems were lengthened or shortened, and all of the costumes were cleaned and pressed.

1. Two hundred invitations to the opening of the student art show were misplaced by my absentminded friend Joe.

2. No loyalty at all was shown by the dog to his owner, who had mistreated him.

3. It can be concluded that a college education provides a significant economic advantage.

4. The new car was purchased without serious thought about how we would make the monthly payments.

5. Home equity loans were explained to me by the assistant manager.

Editing for Standard English

If English is not your native language or if your speech has been influenced by a nonstandard dialect, Part VI will alert you to a number of possible problems caused by language interference. Language interference occurs when the rules of your native language or your spoken dialect differ from the rules of standard English.

As you probably know, many people speak two varieties of English—standard English, used in academic and business situations, and a nonstandard dialect, spoken with close acquaintances who share a regional or social heritage. Except when used deliberately for effect, nonstandard dialects should not appear in written English.

The rules of standard English are based on the speech and writing of educated persons such as journalists, television news commentators, national politicians, poets, novelists, historians, and scholars. Some of the most basic of these rules appear in the following sections. Others appear in the Glossary of Usage or elsewhere in this handbook.

28

Use the -s form of a verb when standard English requires it.

In some nonstandard dialects, the present-tense verb system differs from that of standard English. Where standard English requires an -s ending, the dialect may omit it.

> **STANDARD**   Bill *travels* to New York once a year.
>
> **NONSTANDARD** Bill *travel* to New York once a year.

Where standard English does not require the -s ending, the dialect may add it.

STANDARD	The facts *support* our hypothesis.	
NONSTANDARD	The facts *supports* our hypothesis.	

28a **In the present tense, use *-s* (or *-es*) endings on verbs that have third-person singular subjects.**

All singular nouns (*child, tree*) and the pronouns *he, she,* and *it* are third-person singular; indefinite pronouns such as *everyone* and *neither* are also third-person singular. When the subject of a sentence is third-person singular, its verb takes an *-s* or *-es* ending in the present tense. (See also 21.)

	SINGULAR		**PLURAL**	
FIRST PERSON	I	love	we	love
SECOND PERSON	you	love	you	love
THIRD PERSON	he/she/it	loves	they	love
	child	loves	parents	love
	everyone	loves		

In some dialects, the *-s* ending required by standard English is omitted.

▶ Ellen taught him what he ~~know~~ *knows* about the paperwork in this

agency.

Sulfur dioxide ~~turn~~ *turns* leaves yellow, ~~dissolve~~ *dissolves* marble, and ~~eat~~ *eats*

away iron and steel.

The subjects *he* and *sulfur dioxide* are third-person singular, so the verbs must end in *-s*.

CAUTION: Do not add the *-s* ending to the verb if the subject is not third-person singular.

The writers of the following sentences, knowing they sometimes dropped *-s* endings from verbs, overcorrected by adding the endings where they don't belong.

▶ I prepares/ program specifications and machine logic

diagrams.

The writer mistakenly concluded that the -s ending belongs on present-tense verbs used with *all* singular subjects, not just *third-person* singular subjects. The pronoun *I* is first-person singular, so its verb does not require the -s.

▶ The dirt floors requires/ continual sweeping.

The writer mistakenly thought that the -s ending on the verb indicated plurality. The -s goes on present-tense verbs used with third-person *singular* subjects.

28b Use *has* (not *have*) with third-person singular subjects.

The present-tense forms of the frequently used verb *have* are listed below.

	SINGULAR		PLURAL	
FIRST PERSON	I	have	we	have
SECOND PERSON	you	have	you	have
THIRD PERSON	he/she/it	has	they	have

In some dialects, *has* does not appear; *have* is used with all subjects.

▶ This respected musician almost always ~~have~~ a message to
^{has}

convey in his work.

As for the retirement income program, it ~~have~~ finally been
^{has}

established.

The subjects *musician* and *it* are third-person singular, so the verb should be *has* in each case.

CAUTION: Do not use *has* if the subject is not third-person singular. The writers of the following sentences were aware that they often wrote *have* when standard English requires *has*. Here they are using what appears to them to be the "more correct" form, but in an inappropriate context.

▶ My business law classes ~~has~~ *have* helped me to understand more about contracts.

I ~~has~~ *have* much to be thankful for.

The subjects of these sentences — *classes* and *I* — are third-person plural and first-person singular, so standard English requires *have*. *Has* is used with third-person singular subjects only.

28c Use *does* and *doesn't* (not *do* and *don't*) with third-person singular subjects.

The present-tense forms of the frequently used verb *do* are listed in the following chart.

	SINGULAR		**PLURAL**	
FIRST PERSON	I	do/don't	we	do/don't
SECOND PERSON	you	do/don't	you	do/don't
THIRD PERSON	he/she/it	does/doesn't	they	do/don't

The use of *don't* instead of the standard English *doesn't* is a feature of many dialects in the United States. Use of *do* for *does* is rarer.

▶ Grandfather really ~~don't~~ *doesn't* have a place to call home.

Does
~~Do~~ she know the correct procedure for setting up the
∧

experiment?

Grandfather and *she* are third-person singular, so the verbs
should be *doesn't* and *does*.

28d Use *is* and *was* (not *are* and *were*) with third-
person singular subjects; use *am* and *was* (not *are* and
were) with first-person singular subjects.

The verb *be* has three forms in the present tense (*am, is, are*)
and two in the past tense (*was, were*).

	SINGULAR		**PLURAL**	
FIRST PERSON	I	am/was	we	are/were
SECOND PERSON	you	are/were	you	are/were
THIRD PERSON	he/she/it	is/was	they	are/were

was
▶ Judy wanted to borrow Tim's notes, but she ~~were~~ too shy to
∧

ask for them.

The subject *she* is third-person singular, so the verb should be
was.

EXERCISE 28–1

Edit the following sentences to conform to the rules of standard
English. If a sentence is correct, write "correct" after it. Answers to
lettered sentences appear in the back of the book. Example:

has
The social worker ~~have~~ so many problems in her own life
doesn't ∧
that she ~~don't~~ know how to advise anyone else.
∧

a. I love to watch Anthony as he leaps off the balance beam and lands lightly on his feet.
b. Do he have enough energy to hold down two jobs while going to night school?
c. The whooping crane have been an endangered species since the late 1930s.
d. Our four children plays one or two instruments each.
e. Even though Maria is in her late twenties, her mother treat her like a child.

1. I certainly misses the good times we used to have.
2. Have there ever been a time in your life when you were too depressed to get out of bed?
3. The supervisor always answer any questions the employees have.
4. Today a modern school building covers most of the old grounds.
5. Because of his shyness, Jeff rarely ask questions or volunteer answers.

29

Use *-ed* endings on regular verbs when standard English requires them.

All verbs have three principal parts: the infinitive, the past-tense form, and the past participle. A verb is regular if both its past-tense and past-participle forms are created by adding *-ed* or *-d* to the infinitive.

INFINITIVE	PAST TENSE	PAST PARTICIPLE
talk	talked	talked
smoke	smoked	smoked
paint	painted	painted
end	ended	ended

A verb is irregular if its past-tense and past-participle forms do not follow the above pattern: *ring, rang, rung; bring, brought, brought; choose, chose, chosen.* (See 27a and 47c.)

Regular verbs ordinarily cause few problems. However, speakers who do not fully pronounce *-ed* endings may omit them in writing. Failure to pronounce *-ed* endings is common in many dialects and in informal speech even in standard English. In speech, such deletions are likely to occur when the *-ed* ending does not add another syllable (*fixed, concerned*) or when the verb appears before a word whose sound blends into the *-ed* sound (*used to, planned to*).

29a Use an *-ed* or *-d* ending to express the past tense of regular verbs.

The past tense is used when the action occurred entirely in the past.

▶ On the day he returned home, Ed ~~fix~~ his brother's
   ^*fixed*

skateboard and his mother's 1955 Thunderbird.

▶ Last summer my counselor ~~advise~~ me to ask my chemistry
   ^*advised*

instructor for help.

29b Use an *-ed* or *-d* ending on past participles of regular verbs.

Past participles are used in three ways: (1) following *have, has,* or *had* to form one of the perfect tenses; (2) following *be, am, is, are, was, were, being,* or *been* to form the passive voice; and (3) as adjectives modifying nouns or pronouns. The perfect tenses are listed on page 201. The passive voice is discussed in 48b, participles in 49c.

▶ John has ~~work~~ *worked* as a clerk-typist for seven years.

Has worked is the present perfect tense (*has* or *have* followed by a past participle).

▶ Though it is not a new phenomenon, wife-beating is ~~publicize~~ *publicized* more frequently.

Is publicized is the passive voice (a form of *be* followed by a past participle).

▶ All aerobics classes end in a cool-down period to loosen ~~tighten~~ *tightened* muscles.

Tightened functions as an adjective modifying the noun *muscles.*

EXERCISE 29–1

Edit the following sentences to conform to the rules of standard English. If a sentence is correct, write "correct" after it. Answers to lettered sentences appear in the back of the book. Example:

After the interview was over, the personnel manager ~~ask,~~ *asked,*

"Weren't you the person I talked to on the phone last

week?"

a. Our captain talked so much at meals that we learn to ignore him.
b. The prosecuting attorney was opposed to any suggestion of plea bargaining.

c. That line of poetry can be express more dramatically.
d. Our church has a close-circuit television.
e. England, France, and the United States had already sign a treaty before the war intensified.

1. The police are use to helping lost tourists.
2. How would you feel if your mother or a love one had been a victim of a crime like this?
3. Staggered working hours have lessen traffic jams and save many motorists gallons of gas.
4. Many people in my hometown have been ask to help with the rally.
5. The ball was pass from one player to the other so fast that even the TV crew miss some of the fouls.

30

Use the articles *a*, *an*, and *the* when standard English requires them.

Except for occasional difficulty in choosing between *a* and *an*, native speakers of English encounter few problems with articles. To speakers whose native language is not English, however, articles can prove troublesome, for the rules governing their use are surprisingly complex. This section summarizes those rules.

The definite article *the* and the indefinite articles *a* and *an* signal that a noun is about to appear. The noun may follow the article immediately or modifiers may intervene (see 47a and 47d):

> the candidate, the exceptionally well-qualified candidate
> a sunset, a spectacular sunset
> an apple, an elegant home

30a Use *an* before a vowel sound, *a* before a consonant sound.

Standard English requires *an*, not *a*, before vowels and vowel sounds: *an eggplant, an hour.* See the Glossary of Usage.

▶ I would be happier digging a ditch or working on ~~a~~ *an* assembly line.

▶ Herb's younger sister is ~~a~~ *an* X-ray technologist.

30b Use the indefinite article *a* (or *an*) with singular count nouns whose specific identity is not known to the reader.

Count nouns refer to persons, places, or things that can be counted: *one girl, two girls; one city, three cities; one apple, four apples.* Mass (or noncount) nouns refer to entities or abstractions that cannot be counted: *lemonade, steel, air, dirt, furniture, patience, knowledge.* Count nouns have singular and plural forms, but mass nouns ordinarily do not.

If the specific identity of a singular count noun is not known to the reader—perhaps because it is being mentioned for the first time, perhaps because its specific identity is unknown even to the writer—the noun should usually be preceded by *a* or *an*. *A* (or *an*) usually means "one among many" but can also mean "any one."

▶ Mary Beth arrived in *a* limousine.

▶ We are looking for *an* apartment close to the lake.

30c Use the definite article *the* with most nouns whose specific identity is known to the reader.

The definite article *the* is used with most nouns whose identity is known to the reader. (For exceptions, see 30d.) Usually the identity will be clear to the reader for one of the following reasons:

1. The noun has been previously mentioned.
2. A phrase or clause following the noun restricts its identity.
3. The noun describes a unique person, place, or thing.

▶ A truck loaded with dynamite cut in front of our van. When
   the
   truck skidded a few seconds later, we nearly plowed into it.
   ∧

The noun *truck* is preceded by *a* when it occurs for the first time. When the noun is mentioned again, it is preceded by *the* since readers know at this point which truck is being discussed.

                the
▶ Bob warned me that gun on the shelf was loaded.
              ∧

The phrase *on the shelf* identifies the gun.

                                              the
▶ During an eclipse, one should not look directly at sun.
                                            ∧

Since there is only one sun in our solar system, the identity is clear.

30d Do not use articles when standard English does not require them.

It is not necessary to mark every noun with an article. This section details the most common situations in which an article is *not* required.

1. Usually an article is not used when another noun-marker has been used instead.

Articles are not the only words to mark nouns. Other noun-markers include possessive nouns (Helen's), numbers, and the following pronouns: *my, your, his, her, its, our, their, whose, this, that, these, those, all, any, each, either, every, few, many, more, most, much, neither, several, some.*

2. *A* (or *an*) is not ordinarily used with mass nouns (those referring to things or abstractions that cannot be counted) or with plural nouns.

▶ Claudia asked her mother for ~~an~~ advice.

▶ As a child I earned money by delivering ~~a~~ newspapers.

3. *The* is not used with plural or mass nouns meaning "all" or "in general."

▶ ~~The~~ ꟻfountains are an expensive element of landscape design.

▶ In some parts of the world, ~~the~~ rice is preferred to all other

grains.

4. *The* is not used with names of persons (Jessica Webner), names of streets, cities, and states (Prospect Street, Detroit, Idaho), names of continents and most countries (Europe, South America, Costa Rica, India), and the proper names of most lakes and single mountains (Lake Geneva, Mount Everest).

EXERCISE 30–1

Articles have been omitted from the following story, adapted from *Zen Flesh, Zen Bones,* compiled by Paul Reps. Insert the articles *a, an*, and *the* where standard English requires them and be prepared to explain the reasons for your choices.

Moon Cannot Be Stolen

Ryokan, who was Zen master, lived simple life in little hut at foot of mountain. One evening thief visited hut only to discover there was nothing in it to steal.

Ryokan returned and caught him. "You may have come long way to visit me," he told prowler, "and you should not return empty-handed. Please take my clothes as gift." Thief was bewildered. He took Ryokan's clothes and slunk away. Ryokan sat naked, watching moon. "Poor fellow," he mused, "I wish I could give him this beautiful moon."

31

Be alert to a variety of differences between standard and nonstandard English.

31a Do not omit needed verbs.

Although standard English allows some linking verbs and helping verbs to be contracted, at least in informal contexts, it does not allow them to be omitted.

Linking verbs, used to link subjects to subject complements, are frequently a form of *be: be, am, is, are, was, were, being, been.* (See 48b.) Some of these forms may be contracted (*I'm, she's, we're*), but they should not be omitted altogether.

are
▶ When we out there in the evening, we often hear the
      ∧
helicopters circling above.

▶ Alvin a man who can defend himself.

    is

    ∧

Helping verbs, used with main verbs, include forms of *be, do,* and *have* or the words *can, will, shall, could, would, should, may, might,* and *must.* (See 47c.) Some helping verbs may be contracted (*he's leaving, we'll celebrate, they've been told*), but they should not be omitted altogether.

    have

▶ We been in Chicago since last Thursday.

    ∧

                    would

▶ Do you know someone who be good for the job?

                    ∧

31b   Use -s endings on most nouns to show plurality.

In some dialects the plural marker -*s* is commonly dropped when a noun is preceded by a number or some other indication of quantity. Speakers of these dialects may feel that the -*s* ending is redundant and therefore unnecessary in such constructions. In standard English, however, the absent -*s* ending is quite conspicuous, especially in writing.

    tourists

▶ For most ~~tourist~~, the first few days in Hawaii are spent in

    ∧

Honolulu.

                    gallons

▶ We could afford only three ~~gallon~~ of gas.

                  ∧

Some nouns form plurals irregularly (*man, men; child, children; deer, deer; goose, geese*). Do not add -*s* endings to these nouns. When in doubt, consult the dictionary.

▶ We spotted six deer~~s~~ during our recent camping trip.

31c Use an apostrophe and an -s to show possession.

Standard English requires an apostrophe and an s (or an s followed by an apostrophe) to show possession: *my friend's house, the students' rights.* Some dialects allow both the apostrophe and the s to be omitted (*my friend house*) because the context usually makes the meaning clear. To speakers of standard English, even those who are tolerant of an occasional dropped apostrophe, the omission of both the apostrophe and the s is distracting. For a full discussion of the apostrophe, see 36.

▶ My union representative accompanied me to the assistant
director's
~~director~~ office.

▶ Sandra gave Joe directions to her ~~cousin~~ *cousin's* house.

31d Avoid double negatives.

Standard English allows two negatives only if a positive meaning is intended: *The runners were not unhappy with their performance.* Double negatives used to emphasize negation are nonstandard.

▶ Management is not doing ~~nothing~~ *anything* to see that the trash is

picked up.

George won't ~~never~~ *ever* forget that day.

I enjoy living alone because I don't have to answer to
~~nobody~~ *anybody*.

The double negatives *not . . . nothing, won't never,* and *don't . . . nobody* are nonstandard.

The word *hardly* is considered a negative, so it should not be used with negatives such as *not* or *never.*

▶ Maxine is so weak she ~~can't~~ ^{can} hardly climb stairs.

EXERCISE 31–1

Edit the following sentences to conform to the rules of standard English. If a sentence is correct, write "correct" after it. Answers to lettered sentences appear in the back of the book. Example:

Marianne doesn't know ~~nothing~~ ^{anything} about computers.

a. The childrens in my neighborhood all walked to school.
b. They skate swiftly, waving and dodging as they drive the pucks toward the opposing team goal.
c. Chris didn't know about Marlo's death because he never listens. He always talking.
d. Though the meals are free, donations are accepted to help pay the operational costs.
e. With the budget deadline approaching, our office hasn't hardly had time to handle routine correspondence.

1. Pedro was standing about ten foot from a rattlesnake.
2. Even though the children were never left no more than five minutes without supervision, they still managed to get into trouble.
3. When Henderson career was on the rise, he developed an expensive lifestyle.
4. My father knew how much we hated those lectures, but they were less painful than one of his spankings.
5. We often don't know whether he angry or just joking.

PART VII

Editing for Punctuation

32

The comma

The comma was invented to help readers. Without it, sentence parts can collide into one another unexpectedly, causing misreadings.

> **CONFUSING** If you cook Elmer will do the dishes.

> **CONFUSING** While we were eating a rattlesnake approached our campsite.

Add commas in the logical places (after *cook* and *eating*), and suddenly all is clear. No longer is Elmer being cooked, the rattlesnake being eaten.

Various rules have evolved to prevent such misreadings and to speed readers along through complex grammatical structures. Those rules are detailed below.

32a Use a comma before a coordinating conjunction joining independent clauses.

When a coordinating conjunction connects two or more independent clauses—word groups that might have been punctuated as separate sentences—a comma must precede it. There are seven coordinating conjunctions in English: *and, but, or, nor, for, so,* and *yet.*

▶ Nearly everyone has heard of love at first sight, but I fell in
love at first dance.

Together the comma and the coordinating conjunction *but* signal that one independent clause has come to a close and that another, equally important, is about to begin.

▶ Along the walls were glass cubicles, and partitions ran down
                                    ∧
the middle of the room.

Without the comma one is likely to think, on first reading, that glass cubicles *and partitions* were along the walls. A comma prevents readers from grouping the words in this misleading way.

EXCEPTION: If the two independent clauses are short and there is no danger of misreading, the comma may be omitted.

The plane took off and we were on our way.

CAUTION: Do *not* use a comma to separate coordinate word groups that are not independent clauses. See 33a.

A good money manager controls expenses and invests surplus dollars to meet future needs.

In this example *controls . . . and invests* is a compound verb; the sentence does not consist of two independent clauses.

32b Use a comma after an introductory clause or phrase.

The most common introductory word groups are clauses and phrases functioning as adverbs. Such word groups usually tell when, where, how, why, or under what conditions the main action of the sentence occurred. See 49a, 49b, and 49c.

▶ Near a small stream at the bottom of the canyon ▲we

discovered an abandoned shelter.

The comma is a useful signal that the introductory phrase is over and that the main part of the sentence is about to begin.

▶ When Irwin was ready to eat ▲his cat jumped onto the table.

Without the comma, readers may have Irwin eating his cat. The comma signals that *his cat* is the subject of a new clause, not part of the introductory one.

EXCEPTION: The comma may be omitted after a short adverb clause or phrase if there is no danger of misreading.

In no time we were at 2,800 feet.

Sentences also frequently begin with phrases describing the noun or pronoun immediately following them. The comma tells readers that they are about to hear that noun or pronoun; therefore, the comma is usually required even when the phrase is short. See 49c.

▶ Knowing that he couldn't outrun a car ▲Kevin took to the

fields.

Excited about the move ▲Alice and Don began packing their

books.

The commas tell readers that they are about to hear the nouns described: *Kevin* in the first sentence, *Alice and Don* in the second.

NOTE: Other introductory word groups include transitions, conjunctive adverbs, and absolute phrases. See 32f and 32g.

EXERCISE 32–1

Add or delete commas where necessary in the following sentences. If a sentence is correct, write "correct" after it. Answers to lettered sentences appear in the back of the book. Example:

> Because it rained all Memorial Day, our picnic was rather
>
> soggy.

a. This summer we hiked in the White Mountains and canoed the Saco River into Maine.
b. The man at the next table complained loudly and the waiter stomped off in disgust.
c. Between the heavy rain and the thick fog, the driving was bad.
d. Nursing is physically, and mentally demanding, yet the pay is low.
e. After I won the hundred-yard dash I found a bench in the park and collapsed.

1. Under Title IV of the Interpersonnel Act of 1970 our office has entered into an agreement with the University of Arkansas.
2. After everyone had eaten Lu and George cut the cake.
3. The temperature was 104 degrees and Eric's car was not equipped with air-conditioning.
4. Knowing how nurses are treated in that hospital she was brave to complain about Dr. Michaels.
5. Instead of eating half a cake or two dozen cookies, I now grab a banana or an orange.
6. He pushed the car beyond the toll gate and dashed a bucket of water on the smoking hood.
7. Lighting the area like a second moon the helicopter circled the scene.
8. While one of the robbers tied Laureen to a chair, and gagged her with an apron, the other emptied the contents of the safe into a knapsack.

9. As cucumbers grow their vines need room to expand.
10. Many musicians of Bach's time played several instruments, but few mastered them as early or played with as much expression as Bach.

32c Use a comma between all items in a series.

When three or more items are presented in a series, those items should be separated from one another with commas. Items in a series may be single words, phrases, or clauses.

> At Dominique's one can order fillet of rattlesnake, bison burgers, or pickled eel.

Although some writers view the comma between the last two items as optional, most agree that it is better to put it in because its omission can result in ambiguity or misreading.

▶ My uncle willed me all of his property, houses , and

warehouses.

Did the uncle will his property *and* houses *and* warehouses — or simply his property, consisting of houses and warehouses? If the former meaning is intended, a comma is necessary to prevent ambiguity.

▶ The activities include a search for lost treasure, dubious

financial dealings, much discussion of ancient heresies ,

and midnight orgies.

Without the comma this sentence is easily misread. The people seem to be discussing orgies, not having them. The comma makes it clear that *midnight orgies* is a separate item in the series.

32d Use a comma between coordinate adjectives not joined by *and.* Do not use a comma between cumulative adjectives.

When two or more adjectives each modify a noun separately, they are coordinate.

> Mother has become a *strong, confident, independent* woman.

Adjectives are coordinate if they can be joined with *and* (strong *and* confident *and* independent) or if they can be scrambled (an independent, strong, confident woman).

Adjectives that do not modify the noun separately are cumulative.

> *Three large gray* shapes moved slowly toward us.

Beginning with the adjective closest to the noun *shapes,* these modifiers lean on one another, piggyback style, with each modifying a larger word group. *Gray* modifies *shapes, large* modifies *gray shapes,* and *three* modifies *large gray shapes.* We cannot insert the word *and* between cumulative adjectives (three *and* large *and* gray shapes). Nor can we scramble them (gray three large shapes).

COORDINATE ADJECTIVES

▶ Robert is a warm▲ gentle▲ affectionate father.

The adjectives *warm, gentle,* and *affectionate* each modify *father* separately. They can be connected with *and* (warm *and* gentle *and* affectionate), and they can be scrambled (an affectionate, warm, gentle father).

CUMULATIVE ADJECTIVES

▶ Ira ordered a rich/chocolate/layer cake.

Ira didn't order a cake that was rich and chocolate and layer: He ordered a *layer cake* that was *chocolate*, a *chocolate layer cake* that was *rich*. These cumulative adjectives cannot be scrambled: a layer chocolate rich cake.

EXERCISE 32-2

Add or delete commas where necessary in the following sentences. If a sentence is correct, write "correct" after it. Answers to lettered sentences appear in the back of the book. Example:

> We gathered our essentials, took off for the great outdoors**,**
> and ignored the fact that it was Friday the 13th.

a. She wore a black silk cape, a rhinestone collar, satin gloves and army boots.
b. I called the fire department, ran downstairs to warn my neighbors, and discovered that they had set the fire on purpose.
c. He was an impossible demanding guest.
d. Juan walked through the room with casual elegant grace.
e. My cat's pupils had constricted to small black shining dots.

1. My brother and I found a dead garter snake, picked it up and placed it on Miss Eunice's doorstep.
2. I could tell from the look of her room that the quiet, neat attractive girl was at heart a slob.
3. For breakfast the children ordered cornflakes, English muffins with peanut butter and cherry Cokes.
4. Movies have often portrayed bootleggers as mean cutthroat racketeers.
5. At one of his concerts, James Galway pulled two cheap tin horns from his pockets and played a different tune on each one simultaneously.
6. Handguns, knives, and other weapons are turning up in locker checks at our junior high school.
7. An ambulance threaded its way through police cars fire trucks and irate citizens.

8. Mark was clad in a luminous orange rain suit and a brilliant white helmet.
9. It was a small unimportant part.
10. My once-timid mother fired the building superintendent, hired a replacement and began serving legal notices against delinquent tenants.

32e Use commas to set off nonrestrictive elements. Do not use commas to set off restrictive elements.

Word groups describing nouns or pronouns (adjective clauses, adjective phrases, and appositives) are restrictive or nonrestrictive. A *restrictive* element defines or limits the meaning of the word it modifies and is therefore essential to the meaning of the sentence. Because it contains essential information, a restrictive element is not set off with commas.

RESTRICTIVE
For camp the children needed clothes *that were washable.*

If you remove a restrictive element from a sentence, the meaning changes significantly, becoming more general than you intended. The writer of the example sentence does not mean that the children needed clothes in general. The intended meaning is more limited: the children needed *washable* clothes.

A *nonrestrictive* element describes a noun or pronoun whose meaning has already been clearly defined or limited. Because it contains nonessential or parenthetical information, a nonrestrictive element is set off with commas.

NONRESTRICTIVE
For camp the children needed sturdy shoes, *which were expensive.*

If you remove a nonrestrictive element from a sentence, the meaning does not change dramatically. Some meaning is lost, to be sure, but the defining characteristics of the person or thing described remain the same as before. The children needed *sturdy shoes,* and these happened to be expensive.

Word groups describing proper nouns are nearly always nonrestrictive: The Illinois River, *which flows through our town,* has reached flood stage. Word groups modifying indefinite pronouns such as *everyone* and *something* are nearly always restrictive: Joe whispered something *that we could not hear.*

Often it is difficult to tell whether a word group is restrictive or nonrestrictive without seeing it in context and considering your meaning. Should you write "The dessert made with fresh raspberries was delicious" or "The dessert, made with fresh raspberries, was delicious"? That depends. If the phrase *made with fresh raspberries* tells readers which of two or more desserts you're referring to, you would omit the commas. If the phrase merely adds information about the one dessert served with the meal, you would use the commas.

Adjective clauses

Adjective clauses are patterned like sentences, containing subjects and verbs, but they function within sentences as modifiers of nouns or pronouns. They always follow the word they modify, usually immediately. Adjective clauses begin with a relative pronoun (*who, whom, whose, which, that*) or with a relative adverb (*where, when*).

NONRESTRICTIVE CLAUSE

▶ Ed's country house, which is located on thirteen acres, was
completely furnished with bats in the rafters and mice in the
kitchen.

The clause *which is located on thirteen acres* does not restrict the meaning of *Ed's country house,* so the information is nonessential.

RESTRICTIVE CLAUSE

▶ An office manager for a corporation/ that had government

contracts/ asked her supervisor whether she could

reprimand her co-workers for smoking.

Because the adjective clause *that had government contracts* identifies the corporation, the information is essential.

NOTE: Many writers reserve *which* for nonrestrictive clauses, and *that* for restrictive clauses. See the Glossary of Usage.

Phrases functioning as adjectives

Prepositional or verbal phrases functioning as adjectives may be restrictive or nonrestrictive and are punctuated according to the rules used for adjective clauses.

NONRESTRICTIVE PHRASE

▶ The helicopter, with its 100,000-candlepower spotlight
        ∧
illuminating the area, circled above.
                ∧

The *with* phrase is nonessential because its purpose is not to specify which of two or more helicopters is being discussed.

RESTRICTIVE PHRASE

▶ One corner of the attic was filled with newspapers/ dating

from the turn of the century.

Dating from the turn of the century restricts the meaning of *newspapers,* so the comma should be omitted.

Appositives

An appositive is a noun or noun phrase that renames a nearby noun immediately preceding it. Most appositives are nonrestrictive and should be set off with commas; the few that are restrictive require no commas.

NONRESTRICTIVE APPOSITIVE

▶ Norman Mailer's first novel, *The Naked and the Dead,* was a
best-seller.

The term *first* restricts the meaning to one novel, so the appositive *The Naked and the Dead* is nonrestrictive.

RESTRICTIVE APPOSITIVE

▶ The song "Fire It Up" was blasted out of amplifiers ten feet
tall.

Once they've read *song,* readers still don't know precisely which song the writer means. The appositive following *song* restricts its meaning.

EXERCISE 32–3

Add or delete commas where necessary in the following sentences. If a sentence is correct, write "correct" after it. Answers to lettered sentences appear in the back of the book. Example:

My youngest sister, who plays left wing on the team, now

lives at The Sands, a beach house near Los Angeles.

a. We bought a home in Upper Marlboro where my husband worked as a mail carrier.
b. Ms. Taylor who works in accounting will be joining our carpool.
c. The woman running for the council seat in the fifth district had a long history of community service.
d. Shakespeare's tragedy, *King Lear,* was given a splendid performance by the actor, Laurence Olivier.
e. The man, whom you recommended to us, is an excellent addition to our staff.

1. I had the pleasure of talking to a woman who had just returned from India where she had lived for ten years.
2. Ignoring several openings, Mary waited for a job, with no overtime, to become available.
3. Ms. Smith's favorite is the youngest brother, Tommie.
4. Greg's cousin Albert lives in Huntington Beach. [*Greg has more than one cousin.*]
5. The elderly gentleman waiting for a prescription is Mr. Riley.
6. The second phone number 383-1351, is used for business.
7. *Where the Wild Things Are,* the 1964 Caldecott Medal winner, is my nephew's favorite book.
8. Students, who sign up for Children's Literature and expect an easy A, have usually revised their expectations by the end of the first week.
9. On Christmas morning, the children wildly excited about their gifts forgot their promises not to wake their parents.
10. Going on an archeological dig which has always been an ambition of mine seems out of the question this year.

32f Use commas to set off transitions, conjunctive adverbs, and parenthetical expressions.

Transitions are bridges between sentences or parts of sentences. *For example, in other words, in fact, in the first place,* and *as a matter of fact* are common examples.

▶ As a matter of fact, American football was established by
                    ∧
fans who wanted to play a more organized game of rugby.

▶ Celery, for example, contains more sodium than most
    ∧   ∧
people would imagine.

Conjunctive adverbs include *however, therefore, further-more, moreover, nevertheless, thus,* and *consequently.* When such words are used between independent clauses, they are preceded by a semicolon and are usually followed by a comma. (See 34.) Otherwise they are usually separated from the rest of the sentence with commas.

▶ The prospective babysitter was very kind; however, she was
                                                   ∧
busy every Saturday for a month.

▶ The major benefit of flex-time to working parents, however,
                                                 ∧   ∧
is the opportunity to spend more time with their children.

EXCEPTION: If a transition or conjunctive adverb blends smoothly with the rest of the sentence, calling for little or no pause in reading, it does not need to be set off with a comma. Expressions such as *also, at least, certainly, consequently, indeed, of course, moreoever, no doubt, perhaps, then,* and *therefore* do not necessarily call for a pause.

Bill's typewriter is broken; you will *therefore* need to borrow Sue's.

Expressions that are distinctly parenthetical should be set off with commas. Providing supplemental comments or information, they interrupt the flow of a sentence or appear as afterthoughts.

▶ Evolution, so far as we know, doesn't work this way.
          ∧   ∧

▶ The bass weighed about twelve pounds, give or take a few
ounces.

32g Use commas to set off absolute phrases.

An absolute phrase, which modifies the whole sentence, usually consists of a noun followed by a participle or participial phrase. (See 49e.)

▶ Brenda was forced to rely on public transportation, her car
having been wrecked the week before.

▶ Her tennis game at last perfected, Chris won the cup.

32h Use commas to set off contrasted elements.

▶ Jane talks to me as an adult and friend, not as her little
sister.

▶ Celia, unlike Robert, had no loathing for dance contests.

32i Use commas to set off nouns of direct address, the words *yes* and *no*, interrogative tags, and mild interjections.

▶ Forgive us, Dr. Spock, for spanking Brian.

▶ Yes, the loan will probably be approved.

▶ The film was faithful to the book, wasn't it?

▶ Well, cases like these are difficult to decide.

32j Use commas with expressions such as *he said* to set off direct quotations. (See also 37e.)

▶ Naturalist Arthur Cleveland Bent remarked, "In part the peregrine declined unnoticed because it is not adorable."

▶ "Convictions are more dangerous foes of truth than lies," wrote philosopher Friedrich Nietzsche.

32k Use commas with dates, addresses, and titles.

In dates, the year is set off from the rest of the sentence with a pair of commas.

▶ On December 12, 1890, orders were sent out for the arrest of Sitting Bull.

EXCEPTIONS: If the date is inverted, commas are not needed.

On 15 April 1983 Congress voted on important legislation.

If only the month and year are given, commas are not needed.

January 1982 was an extremely cold month.

The elements of an address or place name are followed by commas. A zip code, however, is not preceded by a comma.

▶ John Lennon was born in Liverpool, England, in 1940.

▶ Please send the package to Greg Tarvin at 708 Spring Street, Washington, Illinois 61571.

If a title follows a name, separate it from the rest of the sentence with a pair of commas.

▶ Sandra Barnes, M.D., performed the surgery.

EXERCISE 32–4: Review

Add or delete commas where necessary in the following sentences. If a sentence is correct, write "correct" after it. Answers to lettered sentences appear in the back of the book. Example:

Although we invited him to the party, Gerald decided to spend another late night in the computer room.

a. Each morning the seventy-year-old woman cleans the barn, shovels manure and spreads clean hay around the milking stalls.
b. Good technique does not guarantee however, that the power you develop will be sufficient for Kyok Pa competition.
c. My only brother, George, worked as a congressional aide last summer.
d. We pulled into the first apartment complex we came upon, and slowly patrolled the parking lots.

e. We wondered how our overweight grandmother could have been the pretty bride in the picture but we kept our wonderings to ourselves.

1. Mr. Mundy was born on July 22, 1939 in Arkansas, where his family had lived for four generations.
2. The coach having bawled us out thoroughly, we left the locker room with his last harsh words ringing in our ears.
3. The students of Highpoint are required to wear dull green, polyester pleated skirts.
4. Draped in scarlet, green, and navy blankets the horses threaded their way through town.
5. Siddhartha decided to leave his worldly possessions behind and live in the forest by a beautiful river.
6. Julia lives in Sawbridgeworth, Hertfordshire, England for most of the year.
7. "Yes Virginia, there is a Santa Claus," said the editor.
8. Thermography, most experts agree, is safer than mammography.
9. It has been reported that the Republican who suggested Eisenhower as a presidential candidate meant Milton, not Ike.
10. "The last flight" she said with a sigh "went out five minutes before I arrived at the airport."

33

Unnecessary commas

33a Do not use a comma between compound elements that are not independent clauses.

Though a comma should be used before a coordinating conjunction joining independent clauses (see 32a), this rule should not be extended to other compound word groups.

▶ The director led the cast members to their positions/and

gave an inspiring last-minute pep talk.

The word group following *and* is not an independent clause because it lacks a subject; *and* connects the verbs *led* and *gave*.

▶ Jake still doesn't realize that his illness is serious/and that

he will have to alter his diet to improve.

The word group following *and* is not an independent clause. *And*
connects two subordinate clauses, each beginning with *that*.

33b Do not use a comma to separate the subject from
the verb or the verb from its object or complement.

A sentence should flow from subject to verb to object without
unnecessary pauses. Commas may appear between these major sentence elements only when a specific rule calls for them.

▶ Abiding by the 55-mile-per-hour speed limit/can save

considerable gasoline.

The gerund phrase *Abiding by the 55-mile-per-hour speed limit*
is the subject of the verb *can save*, and it should not be separated from that verb. In fact, a comma here would lead to misreading, for readers would expect a sentence like this one, opening with a participial phrase: *Abiding by the 55-mile-per-hour
speed limit, we can save considerable gasoline.*

▶ Fran explained to Mr. Dospril/that she was busy and would

have to see him later.

The *that* clause is the direct object of the verb *explained*. The writer has mistakenly used a comma to separate the verb from its object.

33c Do not use a comma before the first or after the last item in a series.

Though commas are required between items in a series (32c), do not place them either before or after the series.

▶ Other causes of asthmatic attacks are/ stress, change in

temperature, humidity, and cold air.

▶ Ironically, this job that appears so glamorous, carefree, and

easy/ carries a high degree of responsibility.

33d Do not use a comma between cumulative adjectives or between an adjective and the noun that follows it.

Though commas are required between coordinate adjectives (those that can be separated with *and*), they do not belong between cumulative adjectives (those that cannot be separated with *and*). For a full discussion, see 32d.

▶ In the corner of the closet we found an old/ maroon hatbox

from Sears.

A comma should never be used to separate an adjective from the noun that follows it.

▶ It was a senseless, dangerous/mission.

33e Do not use commas to set off restrictive or mildly parenthetical elements.

Restrictive elements are adjectival modifiers or appositives necessary for identifying the nouns they follow. For a full discussion, see 32e.

▶ Drivers/who think they own the road/make cycling a

dangerous sport.

The modifier *who think they own the road* restricts the drivers being discussed, identifying the exact group the sentence is about. The writer who puts commas around this modifier falsely suggests that all drivers think they own the road.

▶ Margaret Mead's book/*Coming of Age in Samoa*/stirred up

considerable controversy when it was published.

Since Margaret Mead wrote more than one book, the appositive contains information essential to the meaning of the sentence.

Although commas should be used with distinctly parenthetical expressions (see 32f), do not use them to set off elements that are only mildly parenthetical.

▶ As long as patients are treated in a professional yet

compassionate manner, most/eventually/learn to deal with

their illness.

33f Do not use a comma to set off a concluding adverbial clause that is essential to the meaning of the sentence.

When adverb clauses introduce a sentence, they are nearly always followed by a comma (see 32b). When they conclude a sentence, however, they are not set off by commas if their content is essential to the meaning of the earlier part of the sentence. Adverb clauses beginning with *after, as soon as, before, because, if, since, unless, until,* and *when* are usually essential.

▶ Don't visit Paris at the height of the tourist season/unless

you have booked hotel reservations.

The *unless* clause is essential. Without it, the sentence would be advising us to avoid Paris at the height of the tourist season even if we had booked reservations.

When a concluding adverb clause is nonessential, it should be preceded by a comma. Clauses beginning with *although, even though, though,* and *whereas* are usually nonessential.

The lecture seemed to last only a short time, although the clock said it had gone on for more than an hour.

33g Do not use a comma before a parenthesis.

▶ At MCI Sylvia began at the bottom/ (with only three and a

half walls and a swivel chair), but within five years she had

been promoted to supervisor.

33h Do not use a comma after *such as* or *like.*

▶ Many shade-loving plants, such as⁄begonias, impatiens, and coleus, can add color to a shady garden.

33i Do not use a comma before *than.*

▶ Touring Crete was more thrilling for us⁄than visiting the Greek islands frequented by the jet set.

EXERCISE 33 – 1

Delete commas where necessary in the following sentences. If a sentence is correct, write "correct" after it. Answers to lettered sentences appear in the back of the book. Example:

Loretta Lynn has paved the way for artists such as⁄Barbara Mandrell and Janie Fricke.

a. We'd rather spend our money on blue-chip stocks, than speculate on porkbellies.
b. Being prepared for the worst, is one way to escape disappointment.
c. He went out into the cold and hailed a cab.
d. My father said, that he would move to California, if I would agree to transfer to UCLA.
e. I quickly accepted the fact that I was, literally, in third-class quarters.

1. The man, who escaped, was the one we wanted.
2. He wore a thick, black, wool coat over army fatigues and a spotted, T-shirt.

3. Often public figures, (Michael Jackson is a good example) go to great lengths to guard their private lives.
4. She loved early spring flowers such as, crocuses, daffodils, forsythia, and irises.
5. When he heard the groans, he opened the door, and ran out.
6. Mesquite, the hardest of the softwoods, grows primarily in the Southwest.
7. Dougherty says that the record for arrests would have been better, if he had not pulled the officers away from their regular duties to assist the homicide division.
8. The brass section of our high school band consisted of, four bugles, two trumpets, and one huge tuba.
9. Captain Edward Spurlock observed, that the vast majority of crimes in our city are committed by repeat offenders.
10. Sharecroppers are given a free house, but they pay for everything else.

34

The semicolon

The semicolon is used to separate major sentence elements of equal grammatical rank.

34a Use a semicolon between closely related independent clauses not joined by a coordinating conjunction.

When related independent clauses appear in one sentence, they are ordinarily connected with a comma and a coordinating conjunction (*and, but, or, nor, for, so, yet*). The coordinating conjunction signals the relation between the clauses. If the relation is clear without the conjunction, a writer may choose to connect the clauses with a semicolon instead.

> Injustice is relatively easy to bear; what stings is justice.
> —H. L. Mencken

The semicolon must be used whenever the coordinating conjunction has been omitted between independent clauses. To use merely a comma creates a serious error known as a comma splice. (See 20.)

▶ Evita didn't rise through hard work and dedication/; she

found other means.

▶ Some of the inmates were young and strung out on drugs/;

others looked as if they might kill at any moment.

34b Use a semicolon between independent clauses linked with a conjunctive adverb or transitional expression.

Conjunctive adverbs such as *however, nevertheless, moreover,* and *therefore* and transitional expressions such as *in fact* or *for example* frequently link independent clauses appearing in one sentence. When such words appear between the clauses, they are preceded by a semicolon and are usually followed by a comma.

▶ I learned all the rules and regulations/; however, I never

really learned to control the ball.

When a conjunctive adverb or transitional expression appears in the middle or at the end of the second independent clause, the semicolon goes *between the clauses*, not before the joining word.

▶ Twenty-eight of the applicants had college degrees/; twenty-four of them/, however, were clearly unqualified for the position.

Conjunctive adverbs and transitional expressions should not be confused with the coordinating conjunctions *and, but, or, nor, for, so,* and *yet,* which are preceded by a comma when they link independent clauses. (See 20.)

34c A semicolon may be used between independent clauses containing internal punctuation even when a coordinating conjunction links the clauses.

Ordinarily a semicolon is not used before a coordinating conjunction linking independent clauses. However, if the clauses contain internal punctuation, a semicolon may be used.

> As a vehicle [the Model T] was hard-working, commonplace, and heroic; and it often seemed to transmit those qualities to the persons who rode in it. — *E. B. White*

Though a comma would also be correct in this sentence, the semicolon is more effective, for it indicates the relative weights of the pauses.

34d Use a semicolon between items in a series containing internal punctuation.

▶ Classic science fiction sagas are *Star Trek*, with Mr. Spock and his large pointed ears/; *Battlestar Galactica*, with its

Cylon Raiders/; and *Star Wars*, with Han Solo, Luke

Skywalker, and Darth Vader.

Without the semicolons the reader would have to sort out the major groupings, distinguishing between important and less important pauses according to the logic of the sentence. By inserting semicolons at the major breaks, the writer does this work for the reader.

34e Do not use a semicolon to separate a subordinate clause from the rest of the sentence.

The semicolon should be used only between items of equal grammatical rank. Subordinate clauses are less important grammatically than the independent clauses in which they appear. (See 49b.)

▶ Unless you brush your teeth within ten or fifteen minutes

after eating/, brushing does almost no good.

The *Unless* clause is subordinate. Introductory subordinate clauses are usually followed by a comma (32b), never by a semicolon.

EXERCISE 34 – 1

Add commas or semicolons where needed in the following famous quotations. If a sentence is correct, write "correct" after it. Answers to lettered sentences appear in the back of the book. Example:

If an animal does something , we call it instinct ; if we do the

same thing , we call it intelligence.   — Will Cuppy

a. If fifty million people say a foolish thing it is still a foolish thing.
          — Anatole France

b. When I get a little money I buy books if any is left I buy food and clothes.   —Desiderius Erasmus

c. Don't talk about yourself it will be done when you leave.
                                              —Wilson Mizner

d. The only sensible ends of literature are first the pleasurable toil of writing second the gratification of one's family and friends and lastly the solid cash.   —Nathaniel Hawthorne

e. All animals are equal but some animals are more equal than others.   —George Orwell

1. Everyone is a genius at least once a year a real genius has his original ideas closer together.   —G. C. Lichtenberg

2. When choosing between two evils I always like to try the one I've never tried before.   —Mae West

3. I don't know who my grandfather was I am much more concerned to know what his grandson will be. —Abraham Lincoln

4. America is a country that doesn't know where it is going but is determined to set a speed record getting there.
                                            —Lawrence J. Peter

5. Do not ask me to be kind just ask me to act as though I were.
                                              —Jules Renard

35

The colon

The colon is used primarily to call attention to the words that follow it.

35a Use a colon after an independent clause to direct attention to a list, an appositive, or a quotation.

A LIST

The daily routine should include at least the following: twenty knee bends, fifty sit-ups, fifteen leg lifts, and five minutes of running in place.

To bring law and order to the fish tank, I had several alternatives: I could separate the villain from the victim, I could destroy the evil one, or I could hire a watchdog.

AN APPOSITIVE

My roommate is guilty of two of the seven deadly sins: gluttony and sloth.

Karate teaches respect: respect for your elders, for your country and flag, for your fellow students, for yourself.

A QUOTATION

Consider the words of John F. Kennedy: "Ask not what your country can do for you; ask what you can do for your country."

In a recent interview, Dave Erikson, a member of the Eagle Valley Environmentalists, explained what his group is trying to accomplish: "Most of our efforts are directed toward saving the bald eagle's wintering habitat along the Mississippi River."

For other ways of introducing quotations, see 37e.

35b Use a colon between independent clauses if the second summarizes or explains the first.

Faith is like love: It cannot be forced.

NOTE: When an independent clause follows a colon, it may begin with a lowercase or a capital letter.

35c Use a colon after the salutation in a formal letter, to indicate hours and minutes, to show proportions, and between city and publisher in bibliographic entries.

Dear Sir or Madam:

5:30 P.M. (or p.m.)

Martinis should be mixed about 5:1.

New York: St. Martin's, 1984

35d Do not use a colon before a list unless the list is preceded by an independent clause.

▶ Some important vitamins found in vegetables are / vitamin A,

thiamine, niacin, and vitamin C.

The area to be painted consisted of / three gable ends, trim

work, sixteen windows, and a front and back porch.

The lists in these sentences are not introduced with independent clauses. The list in the first sentence is simply a subject complement following the verb *are;* the list in the second sentence is the object of the preposition *of.*

EXERCISE 35 – 1

Edit the following sentences to correct errors in the use of the comma, the semicolon, or the colon. If a sentence is correct, write "correct" after it. Answers to lettered sentences appear in the back of the book. Example:

Smiling confidently, the young man stated his major goal in

life / to be secretary of agriculture before he was thirty.

a. The second and most memorable week of survival school consisted of five stages: orientation; long treks; POW camp; escape and evasion; and return to civilization.

b. Among the canceled classes were: calculus, physics, advanced biology, and English 101.

c. I entered this class feeling jittery and incapable, I leave feeling poised and confident.

d. Do not volunteer for any leadership position; unless you are certain that you can fulfill all the responsibilities.

e. In the introduction to his wife's book on gardening, E. B. White describes her writing process: "The editor in her fought the writer every inch of the way; the struggle was felt all through the house. She would write eight or ten words, then draw her gun and shoot them down."

1. His only desires were for vengeance; vengeance for his father's death, vengeance for his mother's loss of eyesight, vengeance for his own lost youth.

2. Martin Luther King, Jr., who forged the nonviolent civil rights movement in the United States, had not intended to be a preacher; initially, he had planned to become a lawyer.

3. Severe, unremitting pain is a ravaging force; especially when the patient tries to hide it from others.

4. The office work includes: typing reports and briefing materials; editing drafts for punctuation and grammar; and answering the phone.

5. Delegates came to the convention from all around the globe: from Basel, Switzerland, Waikiki, Hawaii, Nome, Alaska, and Pretoria, South Africa.

6. There are two types of leave: annual leave, which is used for vacations and personal reasons; and sick leave, which is used for medical appointments and illness.

7. I'm from Missouri, you must show me.

8. For some, happiness comes all in one satisfying, glowing piece, others, by patching together little bits of it, manage to salvage enough to keep warm.

9. By 2.30 that afternoon, the odds were 4;1 against him.

10. Historian Robert Kee looks to the past for the source of the political troubles in Ireland; "If blame is to be apportioned for today's situation in Northern Ireland, it should be laid not at the door of men today but of history."

36

The apostrophe

36a Use an apostrophe to indicate that a noun is possessive.

Possessive nouns usually indicate ownership, as in *Tim's hat* or *the lawyer's desk.* Frequently, however, ownership is only loosely implied: *the tree's roots, a day's work.* If you are not sure whether a noun is possessive, try turning it into an *of* phrase: *the roots of the tree, the work of a day.*

1. If the noun does not end in *-s,* add *-'s.*

> Roy managed to climb out on the driver's side.

> Thank you for refunding the children's money.

2. If the noun is singular and ends in *-s,* add *-'s.*

> Lois's sister spent last year in India.

EXCEPTION: If pronunciation would be awkward with the added *-'s,* some writers use only the apostrophe. Either use is acceptable.

> Euripides' plays are among my favorites.

3. If the noun is plural and ends in *-s,* add only an apostrophe.

> Both actresses' jewels were stolen.

4. To show joint possession, use *-'s* (or *-s'*) with the last

noun only; to show individual possession, make all nouns possessive.

> Have you seen Joyce and Greg's new camper?

> John's and Marie's expectations of marriage couldn't be more different.

In the first sentence, Joyce and Greg jointly own one camper. In the second sentence, John and Marie individually have different expectations.

5. If a noun is compound, use *-'s* (or *-s'*) with the last element.

> Her father-in-law's sculpture won first place.

36b Use an apostrophe and -s to indicate that an indefinite pronoun is possessive.

Indefinite pronouns are pronouns that refer to no specific person or thing: *everyone, someone, no one, something.* (See 47b.)

> Someone's raincoat has been left behind.

> This diet will improve almost anyone's health.

36c Use an apostrophe to mark contractions.

In contractions the apostrophe takes the place of missing letters.

> If that's not love, what would you call it?

> Doesn't Frank plan to go on the tour?

That's stands for *that is, doesn't* for *does not.*

36d Use an apostrophe and *-s* to pluralize numbers mentioned as numbers, letters mentioned as letters, words mentioned as words, and abbreviations.

Peggy skated nearly perfect figure 8's.

The bleachers in our section were marked with large red *J*'s.

We've heard enough *maybe*'s.

You must ask to see their I.D.'s.

EXCEPTION: An *-s* alone is often added to the years in a decade: the *1980s.*

36e Avoid common misuses of the apostrophe.

1. Do not use an apostrophe with nouns that are not possessive.

▶ Some ~~outpatient's~~ *outpatients* are given special parking permits.

2. Do not use an apostrophe in the possessive pronouns *its, whose, his, hers, ours, yours,* and *theirs.*

▶ Each area has ~~it's~~ *its* own conference room.

It's means *it is.* The possessive pronoun *its* contains no apostrophe, despite the fact that it is possessive.

▶ This course was taught by a professional florist ~~who's~~ *whose* technique was oriental.

Who's means *who is.* The possessive pronoun is *whose.*

EXERCISE 36 – 1

Edit the following sentences to correct errors in the use of the apostrophe. If a sentence is correct, write "correct" after it. Answers to lettered sentences appear in the back of the book. Example:

Marietta lived above the only bar in town, Smiling ~~Jacks~~ Jack's.

a. In a democracy anyones vote counts as much as mine.
b. He received two A's, three B's, and a C.
c. The puppy's favorite activity was chasing it's tail.
d. *Bubbling Brown Sugar* is one of the best musicals I've ever seen.
e. A crocodiles' life span is about thirteen years.

1. The snow does'nt rise any higher than the horses' fetlocks. [*more than one horse*]
2. For a bus driver, complaints, fare disputes, and robberies are all part of a days work.
3. Each day the menu features a different European countries' dish.
4. After a good nights rest, we headed for the chairlift's.
5. Booties are placed on the sled dogs feet to protect them from sharp rocks and ice. [*more than one dog*]
6. Sue and Ann went to a party for a friend of theirs'.
7. Kevins girl friend often calls late at night.
8. Ethiopians's meals were served on fermented bread.
9. Luck is an important element in a rock musician's career.
10. In the military you will be lucky to acquire a skill thats marketable in the civilian world.

37

Quotation marks

37a Use quotation marks to enclose direct quotations from printed material.

"A foolish consistency is the hobgoblin of little minds," wrote Ralph Waldo Emerson.

In *Walden* Thoreau offers this advice: "As long as possible live free and uncommitted. It makes but little difference whether you are committed to a farm or the county jail."

CAUTION: Do not use quotation marks around indirect quotations. An indirect quotation reports someone's ideas without using that person's exact words.

Ralph Waldo Emerson believed that consistency is the mark of a small mind.

EXCEPTION: Quotation marks are not used around long quotations that have been set off from the rest of the text. Quotations of four lines or more should be set off by indenting ten spaces from the left margin. Two or more lines of poetry are generally handled in this manner as well. See 52e.

37b Use quotation marks to enclose a person's spoken words or unspoken thoughts.

In a husky voice Ali bragged, "My opponent will be on the floor in round four. He'll take a dive in round five. In round nine he'll be all mine."

I thought to myself, "This is a jail, so what does he expect?"

NOTE: In dialogue, begin a new paragraph to mark a change in speaker.

"Mom, his name is Willie, not William. A thousand times I've told you, it's *Willie.*"

"Willie is a derivative of William, Lester. Surely his birth certificate doesn't have Willie on it, and I like calling people by their proper names."

"Yes, it does, ma'am. My mother named me Willie K. Mason."

—Gloria Naylor

If a single speaker utters more than one paragraph, introduce each paragraph with quotation marks, but do not use closing quotation marks until the end of the speech.

37c Use single quotation marks to enclose a quotation within a quotation.

According to Paul Eliott, Eskimo hunters "chant an ancient magic song to the seal they are after: 'Beast of the sea! Come and place yourself before me in the early morning!' "

37d Use quotation marks around the titles of newspaper and magazine articles, poems, short stories, songs, television and radio programs, and chapters or subdivisions of books.

Katherine Mansfield's "The Garden Party" provoked a lively discussion in our short-story class last night.

NOTE: Titles of books, plays, and films and names of magazines and newspapers are put in italics or underlined. See 42a.

37e Use punctuation with quotation marks according to convention.

1. Place periods and commas inside quotation marks.

"This is a stickup," said the well-dressed young couple. "We want all your money."

2. Put colons and semicolons outside quotation marks.

Harold wrote that he was "unable to attend the fundraiser for Ground Zero"; his letter, however, contained a substantial contribution.

3. Put question marks and exclamation points inside quotation marks unless they apply to the sentence as a whole.

Contrary to tradition, bedtime at my house is marked by "Mommy, can I tell you a story now?"

Have you heard the old proverb "Do not climb the hill until you reach it"?

In the first sentence, the question mark applies only to the quoted question. In the second sentence, the question mark applies to the whole sentence.

4. After a word group introducing a quotation, choose a colon, a comma, or no punctuation at all—whichever is appropriate in the context.

If a quotation has been formally introduced, a colon is appropriate. A formal introduction is a full independent clause, not just an expression such as *he said* or *she remarked.*

Freuchen points out that the diet is not as monotonous as it may seem: "When you have meat and meat, and meat again, you learn to distinguish between the different parts of an animal."

If a quotation is introduced with an expression such as *he said* or *she remarked* — or if it is followed by such an expression — a comma is needed.

Robert Frost said, "You can be a little ungrammatical if you come from the right part of the country."

"You can be a little ungrammatical if you come from the right part of the country," Robert Frost said.

When a quotation is blended into the writer's own sentence, either a comma or no punctuation is appropriate, depending on the way in which the quotation fits into the sentence structure.

The future champion could, as he put it, "float like a butterfly and sting like a bee."

Charles Hudson noted that the prisoners escaped "by squeezing through a tiny window eighteen feet above the floor of their cell."

If a quotation appears at the beginning of a sentence, set it off with a comma unless the quotation ends with a question mark or an exclamation point.

"We shot them like dogs," boasted Davy Crockett, who was among Jackson's troops.

"What is it?" I asked, bracing myself.

If a quoted sentence is interrupted by explanatory words, use commas to set off the explanatory words.

"A great many people think they are thinking," wrote William James, "when they are merely rearranging their prejudices."

If two successive quoted sentences from the same source are interrupted by explanatory words, use a comma before the explanatory words and a period after them.

"I was a flop as a daily reporter," admitted E. B. White. "Every piece had to be a masterpiece — and before you knew it, Tuesday was Wednesday."

37f Quotation marks may be used to set off words used as words.

Although words used as words are ordinarily underlined, to indicate italics (see 42d), quotation marks are also acceptable. Just be sure to follow consistent practice throughout a paper.

> The words "flaunt" and "flout" are frequently confused.

> The words *flaunt* and *flout* are frequently confused.

37g Do not use quotation marks to draw attention to familiar slang or to justify an attempt at humor.

▶ Greasers shout at their mothers, cruise the streets at night,

and punch each other out ~~"~~just for fun.~~"~~

EXERCISE 37–1

Add or delete quotation marks as needed and make any other necessary changes in punctuation in the following sentences. If a sentence is correct, write "correct" after it. Answers to lettered sentences appear in the back of the book. Example:

> Bill Cosby once said, "I don't know the key to success, but
>
> the key to failure is trying to please everyone."

a. Fire and Ice is one of Robert Frost's most famous poems.
b. As Emerson wrote in 1849, I hate quotations. Tell me what you know.
c. Joggers have to run up the hills and then back down, but bicyclers, once they reach the top of a hill, get a "free ride" back down.

d. Despite our earlier argument, Debbie approached me after work and said, "How about a game of Ms. Pac-Man, John?"

e. Historians Segal and Stineback tell us that the English settlers considered these epidemics "the hand of God making room for His followers in the "New World"."

1. The dispatcher's voice cut through the still night air: "Scout 41, robbery in progress, alley rear of 58th and Blaine.

2. For the body to turn sugar into glucose, other nutrients in the body must be used. Sugar "steals" these other nutrients from the body.

3. Kara looked hopelessly around the small locked room. "If only I were a flea," she thought, "I could get out of here."

4. My skiing instructor promised us that "we would all be ready for the intermediate slope in one week."

5. After the movie Vicki said, "The reviewer called this flick "trash of the first order." I guess you can't believe everything you read."

6. Joan was a self-proclaimed "rabid Celtics fan"; she went to every home game and even flew to Los Angeles for the playoffs.

7. Who said, "I have sworn upon the altar of God eternal hostility against every form of tyranny"?

8. As David Anable has written: "The time is approaching when we will be able to select the news we want to read from a pocket computer."

9. "Could one define the word 'red,' " asks Wittgenstein, "by pointing to something that was *not red*?"

10. While working at the clinic, I felt like a contestant on that old television program 'Beat the Clock.'

38

End punctuation

38a The period

1. Use a period to end all sentences except direct questions or genuine exclamations.

Everyone knows that a period should be used to end most sentences. The only problems that arise concern the choice between a period and a question mark or between a period and an exclamation point.

If a sentence reports a question instead of asking it directly, it should end with a period, not a question mark.

Celia asked whether the picnic would be canceled.

If a declarative or an imperative sentence is not a genuine exclamation, it should end with a period, not an exclamation point.

After years of working her way through school, Pat finally graduated with high honors.

Fill out the travel form in triplicate and then send it to the main office.

2. Use periods in abbreviations according to convention. A period is conventionally used in abbreviations such as the following:

Dr.	M.A.	A.M. (or a.m.)	i.e.
Mr.	Ph.D.	B.C. (or BC)	e.g.
Ms.	R.N.	A.D. (or AD)	etc.

A period is not used with U.S. Postal Service abbreviations for states: MD, TX, CA.

Ordinarily a period is not used in abbreviations of organization names:

NATO	UNESCO	AFL-CIO	FCC
TVA	IRS	SEC	IBM
USA	NAACP	PUSH	FTC
(or U.S.A.)	UCLA	NBA	NIH

Usage varies, however. When in doubt, consult a dictionary, a style manual, or a publication by the agency in question. Even the yellow pages can help.

38b The question mark

1. Use a question mark after a direct question.

Obviously a direct question should be followed by a question mark:

What is the horsepower of a 747 engine?

If a polite request is written in the form of a question, it too is usually followed by a question mark:

Would you please send me your catalog of lilies?

CAUTION: Do not use a question mark after an indirect question (one that is reported rather than asked directly). Use a period instead.

He asked me who was teaching the mythology course.

2. Questions in a series may be followed by question marks even when they are not complete sentences:

We wondered where Calamity had hidden this time. Under the sink? Behind the furnace? On top of the bookcase?

38c The exclamation point

1. Use an exclamation point after a word group or sentence that expresses exceptional feeling or deserves special emphasis.

The medic shook me and kept yelling, "He's dead! He's dead! Can't you see that?"

2. Do not overuse the exclamation point.

▶ In the fisherman's memory the fish lives on, increasing in

length and weight with each passing year, until at last it is

big enough to shade a fishing boat/.
              ∧

This sentence doesn't need to be pumped up with an exclamation point. It is emphatic enough without it.

▶ Whenever I see Martina lunging forward to put away an

overhead smash, it might as well be me/. She does it just the
                                    ∧

way that I would!

The first exclamation point should be deleted so that the second one will have more force.

EXERCISE 38–1

Add appropriate end punctuation in the following paragraph.

Although I am generally rational, I am superstitious I never walk under ladders or put shoes on the table If I spill the salt, I go into frenzied calisthenics picking up the grains and tossing them over my left shoulder As a result of these curious activities, I've always wondered whether knowing the roots of superstitions would quell my irrational responses Superstition has it, for example, that one should never place a hat on the bed This superstition arises from a time when head lice were quite common and placing a guest's hat on the bed stood a good chance of spreading lice through the host's bed Doesn't this make good sense And doesn't it stand to reason that if I

know that my guests don't have lice I shouldn't care where
their hats go Of course it does It is fair to ask, then, whether I
have changed my ways and place hats on beds Are you kidding
I wouldn't put a hat on a bed if my life depended on it

39

Other punctuation marks: the dash, parentheses, brackets, the ellipsis mark, the slash

39a The dash

When typing, use two hyphens to form a dash (--). Do not put
spaces before or after the dash.

1. Use dashes to set off parenthetical material that deserves
emphasis.

> Everything that went wrong — from the peeping Tom at her
> window to my head-on collision — was blamed on our move.

2. Use dashes to set off appositives that contain commas.

An appositive is a noun or noun phrase that renames a
nearby noun. Ordinarily most appositives are set off with
commas (32e), but when the appositive contains commas, a
pair of dashes helps readers see the relative importance of all
the pauses.

> In my hometown the basic needs of people — food, clothing,
> and shelter — are less costly than in Los Angeles.

3. Use a dash to prepare for a list, a restatement, an ampli-
fication, or a dramatic shift in tone or thought.

( )

Along the wall are the bulk liquids — sesame seed oil, honey, safflower oil, and that half-liquid "peanuts only" peanut butter.

Consider the amount of sugar in the average person's diet — 104 pounds per year, 90 percent more than that consumed by our ancestors.

Everywhere we looked there were little kids — a box of Cracker Jacks in one hand and mommy or daddy's sleeve in the other.

Kiere took a few steps back, came running full speed, kicked a mighty kick — and missed the ball.

4. Do not overuse the dash.

Unless there is a specific reason for using the dash, avoid it. Unnecessary dashes create a choppy effect.

▶ Seeing that our young people learn to use computers as

instructional tools ⫻ for information retrieval ⫻ makes good

sense. Herding them ⫻ sheeplike ⫻ into computer

technology does not.

39b Parentheses

1. Use parentheses to enclose supplemental material, minor digressions, and afterthoughts.

After taking her temperature, pulse, and blood pressure (routine vital signs), the nurse made Becky as comfortable as possible.

The weights James was first able to move (not lift, mind you) were measured in ounces.

2. Use parentheses to enclose letters or numbers labeling items in a series.

Regulations stipulated that only the following equipment could be used on the survival mission: (1) a knife, (2) thirty feet of parachute line, (3) a book of matches, (4) two ponchos, (5) an *E* tool, and (6) a signal flare.

3. Do not overuse parentheses.

Rough drafts are likely to contain more afterthoughts than necessary. As writers head into a sentence, they often think of additional details, occasionally working them in as best they can with parentheses. Usually such sentences should be revised so that the additional details no longer seem to be afterthoughts.

▶ Tucker's Restaurant serves homestyle breakfasts with fresh eggs, buttered toast, ~~(which is still warm)~~, *warm* sausage, bacon, waffles, pancakes, and even kippers.

▶ Researchers have said that ~~ten million (estimates run as high as fifty million)~~ *from ten to fifty million* Americans have hypoglycemia.

39c Brackets

Use brackets to enclose any words or phrases that you have inserted into an otherwise word-for-word quotation.

> *Audubon* reports that "if there are not enough young to balance deaths, the end of the species [California condor] is inevitable."

The *Audubon* article did not contain the words *California condor* in the sentence quoted, since the context made clear what species was meant, so the writer in this example needed to add the name in brackets.

Brackets may also enclose material that substitutes for a word in the original source. The example would be just as correct without the word *species,* since the words *California condor* could substitute for it.

> *Audubon* reports that "if there are not enough young to balance deaths, the end of the [California condor] is inevitable."

The Latin word *sic* in brackets indicates that an error in a quoted sentence appears in the original source.

> According to the review, Suzanne Farrell's performance was brilliant, "exceding [*sic*] the expectations of even her most loyal fans."

Do not overuse *sic,* however, since calling attention to others' mistakes can appear snobbish. The quotation above, for example, might have been paraphrased instead: *According to the review, even Suzanne Farrell's most loyal fans were surprised by the brilliance of her performance.*

39d The ellipsis mark

The ellipsis mark consists of three spaced periods. Use an ellipsis mark to indicate that you have deleted material from an otherwise word-for-word quotation.

> Reuben reports that "when the amount of cholesterol circulating in the blood rises over . . . 300 milligrams per 100, the chances of a heart attack increase dramatically."

Do not ordinarily use the ellipsis mark at the beginning or at the end of a quotation. See 52e.

39e The slash

Use the slash to separate two or three lines of poetry that have been run into your text. Add a space both before and after the slash.

> In the opening lines of "Jordan," George Herbert pokes gentle fun at popular poems of his time: "Who says that fictions only and false hair / Become a verse? Is there in truth no beauty?"

More than three lines of poetry should be handled as block quotations. See 37a and 52e.

The slash may occasionally be used to separate options such as *pass/fail* and *producer/director.* Do not use a space before or after the slash.

> Roger Sommers, the play's producer/director, announced a change in casting.

Be sparing, however, in this use of the slash. In particular, avoid use of *and/or, he/she,* and *his/her.*

EXERCISE 39 – 1

Edit the following sentences for punctuation problems, focusing especially on appropriate use of the dash, parentheses, brackets, ellipsis mark, and the slash. If a sentence is correct, write "correct" after it. Answers to lettered sentences appear in the back of the book. Example:

> Social insects／bees, for example／are able to communicate quite complicated messages to their fellows.

a. We lived in Iowa (Davenport, to be specific) during the early years of our marriage.

b. Pat helped Geoff put the tail on his kite — which was made of scraps from old dresses — and off they went to the park.

c. *Infoworld* reports that "customers without any particular aptitude for computers can easily learn to use it [the Bay Area Teleguide] through simple, three-step instructions located at the booth."

d. Cancer — a disease that strikes without regard to age, race, or religion and causes dread in the most stalwart person, had struck my family.

e. The class stood, faced the flag, placed hands over hearts, and raced through "I pledge allegiance — liberty and justice for all" in less than sixty seconds.

1. Of the three basic schools of detective fiction, the tea-and-crumpet, the hardboiled detective, and the police procedural, I find the quaint, civilized quality of the tea-and-crumpet school the most appealing.

2. The professional pool player needs to contend not only with abstract theories of math and physics but also with concrete details like the nap of the felt (usually running lengthwise) and the resiliency of the rails.

3. There are three points of etiquette in poker: 1. always allow someone to cut the cards, 2. don't forget to ante up, and 3. never stack your chips.

4. "April is the cruelest month . . . ," wrote T. S. Eliot, but we all know that February holds that honor.

5. The old Valentine verse we used to chant said it all: "Roses are red, / violets are blue, / sugar is sweet, / and so are you."

EXERCISE 39 – 2: Review

Punctuate the following letter.

27 Latches Lane
Missoula Missouri 55432
April 16 1988

Dear Rosalie

I have to tell you about the accident We were driving home at around 5 30 PM of course wed be on the Schuylkill Expressway at rush hour when a tan Cutlass smashed us in the rear Luckily we all had our seatbelts fastened Dr Schabbles who was in the back seat and my husband Bob complained of whiplash but really we got off with hardly a scratch

The mother and daughter in the Cutlass however werent as fortunate They ended up with surgical collars and Ace bandages but their car certainly fared better than ours

The driver of the third car involved in the accident confused everyone Although her car was in the front of the line she kept saying I hit the tan car I hit the tan car We didnt understand until she told us that a fourth car had hit her in the rear and had pushed her ahead of all the rest Can you imagine how frustrated we were when we found out that this man the one who had started it all had left the scene of the accident You were the last car in line someone said No you were we answered The policeman had to reconstruct the disaster from the hopeless babble of eight witnesses

Its uncanny Out of 34800 cars on the expressway on April 14 the police keep count you know our car had to be the one in front of that monstrous tan Cutlass

Well I just wanted to send you a report I hope your days are less thrilling than mine

Yours

Marie

Editing for Mechanics

40

Abbreviations

40a Abbreviate titles immediately before and after proper names.

TITLES BEFORE PROPER NAMES	TITLES AFTER PROPER NAMES
Mr. Ralph Meyer	William Albert, Sr.
Ms. Nancy Linehan	Thomas Hines, Jr.
Mrs. Edward Horn	Anita Lor, Ph.D.
Dr. Margaret Simmons	Robert Simkowski, M.D.
The Rev. John Stone	William Lyons, M.A.
St. Joan of Arc	Margaret Chin, LL.D.
Prof. James Russo	Polly Stein, D.D.S

Do not abbreviate a title if it is not used with a proper name.

▶ My history ~~prof.~~ *professor* was a specialist on America's use of the

atomic bomb in World War II.

Avoid redundant titles such as *Dr. Susan Hasselquist, M.D.* Choose one title or the other: *Dr. Susan Hasselquist* or *Susan Hasselquist, M.D.*

40b Use commonly accepted abbreviations for the names of organizations, corporations, and countries.

Familiar abbreviations, often written without periods, are acceptable:

CIA, FBI, AFL-CIO, NAACP
IBM, UPI, CBS
USA, USSR (or U.S.A., U.S.S.R.)

While in Washington the schoolchildren toured the FBI.

The YMCA has opened a new gym close to my office.

NOTE: When using an unfamiliar abbreviation (such as UAW for United Auto Workers) throughout a paper, write the full name followed by the abbreviation in parentheses at the first mention of the name. Then use the abbreviation throughout the rest of the paper.

40c Use the following commonly accepted abbreviations: B.C., A.D., A.M. (or a.m.), P.M. (or p.m.), $, No. (or no.).

40 B.C. (follows the date)	$100
A.D. 44 (precedes the date)	No. 12
4:00 A.M.	

NOTE: Use the abbreviations No. and $ only with specific numbers and amounts. Otherwise, write out the words.

▶ There were an odd ~~no.~~ *number* of seats in the room.

40d Use commonly accepted English and Latin abbreviations in footnotes and bibliographies and in informal writing for comments in parentheses.

cf. (Latin *confer*, "compare")
e.g. (Latin *exempli gratia*, "for example")
et al. (Latin *et alii*, "and others")

etc. (Latin *et cetera*, "and so forth")
i.e. (Latin *id est*, "that is")
N.B. (Latin *nota bene*, "note well")

She hated the slice-and-dice genre of horror movies (e.g., *Happy Birthday to Me, Psycho, Friday the Thirteenth*).

Harold Simms et al., *The Race for Space*

In formal writing use the appropriate English phrases.

▶ Many obsolete laws remain on the books, ~~e.g.~~ a law in

for example
∧

Vermont forbidding an unmarried man and woman to sit less

than six inches apart on a park bench.

40e Do not abbreviate personal names, units of measurement, days of the week, holidays, months, courses of study, divisions of written works, states and countries (except in addresses and except Washington, D.C.). Do not abbreviate Company, Incorporated, and Brothers unless their abbreviated forms are part of an official name.

PERSONAL NAME Charles (not Chas.)

UNITS OF MEASUREMENT pounds (not lb.)

DAYS OF THE WEEK Monday through Friday (not Mon. through Fri.)

HOLIDAYS Christmas (not Xmas)

MONTHS January, February, March (not Jan., Feb., Mar.)

COURSES OF STUDY political science, psychology (not poli. sci., psych.)

DIVISIONS OF WRITTEN WORKS chapter, page (not ch., p.)

STATES AND COUNTRIES   Massachusetts, New York (not MA or Mass., NY)

PARTS OF A BUSINESS NAME   Adams Lighting Company (not Adams Lighting Co.); Fletcher and Brothers, Incorporated (not Fletcher and Bros., Inc.)

▶ Eliza promised to buy me one ~~℔~~ *pound* of Godiva chocolate for my birthday, which was last ~~Fri.~~ *Friday.*

EXERCISE 40 – 1

Edit the following sentences to correct errors in abbreviations. If a sentence is correct, write "correct" after it. Answers to lettered sentences appear in the back of the book. Example:

This year ~~Xmas~~ *Christmas* will fall on a ~~Fri.~~ *Friday.*

a. Marlon Mansard, a reporter for CBS, received a congressional citation for his work in Lebanon.

b. My grandmother told me that of all the subjects she studied, she found poli. sci. the most challenging.

c. The Rev. Martin Luther King, Sr., spoke eloquently about his son's work against segregation in the South.

d. Julius Caesar was born in B.C. 100 and died in 44 B.C.

e. Turning to p. 195, Marion realized that she had finally reached the end of ch. 22.

1. Pardulio's Meat Market has every conceivable kind of meat: moose, bear, buffalo, deer, whale, chicken, beef, etc.

2. Three interns were selected to assist the chief surgeon, Dr. Paul Hunter, M.D., in the hospital's first heart-lung transplant.

3. Some historians think that the New Testament was completed by A.D. 100.

4. A no. of govt. officials have been reviewing the records of some small brokerage firms in the area.

5. When she arrived in Poughkeepsie to work at IBM, Pauline was overwhelmed by the sophistication and variety of product prototypes.

41

Numbers

41a Spell out numbers of one or two words. Use figures for numbers that require more than two words to spell out.

▶ Now, some ~~8~~ *eight* years later, Muffin is still with us.

▶ I counted ~~one hundred seventy-six~~ *176* records on the shelf.

If a sentence begins with a number, spell out the number or rewrite the sentence.

▶ ~~150~~ *One hundred fifty* children in our program need expensive dental

treatment.

> Rewriting the sentence will also correct the error and may be less awkward if the number is long: *There are 150 children in our program who need expensive dental treatment.*

EXCEPTIONS: In technical and some business writing, figures are preferred even when spellings would be brief, but usage varies.

When several numbers appear in the same passage, many writers choose consistency rather than strict adherence to the rule.

When one number immediately follows another, spell out one and use figures for the other: three 100-meter events, 125 four-poster beds.

41b Generally, figures are acceptable for dates, addresses, percentages, fractions, decimals, scores, statistics and other numerical results, exact amounts of money, divisions of books and plays, pages, identification numbers, and the time.

DATES July 4, 1776, 56 B.C., A.D. 30

ADDRESSES 77 Latches Lane, 519 West 42nd Street

PERCENTAGES 55% (or 55 percent)

FRACTIONS, DECIMALS ½, 0.047

SCORES 7 to 3, 21 – 18

STATISTICS average age 37, average weight 180

SURVEYS 4 out of 5

EXACT AMOUNTS OF MONEY $105.37, $106,000, $0.05

DIVISIONS OF BOOKS volume 3, chapter 4, page 189

DIVISIONS OF PLAYS Act III, scene iii (or Act 3, scene 3)

IDENTIFICATION NUMBERS serial number 10988675

TIME OF DAY 4:00 P.M., 1:30 A.M.

▶ Several doctors put up ~~two hundred fifty-five thousand~~ *$255,000* ~~dollars~~ for the construction of a golf course.

▶ Though I was working on a ~~nineteen thirty-nine~~ *1939* sewing machine, my costume turned out well.

NOTE: When not using A.M. or P.M., write out the time in words (*four o'clock in the afternoon, twelve noon, seven in the morning*).

EXERCISE 41 – 1

Edit the following sentences to correct errors in the use of numbers.
If a sentence is correct, write "correct" after it. Answers to lettered
sentences appear in the back of the book. Example:

By the end of the evening Brandon had only ~~three dollars~~ $3.06
~~and six cents~~ left.

a. On a normal day I spend at least 4 to 5 hours working on computers.
b. The president of Forti Motor Company announced that all shifts
   would report back to work at the Augusta plant on June 6, 1988.
c. The score was tied at 5 – 5 when the momentum shifted and
   carried the Standards to a decisive 12 – 5 win.
d. We ordered three four-door sedans for company executives.
e. In nineteen eighty-seven, only one hundred twelve male high school
   students in our state planned to make a career of teaching.

1. One of my favorite scenes in Shakespeare is the property division
   scene in Act I of *King Lear.*
2. The president's plane will arrive in Houston at 6:30 P.M.
3. 12 percent of all American marriages occur in June.
4. After her 5th marriage ended in divorce, Melinda decided to give
   up her quest for the perfect husband.
5. The results of the vote were thirty-four in favor, one hundred
   eighty-nine against.

42

Italics (underlining)

In handwritten or typed papers <u>underlining</u> represents *italics,* a slanting typeface used in printed material.

42a Underline the titles of books, plays, films, long poems, musical compositions, works of visual art, magazines, newspapers, and pamphlets.

TITLES OF BOOKS   *The Great Gatsby, David Copperfield*

PLAYS   *Julius Caesar, Death of a Salesman*

FILMS   *The French Connection, Star Wars*

LONG POEMS   T. S. Eliot's *The Waste Land*, Milton's *Paradise Lost*

MUSICAL COMPOSITIONS   Handel's *Messiah*, Gershwin's *Porgy and Bess*

WORKS OF VISUAL ART   Rodin's *The Thinker*, da Vinci's *The Last Supper*

MAGAZINES   *Time, Scientific American*

NEWSPAPERS   The *New York Times*, The *Boston Globe*

PAMPHLETS   Thomas Paine's *Common Sense*

The titles of other works, such as short stories, essays, songs, and short poems, are enclosed in quotation marks.

NOTE: Do not underline the Bible or the titles of books in the Bible (Genesis, not *Genesis*); the titles of legal documents (the Constitution, not *Constitution*); or the titles of your own papers.

42b Underline the names of spacecraft, aircraft, ships, and trains.

Apollo VIII, Spirit of St. Louis, Queen Elizabeth II, Silver Streak

▶ The success of the Soviet's <u>Sputnik</u> galvanized the U.S.
space program.

42c Underline foreign words used in an English sentence.

▶ Although Joe's method seemed to be successful, I decided to
establish my own <u>modus operandi.</u>

EXCEPTION: Do not underline foreign words that have become
part of the English language — "dilemma," "bourgeois," and
"karate," for example.

42d Underline words mentioned as words, letters mentioned as letters, and numbers mentioned as numbers.

▶ Tim assured us that the howling probably came from his
bloodhound, Hill Billy, but his <u>probably</u> stuck in our minds.

▶ Sarah called her father by his given name, Johnny, but she
was unable to pronounce <u>J.</u>

▶ A big <u>3</u> was painted on the door.

NOTE: Quotation marks may be used instead of underlining
to set off words mentioned as words. See 37f.

42e Avoid excessive underlining for emphasis.

The best strategies for achieving emphasis are rhetorical. Underlining to highlight words or ideas is a shortcut and should be used sparingly.

▶ Tennis is a sport that has become an <u>addiction</u>.

EXERCISE 42–1

Edit the following sentences to correct errors in the use of italics. If a sentence is correct, write "correct" after it. Answers to lettered sentences appear in the back of the book. Example:

<u>Leaves of Grass</u> by Walt Whitman was quite controversial

when it was published a century ago.

a. Howard Hughes commissioned the Spruce Goose, a beautifully built but thoroughly impractical wooden aircraft.
b. The old man *screamed* his anger, *shouting* to all of us, "I will not leave my money to you worthless lay-abouts!"
c. Even though it is almost always hot in Mexico in the summer, you can usually find a cool spot on one of the park benches in the town's zócalo.
d. I will never forget the way he whispered the word *finished.*
e. One of my favorite novels is George Eliot's "Middlemarch."

1. Bernard watched as Eileen stood transfixed in front of Vermeer's Head of a Young Girl.
2. The preacher was partial to quotations from Exodus.
3. I learned the Latin term ad infinitum from an old nursery rhyme about fleas: "Great fleas have little fleas upon their back to bite 'em, / Little fleas have lesser fleas and so on ad infinitum."
4. After we saw *The Untouchables*, Grandfather told me that he had met Al Capone years ago in Chicago.
5. In her first calligraphy lesson, Susanne learned how to make a Romanesque B.

43

Spelling

You learned to spell from repeated experience with words in both reading and writing, but especially in writing. Words have a look, a sound, and even a feel to them as the hand moves across the page. From your experience with words, you have no doubt developed a "suspicion quotient," an ability to spot particularly tricky words that are worth looking up. Is it *license* or *liscence* or *lisence?* You can probably tell when a word doesn't look quite right. The solution in such cases is obvious: Look up the word in a dictionary.

To develop your suspicion quotient, you can practice with a list of troublesome words, such as the one at the end of this section. Of course, the most effective list for you is a compilation of the words you've actually misspelled.

You can improve your spelling by working at it. Visualize a difficult word. Or, after looking it up in the dictionary, practice writing the word a number of times to give yourself the experience of writing it correctly and remembering it. Some people use mnemonics (memory aids) to help them with habitually misspelled words. For example, *commitment* and *committee* are two words that often give people trouble because of the *t* or *t*'s in the middle. You might remember that commitment is a single thing and then associate that singleness with one *t;* a committee, on the other hand, involves more than one person, so you might remember that the word has more than one *t.* Obviously, your own memory devices for words will be the most effective techniques for you.

Pronouncing a word carefully before writing it can also help your spelling. Don't add extra syllables. Many people say *ath-e-lete* and so misspell the word by adding an extra *e* in the middle. Likewise, don't omit necessary syllables. People often slur syllables in a word and therefore omit them in writing the word. A good example is the word *incidentally*, which people often pronounce *incidently* and so misspell.

If you have a severe spelling problem, perhaps caused by dyslexia, a word processor with a spelling checker is an almost indispensable aid. Be aware of the limitations of computer programs, however. They will not tell you how to spell words not listed in their dictionaries; nor will they help you catch words commonly confused, such as *accept* and *except* or *passed* and *past*. For many words, you will still need to turn to the dictionary.

43a Become familiar with your dictionary.

A good desk dictionary—such as *The American Heritage Dictionary of the English Language, The Random House College Dictionary,* or *Webster's New Collegiate* or *New World Dictionary of the American Language*—is an indispensable writer's aid. By reading or at least skimming your dictionary's guide to its use, which usually appears at the front of the book, you will discover many new reasons for turning to the dictionary for help.

A sample dictionary entry, taken from *The American Heritage Dictionary,* appears on page 292. Labels show where various kinds of information about a word can be found in that dictionary.

Spelling, word division, pronunciation

The main entry (*pre·vent* in the sample entry) shows the correct spelling of the word. When there are two correct spellings of a word (*preventable, preventible*), both are given, with the preferred spelling appearing first.

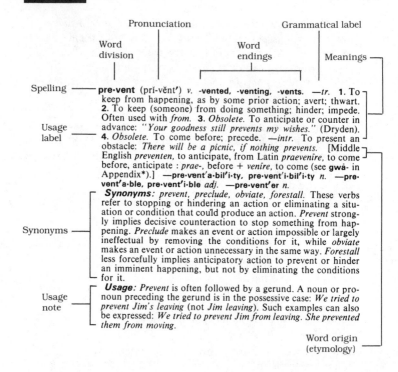

Pronunciation

Grammatical label

Word division

Word endings

Meanings —

Spelling ——— **pre·vent** (pri-věnt′) *v.* -vented, -venting, -vents. —*tr.* **1.** To keep from happening, as by some prior action; avert; thwart. **2.** To keep (someone) from doing something; hinder; impede. Often used with *from.* **3.** *Obsolete.* To anticipate or counter in advance: *"Your goodness still prevents my wishes."* (Dryden). **4.** *Obsolete.* To come before; precede. —*intr.* To present an obstacle: *There will be a picnic, if nothing prevents.* [Middle English *preventen,* to anticipate, from Latin *praevenire,* to come before, anticipate : *prae-*, before + *venire,* to come (see **gwā-** in Appendix*).] —**pre·vent′a·bil′i·ty, pre·vent′i·bil′i·ty** *n.* —**pre·vent′a·ble, pre·vent′i·ble** *adj.* —**pre·vent′er** *n.*

Usage label

Synonyms: *prevent, preclude, obviate, forestall.* These verbs refer to stopping or hindering an action or eliminating a situation or condition that could produce an action. *Prevent* strongly implies decisive counteraction to stop something from happening. *Preclude* makes an event or action impossible or largely ineffectual by removing the conditions for it, while *obviate* makes an event or action unnecessary in the same way. *Forestall* less forcefully implies anticipatory action to prevent or hinder an imminent happening, but not by eliminating the conditions for it.

Synonyms ———

Usage: *Prevent* is often followed by a gerund. A noun or pronoun preceding the gerund is in the possessive case: *We tried to prevent Jim's leaving* (not *Jim leaving*). Such examples can also be expressed: *We tried to prevent Jim from leaving. She prevented them from moving.*

Usage note

Word origin (etymology) —

The main entry also shows how the word is divided into syllables. The dot between *pre* and *vent* separates the word's two syllables. When a word is compound, the main entry shows how to write the word: as one word (*crossroad*), as a hyphenated word (*cross-stitch*), or as two words (*cross section*).

The word's pronunciation is given just after the main entry. The accents indicate which syllables are stressed; the other marks are explained in the dictionary's pronunciation key. In some dictionaries this key appears at the bottom of every page or every other page.

Word endings and grammatical labels

When a word takes endings to indicate grammatical functions (called *inflections*), the endings are listed in boldface, as with *-vented, -venting,* and *-vents* in the sample entry.

Labels for the parts of speech and for other grammatical terms are abbreviated. The most commonly used abbreviations are these:

n.	noun	adj.	adjective
pl.	plural	adv.	adverb
sing.	singular	pron.	pronoun
v.	verb	prep.	preposition
tr.	transitive verb	conj.	conjunction
intr.	intransitive verb	interj.	interjection

Meanings, word origin, synonyms, and antonyms

Each meaning for the word is given a number. Occasionally a word's use is illustrated in a quoted sentence, as with the sentence by Dryden in the sample entry.

The origin of the word, called its *etymology,* appears in brackets after the list of meanings (in some dictionaries it appears before the meanings).

Synonyms, words similar in meaning to the main entry, are frequently listed. In the sample entry, the dictionary draws distinctions in meaning among the various synonyms. Antonyms, which do not appear in the sample entry, are words having a meaning opposite from that of the main entry.

Usage

Usage labels indicate when, where, or under what conditions a particular meaning for a word is appropriately used. Common labels are *informal* (or *colloquial*), *slang, nonstandard,* dialect, obsolete, archaic, poetic, and British. In the sample entry, two meanings of *prevent* are labeled as *obsolete* because they are no longer in use.

Dictionaries sometimes include usage notes as well. In the sample entry, the dictionary offers advice on a grammatical problem that sometimes arises following the verb *prevent*. Such advice is based on the opinions of many experts and on actual usage in current magazines, newspapers, and books.

43b Discriminate between words that sound alike but have different meanings.

Pronunciation can be a useful guide to spelling, but don't rely too heavily on it. As you know by now, words are not always spelled as they sound, especially in English. Think of the different sounds for *-ough* in the following words: *rough, thorough, through, slough*. Other sets of words that cause spelling troubles are homophones, words sounding alike but having different meanings and spellings.

HOMOPHONES (WORDS WITH SIMILAR PRONUNCIATION AND DIFFERENT MEANINGS)

accept (to receive)
except (to take or leave out)

affect (v., to exert an influence)
effect (v., to accomplish; n., result)

ascent (a climb)
assent (agreement)

brake (something used to stop movement)
break (to split or smash into pieces)

capital (seat of government)
capitol (building in which a legislative body meets)

cite (to quote)
sight (vision)
site (position, place)

complement (something that completes)
compliment (praise)

coarse (of ordinary or inferior quality)
course (path, policy chosen)

desert (v., to withdraw from; n., uninhabited and arid land)
dessert (sweet course at the end of a meal)

discreet (prudent, tactful)
discrete (constituting a separate entity)

elicit (to draw or bring out)
illicit (illegal)

eminent (famous, respected)
immanent (indwelling, inherent)
imminent (ready to take place)

formally (in a customary manner)
formerly (in time past)

hole (hollow place)
whole (entire, unhurt)

its (of or belonging to it)
it's (contraction for *it is*)

lead (n., metal; v., to guide)
led (past tense of the verb *lead*)

loose (free, not securely attached)
lose (to fail to keep, to be deprived of)

manner (way)
manor (house)

pair (set of two)
pare (to prepare, trim)
pear (a fruit)

passed (past tense of the verb *pass*)
past (belonging to a former time)

principal (most important; a person who has authority)
principle (a general or fundamental truth)

rain (water falling in drops)
reign (to rule)
rein (restraining influence)

raise (to lift)
raze (to destroy, to lay level with the ground)

stationary (standing still)
stationery (writing paper)

straight (free from curves, bends, or angles)
strait (narrow space or passage)

than (conj., used to compare)
then (adverb of time)

their (belonging to them)
they're (contraction of *they are*)
there (that place or position)

to (prep., toward)
too (also, excessively)
two (one more than one in number)

weather (state of the atmosphere)
whether (indicating a choice between alternatives)

who's (contraction of *who is*)
whose (possessive of *who*)

your (possessive of *you*)
you're (contraction of *you are*)

43c Be aware of the major spelling rules.

1. Use *i* before *e* except after *c* or when sounded like *ay*, as in *neighbor* and *weigh*.

I BEFORE E	relieve, believe, sieve, frieze
E BEFORE I	receive, deceive, sleigh, freight, eight
EXCEPTIONS	seize, either, weird, height, foreign, leisure

2. Generally, drop a final silent *e* when adding a suffix that begins with a vowel. Keep the final *e* if the suffix begins with a consonant.

desire, desiring; remove, removable

achieve, achievement; care, careful

Words such as *argument, truly,* and *changeable* are exceptions.

3. When adding -*s* or -*ed* to words ending in *y*, ordinarily change *y* to *i* when the *y* is preceded by a consonant but not when it is preceded by a vowel.

comedy, comedies; dry, dried

monkey, monkeys; play, played

With proper names ending in *y*, however, do not change the *y* to *i* even if it is preceded by a consonant: *Dougherty, the Doughertys.*

4. If a final consonant is preceded by a single vowel *and* the consonant ends a one-syllable word or a stressed syllable, double the consonant when adding a suffix beginning with a vowel.

bet, betting; commit, committed; occur, occurrence

5. Add -*s* to form the plural of most nouns; add -*es* to singular nouns ending in -*s, -sh, -ch,* and -*x.*

table, tables; paper, papers

church, churches; dish, dishes

Ordinarily add *-s* to nouns ending in *-o* when the *o* is preceded by a vowel. Add *-es* when it is preceded by a consonant.

> radio, radios; video, videos

> hero, heroes; tomato, tomatoes

To form the plural of a hyphenated compound word, add the *-s* to the chief word even if it does not appear at the end.

> mother-in-law, mothers-in-law

NOTE: English words derived from other languages such as Latin or French sometimes form the plural as they would in their original language.

> medium, media; criterion, criteria; chateau, chateaux

43d Learn the following commonly misspelled words.

absence	although	arithmetic
academic	altogether	arrangement
accidentally	always	ascend
accommodate	amateur	association
accomplish	among	athlete
accumulate	analyze	athletics
achievement	annual	attendance
acknowledge	answer	audience
acquaintance	apology	bachelor
acquire	apparently	basically
across	appearance	beginning
address	appropriate	believe
aggravate	arctic	benefited
all right	argument	brilliant
almost	arising	Britain

bureau
business
cafeteria
calendar
candidate
category
cemetery
changeable
changing
characteristic
chosen
column
coming
commitment
committed
committee
comparative
competitive
conceivable
conference
conferred
conqueror
conscience
conscientious
conscious
convenient
courteous
criticism
criticize
curiosity
dealt
decision
definitely
descendant
describe
description
despair
desperate
develop
dictionary

dining
disagree
disappear
disappoint
disastrous
dissatisfied
eighth
eligible
eliminate
embarrass
eminent
emphasize
entirely
entrance
environment
equivalent
especially
exaggerated
exhaust
existence
experience
explanation
extraordinary
extremely
familiar
fascinate
February
foreign
forty
fourth
friend
government
grammar
guard
guidance
harass
height
humorous
illiterate
imaginary

imagination
immediately
incidentally
incredible
indefinitely
indispensable
inevitable
infinite
intelligence
interesting
irrelevant
irresistible
knowledge
laboratory
legitimate
license
lightning
literature
loneliness
maintenance
maneuver
marriage
mathematics
mischievous
necessary
nevertheless
noticeable
obstacle
occasion
occasionally
occur
occurred
occurrence
optimistic
original
outrageous
pamphlet
parallel
particularly
pastime

perform	quantity	sincerely
performance	quiet	soliloquy
permissible	quite	sophomore
perseverance	quizzes	specimen
perspiration	receive	strictly
phenomenon	recognize	subtly
physically	recommend	succeed
picnicking	reference	surprise
playwright	referred	temperature
politics	regard	thorough
practically	religion	tragedy
precede	repetition	transferred
precedence	restaurant	tries
preference	rhythm	truly
preferred	rhythmical	Tuesday
prejudice	ridiculous	unanimous
preparation	roommate	unnecessarily
prevalent	sandwich	until
primitive	schedule	usually
privilege	secretary	vacuum
probably	seize	vengeance
proceed	separate	villain
professor	sergeant	weird
prominent	several	whether
pronunciation	similar	writing

EXERCISE 43–1

Correct any spelling mistakes in the following list of words. If a word is correct, write "correct" after it. (Use a dictionary when in doubt.)

ellusive	beaurocrat	twelth
percieve	erasible	annoint
maladies	inconsistent	ryme
beautiful	pulleys	traceable
anullment	nuclear	retrieveable
retirment	promoteable	skis
lonley	vidio	

44

The hyphen

44a Consult the dictionary to determine whether a compound word should be treated as a hyphenated compound (*water-repellent*), one word (*waterproof*), or two words (*water table*); if the compound word is not in the dictionary, treat it as two words.

▶ Grandma kept a small note book in her apron pocket.

▶ We could see the forest fire clearly from the look out on top of the mountain.

▶ Alice walked through the looking glass into a backward world.

Use a hyphen to connect two or more words functioning together as an adjective before a noun.

▶ Mrs. Douglas gave Mary a seashell and some newspaper–
wrapped fish to take home to her mother.

Priscilla Hobbes is not yet a well–known candidate.

Newspaper-wrapped and *well-known* are adjectives used before the nouns *fish* and *candidate*.

Generally, do not use a hyphen when such compounds follow the noun.

▶ After our television campaign, Priscilla Hobbes will be well/ known.

Do not use a hyphen to connect *-ly* adverbs to the words they modify.

▶ A slowly/moving truck tied up traffic.

NOTE: In a series, hyphens are suspended.

Do you prefer first-, second-, or third-class tickets?

44b Hyphenate the written form of fractions and of compound numbers from twenty-one to ninety-nine.

▶ One‑fourth of my income goes to pay off the national debt.

44c Use the hyphen with the prefixes *all-*, *ex-*, and *self-* and with the suffix *-elect*.

▶ The charity is funneling more money into self‑help projects.

▶ Anne King is our club's president‑elect.

44d The hyphen is used in some words to avoid ambiguity or to separate awkward double or triple letters.

Without the hyphen there would be no way to distinguish between words such as *re-creation* and *recreation*.

Bicycling in the country is my favorite recreation.

The film was praised for its astonishing re-creation of nineteenth-century London.

Hyphens are sometimes used to separate awkward double or triple letters in compound words (*anti-intellectual, cross-stitch*). Always check a dictionary for the standard form of the word.

44e If a word must be divided at the end of a line, divide it correctly.

1. Divide words between syllables.

▶ When I returned from overseas, I didn't ~~reco~~ *recog-*
nize
~~gnize~~ one face on the magazine covers.

2. Never divide one-syllable words.

▶ He didn't have the courage or the ~~stren~~
strength
~~gth~~ to open the door.

3. Never divide a word so that a single letter stands alone at the end of a line or fewer than three letters begin a line.

▶ She'll bring her brother with her when she comes ~~a~~
again
~~gain~~.

▶ As audience to *The Mousetrap*, Hamlet is a ~~watch~~
watcher
~~er~~ watching watchers.

4. When dividing a compound word at the end of a line, either make the break between the words that form the compound or put the whole word on the next line.

▶ My niece is determined to become a long-~~dis-~~

distance
~~tance~~ runner when she grows up.
^

EXERCISE 44–1

Edit the following sentences to correct errors in hyphenation. If a sentence is correct, write "correct" after it. Answers to lettered sentences appear in the back of the book. Example:

Zola's first readers were scandalized by his slice—of—life
                                                        ^ ^

novels.

a. Gold is the seventy-ninth element in the periodic table.
b. The swiftly-moving tugboat pulled alongside the barge and directed it away from the oil spill in the harbor.
c. Many states are adopting laws that limit property taxes for homeowners.
d. Two thirds of the House voted for the amendment.
e. He did fifty push-ups in two minutes and then collapsed.

1. We knew we were driving too fast when our tires skidded over the rain slick surface.
2. Many people protested when the drinking age was lowered from twenty-one to twenty.
3. Instead of an old Victorian, we settled for a modern split-level surrounded by maples.
4. One-quarter of the class signed up for the debate on U.S. foreign aid to Latin America.
5. At the end of *Macbeth*, the hero feels himself profoundly a-lone.

45

Capital letters

In addition to the following rules, a good dictionary can often tell you when to use capital letters.

45a Capitalize proper nouns and words derived from them; do not capitalize common nouns.

Proper nouns are the names of specific persons, places, and things. All other nouns are common nouns. The following types of words are usually capitalized: names for the deity, religions, religious followers, sacred books; words of family relationship used as names; particular places; nationalities and their languages, races, tribes; educational institutions, departments, degrees, particular courses; government departments, organizations, political parties; and historical movements, periods, events, documents.

PROPER NOUNS	COMMON NOUNS
God (used as a name)	a god
Book of Jeremiah	a book
Grandmother Bishop	my grandmother
Father (used as a name)	my father
Lake Superior	a picturesque lake
the Capital Center	a center for advanced studies
the South	a southern state
Japan, a Japanese garden	an ornamental garden
University of Wisconsin	a good university
Geology 101	geology
Environmental Protection Agency	a federal agency

PROPER NOUNS	COMMON NOUNS
Phi Kappa Psi	a fraternity
a Democrat	an independent
the Enlightenment	the eighteenth century
the Declaration of Independence	a treaty

Months, holidays, and days of the week are treated as proper nouns; the seasons and numbers of the days of the month are not.

> Our academic year begins on a Tuesday in early September, right after Labor Day.

> My mother's birthday is in early summer, on the thirteenth of June.

Names of school subjects are capitalized only if they are names of languages. Names of particular courses are capitalized.

> This semester Austin is taking math, geography, geology, French, and English.

> Professor Anderson offers Modern American Fiction 501 to graduate students.

CAUTION: Do not capitalize common nouns to make them seem important: *Our company is currently hiring computer programmers* (not *Company, Computer Programmers*).

45b Capitalize titles of persons when used as part of a proper name but usually not when used alone.

> Professor Margaret Barnes; Dr. Harold Stevens; John Scott Williams, Jr.; Anne Tilton, LL.D.

District Attorney Marshall was reprimanded for badgering the witness.

The district attorney was elected for a two-year term.

Usage varies when the title of an important public figure is used alone: The president (or the President) vetoed the bill.

45c   Capitalize the first, last, and all major words in titles and subtitles of works such as books, articles, and songs.

In both titles and subtitles, major words such as nouns, verbs, adjectives, and adverbs should be capitalized. Minor words such as articles, prepositions, and coordinating conjunctions are not capitalized unless they are the first or last word of a title or subtitle. Capitalize the second part of a hyphenated term in a title if it is a major word but not if it is a minor word.

> *The Country of the Pointed Firs*
> *The Impossible Theater: A Manifesto*
> *The F-Plan Diet*

Capitalize chapter titles and the titles of other major divisions of a work following the same guidelines used for titles of complete works.

> "Work and Play" in Santayana's *The Nature of Beauty*

45d   Capitalize the first word of a sentence.

When lightning struck the house, the chimney collapsed.

Capitalize the first word in every line of poetry unless the poet uses a different convention.

> When I consider everything that grows
> Holds in perfection but a little moment   — *Shakespeare*

> it was the week   that
> i felt the city's narrow breezes rush about
> me   — *Don L. Lee*

45e Capitalize the first word of a quoted sentence unless it is blended into the sentence that introduces it.

> In *Time* magazine Robert Hughes writes, "There are only about sixty Watteau paintings on whose authenticity all experts agree."

> Russell Baker has written that in our country "it is sport that is the opiate of the masses."

If a quoted sentence is interrupted by explanatory words, do not capitalize the first word after the interruption.

> "If you wanted to go out," he said sharply, "you should have told me."

45f Do not capitalize the first word after a colon unless it begins an independent clause, in which case capitalization is optional.

> Most of the bar's patrons can be divided into two groups: the occasional after-work socializers and the nothing-to-go-home-to regulars.

> This we are forced to conclude: the [*or* The] federal government is needed to protect the rights of minorities.

45g Capitalize abbreviations for departments and agencies of government, other organizations, and corporations; capitalize trade names and the call letters of radio and television stations.

EPA, FBI, OPEC, IBM, Xerox, WCRB, WOR-TV

EXERCISE 45 – 1

Edit the following sentences to correct errors in capitalization. If a sentence is correct, write "correct" after it. Answers to lettered sentences appear in the back of the book. Example:

> On our trip to the West we visited the ~~g~~*G*rand ~~c~~*C*anyon and the ~~g~~*G*reat ~~s~~*S*alt ~~d~~*D*esert.

a. District attorney Johnson was disgusted when the jurors turned in a verdict of not guilty after only one hour of deliberation.
b. *The Witches of Eastwick* is a strange novel and an even stranger film.
c. W. C. Fields's epitaph reads, "On the whole, I'd rather be in Philadelphia."
d. Refugees from central America are finding it more and more difficult to cross the rio Grande into the United States.
e. I want to take Environmental Biology 103, one other Biology course, and one English course.

1. "Forbidding people things they like or think they might enjoy," contends Gore Vidal, "Only makes them want those things all the more."
2. Whenever my brother took us to the movies, he gave us three choices: A brainless beach party flick, a foreign fluff film, or a blood-and-lust adventure movie.
3. In our family, aunt Sandra was notorious for her biting tongue.
4. Historians have described Robert E. Lee as the aristocratic south personified.
5. My brother is a Doctor and my sister-in-law is an Attorney.

46

Manuscript preparation

By following standard guidelines in preparing manuscripts, a writer fulfills the reader's expectations about how a paper should look. Decisions about where to put the title, where to number the pages, and how much margin to leave become easier for the writer, and the paper is more legible for the reader. If your instructor provides formal guidelines, follow them; otherwise, use the guidelines given in this section.

Materials

For a typed paper use $8\frac{1}{2}'' \times 11''$, 20-pound typing paper, not onionskin. Some instructors allow erasable or corrasable bond, but ink smears easily on this coated paper, so you should probably avoid it. Use a fresh ribbon, and clean the typewriter keys before you begin. Use Liquid Paper or some other white correction fluid to eliminate errors completely. Allow the liquid to dry and then type over the error. Do not type hyphens, *x*'s, or slashes through a mistake, and do not strike over a mistake without first erasing it or whiting it out. Some instructors will accept a line through the mistake with the correction neatly written or typed above. Use a caret (∧) to indicate where the correction should be inserted. Make the finished page as neat and legible as possible. If a mistake is substantial (more than one line of type), retype the page.

For a paper typed on a word processor, make sure that the print quality and the paper quality meet your instructor's standards. If the paper emerges from the printer in a continuous sheet, separate the pages, remove the feeder strips from the sides of the paper, and assemble the pages in order.

Before you consider submitting a handwritten paper, make sure that your instructor will accept work that is not typewritten. Use 8½″ × 11″, wide-ruled white paper, and write on only one side of the sheet. Do not use legal-size paper or sheets torn from a notebook. Again, the aim is legibility and neatness. If your handwriting is difficult to read, make an effort to type the paper or have it typed. If you must submit a handwritten paper, make your handwriting as clear as possible. Most instructors ask students to skip one line between each line of writing. Use blue or black ink (not pencil) and be sure to use an ink eraser when correcting mistakes. Never scribble over mistakes. Rewrite the page if an error is substantial.

Title and identification

College papers normally do not require a separate title page. Unless instructed otherwise, place your name, the instructor's name, the course number, and the date on separate lines, double-spacing between lines. Type this heading against the left margin about one inch from the top. Double-space after the heading and center the title of the paper in the width of the page. If the title has two or more lines, double-space between the lines and double-space twice after the title to begin the body of the paper. Capitalize the first and last words of the title and subtitle and all other words except articles, prepositions, and coordinating conjunctions (see 45c). Do not underline the title or put it in quotation marks, and do not use a period after the title. If you mention another work in your title, underline the title of that work if it is a book, long poem, play, and so on, or enclose it in quotation marks if it is a poem, essay, short story, or other shorter work. (See 37d and 42a.)

For a research paper, a title page may or may not be required. See page 404 for an example.

Margins, spacing, and indentation

Leave margins of at least one inch but no more than an inch and a half at the top, bottom, and sides of the paper.

Double-space between lines in a typewritten paper, and indent the first line of each paragraph five spaces from the left margin.

For quotations of longer than four typed lines of prose or longer than three lines of verse, indent each line ten spaces from the left margin. Double-space between the body of the paper and the quotation, and double-space the lines of the quotation. (See 52e.)

Pagination

Number all pages at the upper right-hand corner of the page, one-half inch below the top edge. (If you have a separate title page, the title page is uncounted and unnumbered.) Use arabic numerals (1, 2, 3, and so on). Do not put a period after the number and do not enclose the number in parentheses.

If there are endnotes, begin them on a separate page after the text of the paper and continue to number these pages. Do the same if there is a list of works cited. If you include an outline, you can number the outline pages with small roman numerals (i, ii, iii, and so on).

Punctuation and typing

In typing the paper leave one space after words, commas, and semicolons and between the dots in ellipses. Leave two spaces after periods, question marks, and exclamation points. Usage is divided concerning spacing after a colon. Many authorities recommend two spaces, but the 1984 *MLA Handbook for Writers of Research Papers* recommends one space.

To form a dash, type two hyphens with no space between them. Do not put a space between a word and a dash.

Proofreading

Misspelled words, incorrect hyphenation, and errors in grammar and punctuation detract from the overall effect of a paper; if there are too many of these errors, readers will lose patience. Your ideas deserve clear and correct expression. Proofread the final draft of the paper and then proofread it again.

Grammar Basics

47

Parts of speech

There are eight parts of speech: noun, pronoun, verb, adjective, adverb, preposition, conjunction, and interjection. Many words can function as more than one part of speech. For example, depending on its use in a sentence, the word *paint* can be a noun (*The paint is wet*) or a verb (*Please paint the ceiling next*).

47a Nouns

As every schoolchild knows, a noun is the name of a person, place, or thing. In addition, grammarians describe a noun as follows:

> the kind of word that is often marked with an article (*a spoon, an apple, the newspaper*);

> the kind of word that can be pluralized (*one cat, two cats*) or made possessive (*the cat's paw*);

> the kind of word that when derived from another word typically takes one of these endings: play*er*, just*ice*, happi*ness*, divis*ion*, guid*ance*, refer*ence*, pave*ment*, child*hood*, king*dom*, agen*cy*, tour*ist*, sincer*ity*, censor*ship*;

> the kind of word that can fill one of these slots in a sentence: subject, direct object, indirect object, subject complement, object complement, and object of the preposition. (See 48a and 48c.)

Nouns, in other words, may be identified as much by their form and function as by their meaning.

Nouns may occasionally be used as adjectives modifying other nouns (*school* bus, *Wanda's* office). Because they have a dual function, nouns used in this manner may be called *noun/adjectives.*

Nouns are classified for a variety of purposes. When capitalization is the issue, we speak of *proper* versus *common nouns* (see 45a). If the problem is one of word choice, we may speak of *concrete* versus *abstract nouns* (see 18b). The distinction between *mass nouns* and *count nouns* is useful primarily for nonnative speakers of English (see 30b). The term *collective noun* refers to a set of nouns that may cause problems with subject-verb or pronoun-antecedent agreement (see 21e and 22c).

EXERCISE 47 – 1

Underline the nouns (and noun/adjectives) in the following sentences. Answers to lettered sentences appear in the back of the book. Example:

Pride is at the bottom of all great mistakes.

a. The cat in gloves catches no mice.
b. Repetition does not transform a lie into truth.
c. Our national flower is the concrete cloverleaf.
d. The ultimate censorship is the flick of the dial.
e. Figures won't lie, but liars will figure.

1. Conservatism is the worship of dead revolutions.
2. The winds and the waves are always on the side of the ablest navigators.
3. You can't make a silk purse out of a sow's ear.
4. A scalded dog fears even cold water.
5. Prejudice is the child of ignorance.

47b Pronouns

There are thousands of nouns, and new ones come into the language every year. This is not true of pronouns, which number about one hundred and are extremely resistant to change. Most of the pronouns in English are listed in this section.

A pronoun is a word used for a noun. A pronoun usually substitutes for a specific noun, known as its *antecedent.*

When Susan opened the door, *she* pretended surprise.

The noun *Susan* is the antecedent of the pronoun *she.*

Although most pronouns function as substitutes for nouns, some can function as adjectives modifying nouns.

This new car was *my* birthday present.

This modifies the noun *car,* and *my* modifies the noun *present.* Because they have the form of a pronoun and the function of an adjective, such pronouns may be called *pronoun/adjectives.*

Pronouns are classified as personal, possessive, intensive or reflexive, relative, interrogative, demonstrative, and indefinite.

Personal pronouns refer to specific persons or things. They are singular or plural in form, and they always function as noun equivalents.

SINGULAR PERSONAL PRONOUNS   I, me, you, he, him, she, her, it

PLURAL PERSONAL PRONOUNS   we, us, you, they, them

Possessive pronouns indicate ownership. Like personal pronouns, they are singular or plural in form.

SINGULAR POSSESSIVE PRONOUNS   my, mine, your, yours, his, her, hers, its

PLURAL POSSESSIVE PRONOUNS   our, ours, your, yours, their, theirs

Some of these possessive pronouns function as adjectives modifying nouns: *my, your, his, her, its, our, their.*

Intensive pronouns emphasize a noun or another pronoun (The congresswoman *herself* met us at the door). *Reflexive pronouns,* which have the same form as intensive pronouns, name a receiver of an action identical with the doer of the action (Paula cut *herself*). Intensive and reflexive pronouns are singular or plural in form.

SINGULAR INTENSIVE AND REFLEXIVE PRONOUNS   myself, yourself, himself, herself, itself

PLURAL INTENSIVE AND REFLEXIVE PRONOUNS   ourselves, yourselves, themselves

Relative pronouns introduce subordinate clauses functioning as adjectives (The man *who robbed us* was never caught). In addition to introducing the clause, the relative pronoun, in this case *who,* points back to the noun or pronoun that the clause modifies (*man*). (See 49b.)

RELATIVE PRONOUNS   who, whom, whose, which, that

Interrogative pronouns introduce questions (*Who* is expected to win the election?).

INTERROGATIVE PRONOUNS   who, whom, whose, which, what

Demonstrative pronouns are used to identify nouns. Frequently they function as adjectives (*This* chair is my favorite), but they may also function as noun equivalents (*This* is my favorite chair).

DEMONSTRATIVE PRONOUNS this, that, these, those

Indefinite pronouns are used for general rather than specific references. Some are always singular (*everyone, each, none*); others are always plural (*both, many*). Most indefinite pronouns function as noun equivalents, but some can also function as adjectives.

all	anything	everyone	nobody	several
another	both	everything	none	some
any	each	few	no one	somebody
anybody	either	many	nothing	someone
anyone	everybody	neither	one	something

EXERCISE 47–2

Underline the pronouns (and pronoun/adjectives) in the following sentences. Answers to lettered sentences appear in the back of the book. Example:

Beware of persons <u>who</u> are praised by <u>everyone</u>.

a. Admonish your friends in private; praise them in public.
b. Watch the faces of those who bow low.
c. I have written some poetry that I myself don't understand.
d. A skeptic is a person who would ask God for his I.D.
e. No one can be hanged for thinking.

1. Doctors can bury their mistakes, but architects can only advise their clients to plant vines.
2. God made us, but we admire ourselves.
3. We will never have friends if we expect to find them without fault.
4. If a man bites a dog, that is news.
5. Anyone who serves God for money will serve the devil for better wages.

47c Verbs

The verb of a sentence usually expresses action (*jump, think*) or being (*is, become*). It is composed of a main verb possibly preceded by one or more helping verbs:

> MV
> The best fish *swim* near the bottom.

> HV   MV
> A marriage *is* not *built* in a day.

> HV HV   MV
> Even God *has been defended* with nonsense.

Notice that words can intervene between the helping and the main verb (*is* not *built*).

There are twenty-three helping verbs in English. Nine of them, called *modals*, function only as helping verbs, never as main verbs:

> *can, will, shall, should, could, would, may, might, must*

The others may function either as helping verbs or as main verbs:

> have, has, had
> do, does, did
> be, am, is, are, were, being, been

The main verb of a sentence is always the kind of word that would change form if put into these test sentences:

> **INFINITIVE FORM**   Today I (*walk, ride*).

-S FORM	Today he/she/it (*walks, rides*).
PAST TENSE	Yesterday I (*walked, rode*).
PAST PARTICIPLE	I have (*walked, ridden*) many times before.
PRESENT PARTICIPLE	I am (*walking, riding*) right now.

If a word doesn't change form when slipped into these test sentences, you can be certain that it is not a main verb. For example, the noun *revolution,* though it may seem to suggest an action, can never function as a main verb. Just try to make it behave like one (*Today I revolution . . . Yesterday I revolutioned . . .*) and you'll see why.

When both the past-tense and the past-participle forms of a verb end in *-ed,* the verb is regular (*walked, walked*). Otherwise, the verb is irregular (*rode, ridden*). See 30.

The verb *be* is highly irregular, having eight forms instead of the usual five: the infinitive *be,* the present-tense forms *am, is,* and *are,* the past-tense forms *was* and *were,* the present participle *being,* and the past participle *been.*

Helping verbs combine with the various forms of main verbs to create tenses. For a chart of the major tenses, see 27c.

EXERCISE 47–3

Underline the verbs in the following sentences, including helping verbs. Answers to lettered sentences appear in the back of the book. Example:

> <u>Throw</u> a lucky man into the sea, and he <u>will emerge</u> with a
>
> fish in his mouth.

a. Great persons have not commonly been great scholars.
b. Without the spice of guilt, can sin be fully savored?

c. There are many paths to the top of the mountain, but the view is always the same.

d. Birds of a feather flock together.

e. Don't scald your tongue in other people's broth.

1. The king can do no wrong.

2. The road to ruin is always kept in good repair.

3. Clothe an idea in words, and it loses its freedom of movement.

4. Life can only be understood backward, but it must be lived forward.

5. He has every attribute of a dog except loyalty.

47d Adjectives

An adjective is a word used to modify, or describe, a noun or pronoun. An adjective usually answers one of these questions: Which one? What kind of? How many?

> the *lame* elephant [Which elephant?]
>
> *rare, valuable, old* stamps [What kind of stamps?]
>
> *sixteen* candles [How many candles?]

Grammarians also define adjectives according to their form and their typical position in a sentence, as follows:

> the kind of word that usually comes before a noun in a noun phrase (a *frisky* puppy, an *amiable young* man);
>
> the kind of word that can follow a linking verb and describe the subject (the ship was *unsinkable;* talk is *cheap*) (see 48c);
>
> the kind of word that when derived from another part of speech typically takes one of these endings: wonder*ful,* courte*ous,* luck*y,* fool*ish,* pleasur*able,* colon*ial,* defen*sible,* urg*ent,* help*less,* disgust*ing,* friend*ly,* spectacul*ar,* secret*ive.*

The definite article *the* and the indefinite articles *a* and *an* are also classified as adjectives.

Some possessive, demonstrative, and indefinite pronouns can function as adjectives. See 47b.

47e Adverbs

An adverb is a word used to modify, or qualify, a verb (or verbal), an adjective, or another adverb. It usually answers one of these questions: When? Where? How? Why? Under what conditions? To what degree?

> Pull *gently* at a weak rope. [Pull how?]
>
> Read the best books *first.* [Read when?]

Adverbs that modify a verb are also defined according to their form and their typical positions in a sentence, as follows:

> the kind of word that can appear nearly anywhere in a sentence and is often movable (he *sometimes* jogged after work; *sometimes* he jogged after work);
>
> the kind of word that when derived from an adjective typically takes an *-ly* ending (nice, nice*ly*; profound, profound*ly*).

Adverbs modifying adjectives or other adverbs usually intensify or limit the intensity of the word they modify.

> Be *extremely* good, and you will be *very* lonesome.

Adverbs modifying adjectives and other adverbs are not movable. We can't say "Be good *extremely*" or "*Extremely* be good."

The negators *not* and *never* are classified as adverbs. A word such as *cannot* contains a helping verb, *can*, and an adverb, *not*. A contraction such as *can't* contains the helping verb *can* and a contracted form of the adverb *not*.

NOTE: Adverbs can also modify prepositions (Helen left *just* before midnight), prepositional phrases (The budget is *barely* on target), subordinate clauses (We will try to attend, *especially* if you will be there), or whole sentences (*Certainly* Joe did not intend to insult you).

EXERCISE 47 – 4

Underline the adjectives and circle the adverbs in the following sentences. If a word is a noun or pronoun in form but an adjective in function, treat it as an adjective. Also, treat the articles *a, an,* and *the* as adjectives. Answers to lettered sentences appear in the back of the book. Example:

> A little sincerity is a dangerous thing, and a great deal of it
>
> is (absolutely) fatal.

a. Useless laws weaken necessary ones.
b. The American public is wonderfully tolerant.
c. People think too historically.
d. Problems are opportunities in work clothes.
e. Sleep faster. We need the pillows.

1. We cannot be too careful in the choice of our enemies.
2. A wild goose never laid a tame egg.
3. Money will buy a pretty good dog, but it will not buy the wag of its tail.
4. Loquacious people seldom have much sense.
5. An old quarrel can be easily revived.

47f Prepositions

A preposition is a word placed before a noun or pronoun to form a phrase modifying another word in the sentence. The prepositional phrase nearly always functions as an adjective or as an adverb.

The road *to hell* is usually paved *with good intentions.*

To hell functions as an adjective, modifying the noun *road; with good intentions* functions as an adverb, modifying the verb *is paved.*

Prepositional phrases functioning as adjectives usually answer one of the adjective questions: Which one? What kind of? And they nearly always appear immediately following the word they modify. (See 49a.)

Prepositional phrases functioning as adverbs usually answer one of the adverb questions: When? Where? How? Why? Under what conditions? To what degree? Prepositional phrases modifying verbs may appear nearly anywhere in the sentence, and they are often movable.

There are a limited number of prepositions in English. The most common ones are included in the following list:

about	beside	from	outside	toward
above	besides	in	over	under
across	between	inside	past	underneath
after	beyond	into	plus	unlike
against	but	like	regarding	until
along	by	near	respecting	unto
among	concerning	next	round	up
around	considering	of	since	upon
as	despite	off	than	with
at	down	on	through	without
before	during	onto	throughout	
behind	except	opposite	till	
below	for	out	to	

Some prepositions are more than one word long. *Along with, as well as, in addition to, next to,* and *up to* are common examples.

47g Conjunctions

Conjunctions join words, phrases, or clauses, and they indicate the relation between the elements joined.

A coordinating conjunction is used to connect grammatically equal elements. The coordinating conjunctions are *and, but, or, nor, for, so,* and *yet.*

> Poverty is the parent of revolution *and* crime.

> Admire a little ship, *but* put your cargo in a big one.

And connects two nouns; *but* connects two independent clauses.

Correlative conjunctions come in pairs: *either . . . or; neither . . . nor; not only . . . but also; whether . . . or; both . . . and.* Like coordinating conjunctions, they connect grammatically equal elements.

> *Either* Jack Sprat *or* his wife could eat no fat.

A subordinating conjunction introduces a subordinate clause and indicates its relation to the rest of the sentence. (See 49b.) The most common subordinating conjunctions are *after, although, as, as if, because, before, even though, if, in order that, rather than, since, so that, than, that, though, unless, until, when, where, whether,* and *while.*

> *If* triangles had a god, it would have three sides.

A conjunctive adverb may be used with a semicolon to connect independent clauses; it usually serves as a transition between the clauses. The most common conjunctive adverbs are *consequently, finally, furthermore, however, moreover, nevertheless, similarly, then, therefore,* and *thus.*

> When we want to murder a tiger, we call it sport; *however,* when the tiger wants to murder us, we call it ferocity.

47h Interjections

An interjection is a word used to express surprise or emotion (*Oh! Hey! Wow!*).

48

Parts of sentences

Most English sentences flow from subject to verb to any objects or complements. The vast majority of sentences conform to one of these five patterns:

> subject / verb
>
> subject / verb / subject complement
>
> subject / verb / direct object
>
> subject / verb / indirect object / direct object
>
> subject / verb / direct object / object complement

Adverbial modifiers (single words, phrases, or clauses) may be added to any of these patterns, and they may appear nearly anywhere—at the beginning, the middle, or the end.

Predicate is the grammatical term given to the verb plus its objects, complements, and adverbial modifiers.

48a Subjects

The subject of a sentence names who or what the sentence is about. The complete subject is usually composed of a simple subject, always a noun or pronoun, plus any words or word groups modifying the simple subject. To find the complete subject, ask Who? or What?, insert the verb, and finish the question. The answer is the complete subject.

┌──COMPLETE SUBJECT──┐
The purity of a revolution usually lasts about two weeks.

Who or what lasts about two weeks? *The purity of a revolution.*

┌────────COMPLETE SUBJECT────────┐
Historical books that contain no lies are extremely tedious.

Who or what are extremely tedious? *Historical books that contain no lies.*

COMPLETE SUBJECT
In every country the sun rises in the morning.

Who or what rises in the morning? *The sun.* Notice that *in every country the sun* is not a sensible answer to the question. *In every country* is an adverbial phrase modifying the verb *rises.* Since sentences frequently open with such modifiers, it is not safe to assume that the subject must always appear first in a sentence.

To find the simple subject, strip away all modifiers in the complete subject. This includes single-word modifiers such as *the* and *historical,* phrases such as *of a revolution,* and subordinate clauses such as *that contain no lies.*

┌─SS─┐
The purity of a revolution usually lasts about two weeks.

┌─SS─┐
Historical books that contain no lies are extremely tedious.

┌SS┐
In every country *the sun* rises in the morning.

A sentence may have a compound subject containing two or more simple subjects joined with a coordinating conjunction such as *and, but,* or *or.*

┌─ SS ─┐   ┌─ SS ─┐
Much industry and little conscience make us rich.

Occasionally a verb's subject is understood but not present in the sentence. In imperative sentences, which give advice or commands, the subject is understood to be *you.*

[*You*] Hitch your wagon to a star.

Although the subject ordinarily comes before the verb, occasionally it does not. When a sentence begins with *there is* or *there are* (or *there was* or *there were*), the subject follows the verb. The word *there* is an expletive in such constructions, an empty word serving merely to get the sentence started.

┌── SS ──┐
There is *no substitute for victory.*

Occasionally a writer will invert a sentence for effect.

┌─ SS ─┐
Happy is *the nation that has no history.*

Happy is an adjective, so it cannot be the subject. Turn this sentence around and its structure becomes obvious: *The nation that has no history is happy.*

In questions, the subject frequently appears in an unusual position, sandwiched between parts of the verb.

⌐ss⌐
Do *married men* make the best husbands?

Turn the question into a statement, and the words will appear in their usual order: *Married men do make the best husbands.* (*Do make* is the verb.)

EXERCISE 48 – 1

In the following sentences, underline the complete subject and write *ss* above the simple subject(s). If the subject is an understood *you*, insert it in parentheses. Answers to lettered sentences appear in the back of the book. Example:

ss
A little inaccuracy sometimes saves many explanations.

a. A spoiled child never loves its mother.
b. To some lawyers, all facts are created equal.
c. Love your enemies.
d. There is nothing permanent except change.
e. Does hope really spring eternal in the human breast?

1. Habit is overcome by habit.
2. The gardens of kindness never fade.
3. The dog with the bone is always in danger.
4. Fools and their money are soon parted.
5. In golden pots are hidden the most deadly poisons.

48b Verbs

Section 47c explains how to find the verb of a sentence, which consists of a main verb possibly preceded by one or more helping verbs. A sentence's verb may be classified as linking, intransitive, or transitive, depending on the kinds of objects or complements the verb can (or cannot) take.

Linking verbs

Linking verbs link the subject to a subject complement, a word or word group that completes the meaning of the subject by renaming or describing it. If the subject complement *renames* the subject, it is a noun or noun equivalent.

> ┌─────────── s ───────────┐ ┌─v─┐ ┌─sc─┐
> The handwriting on the wall may be a forgery.

If the subject complement *describes* the subject, it is an adjective or adjective equivalent.

> s   v   sc
> Love is blind.

Whenever they appear as main verbs (rather than helping verbs), the forms of *be* — *be, am, is, are, was, were, being,* and *been* — are usually linking. In the preceding sentences, for example, the main verbs are *be* and *is.*

Verbs such as *appear, become, feel, grow, look, make, seem, smell, sound,* and *taste* are sometimes linking, depending on the sense of the sentence.

> ┌─s─┐ ┌─v──┐┌─sc─┐
> At the touch of love, everyone becomes a poet.
>
> ┌──s──┐   ┌v─┐ ┌sc┐
> At first sight, original art often looks ugly.

When you suspect that a verb such as *becomes* or *looks* is linking, check to see if the word or words following it rename or describe the subject. In the sample sentences, *a poet* renames *everyone* and *ugly* describes *art.*

Intransitive verbs

If a verb is not linking, it is either transitive or intransitive, depending on whether it can take a direct object to receive its action. Intransitive verbs cannot take direct objects. Their pattern is always subject/verb.

┌─S─┐ ┌─V─┐
Money talks.

┌──── S ────┐   ┌V┐
Revolutions never go backward.

Nothing receives the actions of talking and going in these sentences, so the verbs are intransitive. Notice that such verbs may or may not be followed by adverbial modifiers. In the second sentence, *backward* is an adverb.

Transitive verbs

A transitive verb takes a direct object, a word or word group that names a receiver of the action.

┌S┐ ┌─V──┐ ┌DO┐
Love will find a way.

In such sentences, the subject and verb alone will seem incomplete. Once we have read "Love will find," for example, we want to know the rest: Love will find what? The answer to the question What? (or Whom?) is the direct object.

Transitive verbs usually appear in the active voice, with the subject doing the action and a direct object receiving the action. Sentences with such a pattern can be transformed into the passive voice, with the subject receiving the action instead.

ACTIVE VOICE   Love will find a way.

PASSIVE VOICE   A way will be found by love.

What was once the direct object (*a way*) has become the subject in the passive-voice transformation, and the original subject appears in a prepositional phrase beginning with *by*. The prepositional phrase is frequently omitted in passive constructions.

PASSIVE VOICE   A way will be found.

Verbs in the passive voice can be identified by their form alone. The main verb is always a past participle such as *found* (see 47c), and a form of *be* (*be, am, is, are, was, were, being, been*) always appears immediately before it (*will be found, had been found, was found*) unless adverbs intervene (*was never found*).

EXERCISE 48–2

Underline the verbs in the following sentences. Then label the verbs as linking, transitive, or intransitive. Answers to lettered sentences appear in the back of the book. Example:

> *intrans.*
> We lived for days on nothing but food and water.

a. All roads lead to Rome.
b. Fear is the mother of morality.
c. I have lived and loved.
d. Hate the sin and love the sinner.
e. Not every day can be a feast of lanterns.

1. To a mouse, a cat is a lion.
2. Wrong must not win by technicalities.
3. He leaped from the frying pan into the fire.
4. I am one individual on a small planet in a little solar system in one of the galaxies.
5. Before marriage, keep your eyes wide open; afterward, keep them half shut.

48c   Objects and complements

In addition to subjects and verbs, many sentences contain objects or complements. Linking verbs take subject complements, and transitive verbs take direct objects (see 48b). In addition, transitive verbs sometimes take indirect objects or object complements.

Subject complements

A subject complement completes the meaning of the subject by either renaming or describing it.

```
   ┌─s─┐ V ┌──────sc──────┐
   History is a bucket of ashes.
   ┌───────s───────┐    ┌─V─┐┌─sc─┐
   Second thoughts often prove wisest.
```

The simple subject complement is nearly always a noun (or pronoun) or an adjective (sometimes called a *predicate noun* or *predicate adjective*). When it is a noun or pronoun such as *bucket*, the complete subject complement renames the subject (*a bucket of ashes* renames *history*). When it is an adjective such as *wisest*, the subject complement describes the subject (*wisest thoughts*).

Subject complements appear only with linking verbs. If the main verb is a form of *be* (*be, am, is, are, was, were, being, been*), the verb is probably linking. Verbs such as *appear, become, feel, grow, look, make, prove, seem, smell, sound,* and *taste* are sometimes linking and sometimes not. (See 48b.)

Direct objects

A direct object, which occurs only with transitive verbs (see 48b), completes the meaning of the verb by naming the receiver of the action.

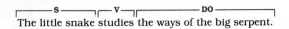

The little snake studies the ways of the big serpent.

The simple direct object is always a noun or pronoun (such as *ways*). To find the complete direct object, read the subject and verb and then ask What? or Whom? The little snake studies what? *The ways of the big serpent.*

The questions What? and Whom? are not, however, a foolproof test for direct objects, because subject complements can also answer the questions. Consider, for example, this pair of sentences.

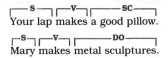

A good pillow and *metal sculptures* both answer the question What? But *a good pillow* is a subject complement because it renames the subject, and *metal sculptures* is a direct object because it receives the action of the verb. The verb *makes* is linking in the first sentence, transitive in the second.

Indirect objects

An indirect object, which usually appears before a direct object, tells to whom or for whom the action of the sentence is done.

     S   V   IO ┌─DO┐   S┌──V──┐ IO┌──DO──┐
You show me a hero, and I will write you a tragedy.

The simple indirect object is always a noun or pronoun. To test for an indirect object, insert the word *to* or *for* before the word or word group in question. If the sentence makes sense, the word or word group is an indirect object.

You show [to] me a hero, and I will write [for] you a tragedy.

An indirect object may be turned into a prepositional phrase using *to* or *for*: *You show a hero to me, and I will write a tragedy for you.*

Only certain transitive verbs take indirect objects. Common examples are *give, ask, bring, find, get, hand, lend, offer, pay, pour, promise, read, send, show, teach, tell, throw,* and *write.*

Object complements

An object complement always follows a direct object, completing its meaning by renaming it or describing it.

```
   ┌─S─┐   ┌─V─┐┌─DO─┐┌────────── OC ──────────┐
   People now call a spade an agricultural implement.
   ┌─S─┐┌─V─┐┌───── DO ─────┐┌─OC─┐
   Love makes all hard hearts gentle.
```

When the object complement *renames* the direct object, it will be a noun or pronoun (such as *implement*). When it *describes* the direct object, it will be an adjective (such as *gentle*).

EXERCISE 48–3

Label the subject complements, direct objects, indirect objects, or object complements in the following sentences. If an object or complement consists of more than one word, bracket and label all of it. Answers to lettered sentences appear in the back of the book. Example:

```
              IO  ┌──DO──┐                      ┌──DO──┐
   Fate gives us our relatives, but we choose our friends.
```

a. Victory has a hundred fathers, but defeat is an orphan.
b. One misfortune always carries another on its back.
c. Lock your door and keep your neighbors honest.

d. All work and no play make Jack a dull boy.
e. Lizzie Borden gave her father forty whacks.

1. Good medicine always tastes bitter.
2. Ask me no questions, and I will tell you no lies.
3. The mob has many heads but no brains.
4. Some folk want their luck buttered.
5. Every bird likes its own nest best.

49

Subordinate word groups

Subordinate word groups include prepositional phrases, subordinate clauses, verbal phrases, appositives, and absolutes. Not all of these word groups are subordinate in quite the same way. Some are subordinate because they are modifiers; others function as noun equivalents, not as modifiers.

49a Prepositional phrases

A prepositional phrase begins with a preposition such as *at, by, for, from, in, of, on, to,* or *with* (47f) and usually ends with a noun or noun equivalent: *on the table, for him, with great fanfare.* The noun or noun equivalent is known as the *object of the preposition.*

Prepositional phrases function either as adjectives modifying a noun or pronoun or as adverbs modifying a verb, an adjective, or another adverb. When functioning as an adjective, a prepositional phrase nearly always appears immediately following the noun or pronoun it modifies:

Variety is the spice *of life.*

Adjective phrases usually answer one or both of the questions Which one? What kind of? If we ask Which spice? or What kind of spice? we get a sensible answer: the spice *of life*.

Adverbial prepositional phrases that modify the verb can appear nearly anywhere in a sentence.

Do not judge a tree *by its bark*.

Tyranny will *in time* lead to revolution.

To the ant, a few drops of rain are a flood.

Adverbial word groups usually answer one of these questions: When? Where? How? Why? Under what conditions?

Do not judge a tree *how? By its bark*.

Tyranny will lead to revolution *when? In time*.

A few drops of rain are a flood *under what conditions? To the ant*.

If a prepositional phrase is movable, you can be certain that it is adverbial; adjectival prepositional phrases are wedded to the words they modify. At least some of the time, adverbials can be moved to other positions in the sentence.

By their fruits you shall know them.

You shall know them *by their fruits*.

NOTE: In questions and subordinate clauses, a preposition may appear after its object.

What are you afraid *of*?

We avoided the clerk *whom* John had warned us *about*.

EXERCISE 49 – 1

Underline the prepositional phrases in the following sentences. Be prepared to explain the function of each phrase. Answers to lettered sentences appear in the back of the book. Example:

A journey <u>of a thousand miles</u> must begin <u>with a single step.</u>

a. Laughter is a tranquilizer with no side effects.
b. One misfortune always carries another on its back.
c. The love of money is the root of all evil.
d. Wall Street begins in a graveyard and ends in a river.
e. You can stroke people with words.

1. A pleasant companion reduces the length of the journey.
2. A society of sheep produces a government of wolves.
3. Some people feel with their heads and think with their hearts.
4. In love and war, all is fair.
5. To my embarrassment, I was born in bed with a lady.

49b Subordinate clauses

Subordinate clauses are patterned like sentences, having subjects and verbs and sometimes objects or complements. But they function within sentences as adjectives, adverbs, or nouns. They cannot stand alone as complete sentences.

Adjective clauses

Like other word groups functioning as adjectives, adjective clauses modify nouns or pronouns. An adjective clause nearly always appears immediately following the noun or pronoun it modifies.

The arrow *that has left the bow* never returns.

Relatives are persons *who live too near and die too seldom.*

To test whether a subordinate clause functions as an adjective, ask the adjective questions: Which one? What kind of? The answer should make sense. Which arrow? The arrow *that has left the bow.* What kind of persons? Persons *who live too near and die too seldom.*

Most adjective clauses begin with a relative pronoun (*who, whom, whose, which,* or *that*), which marks them as grammatically subordinate. In addition to introducing the clause, the relative pronoun points back to the noun that the clause modifies.

The fur *that warms a monarch* once warmed a bear.

Relative pronouns are sometimes "understood":

> The things [that] we know best are the things [that] we haven't been taught.

Occasionally an adjective clause is introduced by a relative adverb, usually *when, where,* or *why.*

> Home is the place *where you slip in the bathtub and break your neck.*

The parts of an adjective clause are often arranged as in sentences (subject/verb/object or complement):

>   **S**   **V** **DO**
> We often forgive the people *who bore us.*

Frequently, however, the object or complement appears first, out of its normal order:

>   **DO** **S** **V**
> We rarely forgive those *whom we bore.*

To determine the subject of a clause, ask Who? or What? and insert the verb. Don't be surprised if the answer is an echo, as in the first adjective clause above: Who bore us? *Who.* To find any objects or complements, read the subject and the verb and then ask Who? Whom? or What? Again, be prepared for a possible echo, as in the second adjective clause above: We bore whom? *Whom.*

Adverb clauses

Adverb clauses usually modify verbs, in which case they may appear nearly anywhere in a sentence — at the beginning, at the end, or somewhere in the middle. Like other adverbial word groups, they tell when, where, why, under what conditions, or to what degree an action occurred or a situation existed.

When the well is dry, we know the worth of water.

Venice would be a fine city *if it were only drained.*

When do we know the worth of water? *When the well is dry.* Under what conditions would Venice be a fine city? *If it were only drained.*

Unlike adjective clauses, adverb clauses are frequently movable. In the sentences above, for example, the adverb clauses can be moved without affecting the meaning of the sentences.

We know the worth of water *when the well is dry.*

If it were only drained, Venice would be a fine city.

When an adverb clause modifies an adjective or an adverb, it is not movable; it must appear next to the word it modifies. In the following examples the *because* clause modifies the adjective *angry,* and the *than* clause modifies the adverb *faster.*

> Angry *because the mayor had not kept his promises,* we worked for his defeat.

> Joan can run faster *than I can bicycle.*

Adverb clauses always begin with a subordinating conjunction such as *although, because, before, if, unless, when, where,* or *while* (47g). Subordinating conjunctions introduce clauses and express their relation to the rest of the sentence.

Adverb clauses are sometimes elliptical, with some of their words being "understood":

> When [it is] painted, the room will look larger.

Noun clauses

Because they do not function as modifiers, noun clauses are not subordinate in the same sense as are adjective and adverb clauses. They are called subordinate only because they cannot stand alone: They must function within another sentence pattern, always as nouns.

A noun clause functions just like a single-word noun, usually as a subject, subject complement, direct object, or object of a preposition.

> ┌────── S ──────┐
> *Whoever gossips to you* will gossip of you.
> ┌────── DO ──────┐
> We never forget *that we buried the hatchet.*

A noun clause usually begins with one of the following subordinating conjunctions: *who, whom, that, what, how, when, where, whether.* The subordinating conjunction may or may not play a significant role in the clause. In the sentences above, for example, *whoever* is the subject of its clause, but *that* does not perform a function in its clause.

As with adjective clauses, the parts of a noun clause may appear out of their normal order (subject/verb/object).

         DO   **S**   **V**
Talent is *what you possess.*

The parts of a noun clause may also appear in normal order.

         S   **V**   **DO**
Genius is *what possesses you.*

EXERCISE 49 – 2

Underline the subordinate clauses in the following sentences. Be prepared to explain the function of each clause. Answers to lettered sentences appear in the back of the book. Example:

When the insects take over the world, we hope that they will

remember our picnics with gratitude.

  a. Though you live near a forest, do not waste firewood.
  b. The gods help those who help themselves.
  c. What is whispered is heard all over town.
  d. The dog that trots finds the bone.
  e. A fraud is not perfect unless it is practiced on clever persons.

  1. What history teaches us is that we have never learned anything from it.
  2. Dig a well before you are thirsty.
  3. Whoever named it necking was a poor judge of anatomy.
  4. If you were born lucky, even your rooster will lay eggs.
  5. Modern poverty is not the poverty that was blessed in the Sermon on the Mount.

49c Verbal phrases

A verbal is a verb form that does not function as the verb of a clause. Verbals include infinitives (the word *to* plus the dictionary form of the verb), present participles (the *-ing* form of the verb), and past participles (the form of the verb that can follow *have*, often ending in *-ed* or *-en*) (see 47c).

INFINITIVE	PRESENT PARTICIPLE	PAST PARTICIPLE
to dream	dreaming	dreamed
to choose	choosing	chosen
to build	building	built
to grow	growing	grown

Instead of functioning as the verb of a clause, a verbal or a verbal phrase functions as an adjective, a noun, or an adverb.

ADJECTIVE	*Stolen* grapes are especially sweet.
NOUN	Continual *dripping* wears away a stone.
ADVERB	Were we born *to suffer?*

Verbals can take objects, complements, and modifiers to form verbal phrases; the phrases usually lack subjects.

Living well is the best revenge.

Governments exist *to protect the rights of minorities.*

The verbal *living* is followed by an adverb modifier, *well;* the verbal *to protect* is followed by a direct object, *the rights of minorities.*

Like single-word verbals, verbal phrases function as adjectives, nouns, or adverbs. In the sentences above, for example, *living well* functions as a noun to fill the subject slot of the sentence, and *to protect the rights of minorities* functions as an adverb, answering the question Why?

Verbal phrases are ordinarily classified as participles, gerunds, and infinitives. This classification is based partly on form (whether the verbal is a present participle, a past participle, or an infinitive) and partly on function (whether the whole phrase functions as an adjective, a noun, or an adverb).

Participial phrases

Participial phrases always function as adjectives. Their verbals are either present participles, always ending in *-ing*, or past participles, frequently ending in *-ed* or *-en* but often appearing in irregular forms (see 27a).

Participial phrases frequently appear immediately following the noun or pronoun they modify.

Congress shall make no law *abridging the freedom of speech or of the press*.

Truth *kept in the dark* will never save the world.

Unlike other adjectival word groups, however, which must always follow the noun or pronoun they modify, participial phrases are often movable. They can precede the word they modify.

Being a philosopher, I have a problem for every solution.

They may also appear at some distance from the word they modify.

History is something that never happened, *written by someone who wasn't there*.

Gerund phrases

Gerund phrases are built around present participles (verb forms ending in *-ing*), and they always function as nouns: usually as subjects, subject complements, direct objects, or objects of a preposition.

┌────── S ──────┐
Justifying a fault doubles it.

┌────── SC ──────┐
The secret of education is *respecting the pupil.*

┌────── DO ──────┐
Kleptomaniacs can't help *helping themselves.*

┌────── OBJ OF PREP ──────┐
The hen is an egg's way of *producing another egg.*

Infinitive phrases

Infinitive phrases, always constructed around *to* plus the dictionary form of the verb (*to call, to drink*), can function as nouns, as adjectives, or as adverbs.

When functioning as a noun, an infinitive phrase may appear in almost any noun slot, usually as a subject, subject complement, or direct object.

┌────── S ──────┐
To side with truth is noble.

┌────── DO ──────┐
Never try *to leap a chasm in two jumps.*

Infinitive phrases functioning as adjectives usually appear immediately following the noun or pronoun they modify.

┌────────────────┐
We do not have the right *to abandon the poor.*

The infinitive phrase limits the meaning of the noun *right*. Which right? *The right to abandon the poor.*

Adverbial infinitive phrases usually qualify the meaning of the verb, telling when, where, how, why, under what conditions, or to what degree an action occurred.

He cut off his nose *to spite his face.*

Here the phrase explains why: Why did he cut off his nose? *To spite his face.*

EXERCISE 49−3

Underline the verbal phrases in the following sentences. Be prepared to explain the function of each phrase. Answers to lettered sentences appear in the back of the book. Example:

Fate tried <u>to conceal him</u> by <u>naming him Smith.</u>

a. The best substitute for experience is being sixteen.
b. Vows made in storms are forgotten in calms.
c. To help a friend is to give ourselves pleasure.
d. Beware of Greeks bearing gifts.
e. Every genius is considerably helped by being dead.

1. The thing generally raised on city land is taxes.
2. To make a crooked stick straight, we bend it the contrary way.
3. He has the gall of a shoplifter returning an item for a refund.
4. Do you want to be a writer? Then write.
5. Being weak, foxes are distinguished by superior tact.

49d Appositive phrases

Though strictly speaking they are not subordinate word groups, appositive phrases function somewhat as adjectives do, to describe nouns or pronouns. Instead of modifying nouns or pronouns, however, appositive phrases rename them. In form they are nouns or noun equivalents.

Appositives are said to be "in apposition" to the nouns or pronouns they rename.

> Politicians, *acrobatics at heart,* can sit on a fence and yet keep both ears to the ground.

Acrobatics at heart is in apposition to the noun *politicians.*

49e Absolute phrases

An absolute phrase modifies a whole clause or sentence, not just one word, and it may appear nearly anywhere in the sentence. It consists of a noun or noun equivalent usually followed by a participial phrase.

> *His words dipped in honey,* the senator mesmerized the crowd.

> The senator, *his words dipped in honey,* mesmerized the crowd.

> The senator mesmerized the crowd, *his words dipped in honey.*

50

Sentence types

Depending on the number and type of clauses they contain, sentences are classified as simple, compound, complex, or compound-complex.

Clauses come in two varieties: independent and subordinate. An independent clause is a full sentence pattern that does not function within another sentence pattern: It contains a subject and verb plus any objects, complements, and modifiers of that verb, and it either stands alone or could stand alone. A subordinate clause is a full sentence pattern that functions within a sentence as an adjective, an adverb, or a noun but that cannot stand alone as a complete sentence. (See 49b.)

50a Simple sentences

A simple sentence is one independent clause with no subordinate clauses.

┌──────────INDEPENDENT CLAUSE──────────┐
Without music, life would be a mistake.

This sentence contains a subject (*life*), a verb (*would be*), a complement (*a mistake*), and an adverbial modifier (*without music*).

A simple sentence may contain compound elements — a compound subject, verb, or object, for example — but it does not contain more than one full sentence pattern. The following sentence is simple because its two verbs (*enters* and *spreads*) share the same subject.

┌───────── INDEPENDENT CLAUSE ─────────┐
Evil enters like a needle and spreads like an oak.

50b Compound sentences

A compound sentence is composed of two or more independent clauses with no subordinate clauses. The independent clauses are usually joined with a comma and a co-ordinating conjunction (*and, but, or, nor, for, so, yet*) or with a semicolon.

┌── INDEPENDENT CLAUSE ─┐   ┌──────INDEPENDENT CLAUSE ──────┐
One arrow is easily broken, but you can't break a bundle of ten.
┌───────── INDEPENDENT CLAUSE──────────┐   ┌─INDEPENDENT–
We are born brave, trusting, and greedy; most of us have
──── CLAUSE────┐
remained greedy.

50c Complex sentences

A complex sentence is composed of one independent clause with one or more subordinate clauses. See 49b.

                  SUBORDINATE
                 ┌── CLAUSE ──────┐
ADJECTIVE   They that sow in tears shall reap in joy.
                 ┌SUBORDINATE CLAUSE┐
ADVERB   If you scatter thorns, don't go barefoot.
                ┌───── SUBORDINATE CLAUSE ──────┐
NOUN   What the scientists have in their briefcases is terrifying.

50d Compound-complex sentences

A compound-complex sentence contains at least two independent clauses and at least one subordinate clause. The following sentence contains two full sentence patterns that can stand alone.

┌INDEPENDENT CLAUSE┐   ┌── INDEPENDENT CLAUSE─┐
Tell me what you eat, and I will tell you what you are.

And each independent clause contains a subordinate clause, making the sentence both compound and complex.

Tell me what you eat, and I will tell you what you are.

EXERCISE 50 – 1

Identify the following sentences as simple, compound, complex, or compound-complex. Be prepared to identify the subordinate clauses and classify them according to their function: adjective, adverb, or noun. (See 49b.) Answers to lettered sentences appear in the back of the book. Example:

> **My folks didn't come over on the Mayflower; they were there**
>
> **to meet the boat.** *compound*

a. The poet is a liar who always speaks the truth.
b. Love your enemies; it will drive them nuts.
c. The frog in the well knows nothing of the ocean.
d. If you don't go to other people's funerals, they won't go to yours.
e. People who sleep like a baby usually don't have one.

1. We often give our enemies the means for our own destruction.
2. Those who write clearly have readers; those who write obscurely have commentators.
3. The impersonal hand of government can never replace the helping hand of a neighbor.
4. Human action can be modified to some extent, but human nature cannot be changed.
5. What has been fashionable once will become fashionable again.

PART X

Special Types of Writing

51

Researching

The requirements of academic research papers vary among the thousands of instructors who assign them, but the overall goal is the same. Instructors want students to *think,* not to go on a treasure hunt for good quotations. Most instructors want their students to conduct research the same way they themselves do: to explore an idea in a systematic way, to interpret what they read, to form a thesis, and to support that thesis with valid and well-documented evidence.

All of this takes time: time for researching and time for drafting and rewriting the essay. Before beginning a research project, you should set a realistic schedule of deadlines. For example, before she began researching the sample research paper that appears on pages 404 – 434, Karen Shaw constructed the following schedule. She received her assignment on October 1, and the due date was November 1.

SCHEDULE	FINISHED BY
1. Take the college's library tour.	October 2
2. Choose a topic and plan a search strategy.	4
3. Locate sources; make bibliography cards.	8
4. Read and take notes.	15
5. Decide on a tentative thesis and outline.	17
6. Draft the paper, using citations where necessary.	22
7. Revise the paper.	25
8. Prepare a list of works cited.	26
9. Type and proofread the final draft.	27

Notice that Shaw built some extra time into her schedule to allow for unexpected delays. Although the due date for the paper was November 1, her schedule called for completing the paper by October 27.

51a Explore your library.

Before you begin researching, walk around the library to find out what it's like. Most libraries provide maps and handouts that describe their services; many conduct orientation programs or have cassette walking tours or slide-cassette shows.

As you explore your library, seek out answers to at least the following questions:

Are the stacks (the shelves on which books are stored) open or closed? In other words, can you go to the books directly, or must you request them at a desk?

Are some books, periodicals, and reference materials located in special rooms or even special buildings?

Is there a traditional card catalog in rows of drawers, or are the library's holdings cataloged on microfiche or microfilm or on a computer? Where is the catalog located?

Where is the reference section?

Where are the periodical indexes?

How and where are periodicals stored? If some periodicals are on microfilm or microfiche, where are the machines for reading them? Do some of these machines print copies as well?

Does the library own films, videotapes, slide-sound sets, records, or floppy disks, and where are they cataloged?

Is there a computer search service? (At some libraries you can buy time on a computer to search one or more of the hundreds of computer databases available.)

As you get to know your library, don't forget the library staff. Librarians are information specialists who can save you time by helping you define what you are looking for and then telling you where to find it. Librarians, especially those in college and university libraries, are educators. Feel free to tell them about your information needs, not just to ask where to find the encyclopedias.

51b Choose a suitable topic.

A good topic fits the assignment, takes you to a variety of sources, and allows you to support a conclusion. It is also narrow enough to allow in-depth analysis.

You should avoid a topic if it is too broad or too narrow, if it depends too heavily on a single source, or if it leads you into scholarly territory clearly beyond your abilities. Above all, avoid topics without a point or a purpose. An unfocused collection of facts about Eskimos, for example, will not make an acceptable essay. On the college level, you are ordinarily expected to reach a conclusion: that the Eskimos' traditional marital customs contributed to their ability to survive in a harsh land, for example, or that the current educational policies of the Bureau of Indian Affairs are damaging to Eskimo children.

Finding a topic

If you have not been assigned a specific topic, you might choose a subject in which you have a personal interest, perhaps because of your experience, hobbies, college courses, or career plans. Or you might develop new interests by browsing through certain library references. For example, *Hot Topics* lists recent articles on controversial social issues and current events, and *Editorial Research Reports* contains digests of recent articles and editorials on debatable issues. You can discover more good topics by skimming through current magazines such as

Newsweek, Psychology Today, Scientific American, and *Smithsonian* or by consulting specialized periodicals in your field. Scholarly controversies encountered in college courses are yet another potential source of topics; ask your professors for suggestions.

Narrowing the topic

Your research will not move efficiently until you have narrowed your topic to a manageable size. Even before you visit the library, you can limit the scope of your investigation. If your general subject is "violence on television," for instance, you might limit yourself to violence in programs directed at children; or you might restrict the topic even further, perhaps to violence in Saturday morning cartoons.

Once inside the library, you will discover a number of ways to narrow your topic. By reading encyclopedia articles or by scanning the headings and subheadings in the card catalog (or in the *Library of Congress Subject Headings;* see pp. 364 – 365), you will get a sense of your topic's natural subdivisions. For current topics, check the subheadings and titles in periodical indexes such as *Readers' Guide to Periodical Literature* or *Magazine Index* (see pp. 366 – 367) or consult the pamphlet file. Without reading a single article it is possible to narrow your topic drastically just by reading subheadings and titles.

As you begin reading books and articles and become more knowledgeable, you may be able to narrow your topic even further and at the same time decide what approach you will take in your paper—or even decide on a tentative thesis.

51c Follow a search strategy.

A search strategy is a systematic plan for tracking down source materials. To create a search strategy, you'll need to ask yourself two questions.

What kinds of source materials should I consult?

In what order should I consult them?

A good search strategy usually moves from general reference works such as encyclopedias to specific books (located through the card catalog) and specific magazine and newspaper articles (located through periodical indexes). But be prepared to modify this strategy in light of your topic, your library resources, your level of expertise, and the amount of time you are able to spend researching.

To research the topic of apes and language, Karen Shaw, whose paper appears on pages 404 – 434, decided to begin with books. Because she was working in a relatively small library, she suspected she might need to request books from neighboring libraries, which would take some time. She began, then, by checking out a few books and ordering others through interlibrary loans. She held off on reading the books, though, because she didn't have time to read them all cover to cover. Before she could read selectively, she needed an overview of her subject.

For an overview Shaw might have turned to a specialized encyclopedia, but because her topic was fairly current, she decided to try magazines instead. Her librarian recommended the *Magazine Index* as the fastest way to locate magazine articles on her topic.

After reading several magazine articles, Shaw became intrigued by the differing opinions of two key researchers, Herbert Terrace and Francine Patterson. With the Terrace-Patterson controversy in mind, she took another look at the books she had collected. She decided that two books, one by Terrace and another by Patterson, were worth reading in their entirety; as for the others, only certain chapters dealt with the key issues raised by Terrace and Patterson, so Shaw focused primarily on those chapters. Because Shaw had planned her search strategy carefully, most of her reading was relevant to her final approach to the topic.

As you survey the possible sources of information listed on the following pages, try to develop an organized search strategy appropriate to your topic. Remember that if you run into problems, a reference librarian will be glad to help.

Reference works

Often you'll want to begin by reading background information in a general encyclopedia, a specialized encyclopedia, or a biographical reference. Later in your research, you may need to turn to other reference works such as atlases, almanacs, or unabridged dictionaries.

GENERAL ENCYCLOPEDIAS Articles in general encyclopedias introduce the topic to you, give you a sense of how broad or narrow it is, and usually end with a bibliography of books for further reading. Although general encyclopedias are a good place to begin your research, do not rely too heavily on them. Ordinarily you should not use information from general encyclopedias directly in your finished paper because you will find more specific information later during your search.

Here is a brief list of general encyclopedias frequently used on the college level.

> *Academic American Encyclopedia.* 21 vols. 1983. Yearbooks.
> *Collier's Encyclopedia.* 24 vols. 1981.
> *Encyclopedia Americana.* 30 vols. New printing yearly. Yearbooks.
> *The New Encyclopaedia Britannica.* 32 vols. 1985. In three parts: *Propaedia*, a one-volume "Outline of Knowledge"; twelve-volume *Micropaedia* with brief entries; seventeen-volume *Macropaedia* of long articles, with bibliographies. Two-volume index. Yearbooks.

SPECIALIZED ENCYCLOPEDIAS For topics that fall within a particular academic discipline, turn to a specialized encyclopedia for an overview. As you read, look for areas in which experts take different positions or where trends, attitudes, beliefs, or circumstances are changing; your finished paper could demonstrate your support for one of the positions or explain the causes or effects of the changes.

Following is a list of specialized encyclopedias covering a number of disciplines.

The Dance Encyclopedia. 1967.
Encyclopedia of Anthropology. 1976.
Encyclopedia of Banking and Finance. 1983.
The Encyclopedia of Biological Sciences. 1981.
Encyclopedia of Computers and Data Processing. 1978.
Encyclopedia of Crime and Justice. 4 vols. 1983.
The Encyclopedia of Management. 1982.
The Encyclopedia of Philosophy. 8 vols. 1967.
Encyclopedia of Psychology. 4 vols. 1984.
Encyclopedia of World Architecture. 1982.
Encyclopedia of World Art. 16 vols. 1959 – 68. Supplement 1983.
An Encyclopedia of World History. 1972.
Encyclopedia of World Literature in the 20th Century. 4 vols. 1981 – 86.
Grzimek's Animal Life Encyclopedia. 13 vols. 1972 – 75.
Harvard Guide to American History. 2 vols. 1974.
International Encyclopedia of the Social Sciences. 17 vols. plus supplement. 1968.
McGraw-Hill Dictionary of Modern Economics. 1983.
McGraw-Hill Encyclopedia of Science and Technology. 15 vols. 1982.
McGraw-Hill Encyclopedia of World Drama. 5 vols. 1984.
The New Grove Dictionary of Music and Musicians. 20 vols. 1980.
The Oxford Companion to American Literature. 1983.
The Oxford Companion to English Literature. 1985.
Reference Encyclopedia of the American Indian. 1978.
Short Story Index: 1900 – 1949. 1956. Supplements through 1978.

BIOGRAPHICAL REFERENCES If your subject is a person, a good place to begin is with a biographical reference such as one of the following.

> *Contemporary Authors.* 1972 – .
> *Current Biography.* 1940 – .
> *Dictionary of American Biography.* 17 vols. plus supplements. 1927 – 84.
> *Dictionary of Literary Biography.* 38 vols. plus supplements. 1978.
> *McGraw-Hill Encyclopedia of World Biography.* 12 vols. 1973.
> *Notable American Women, 1607 – 1950.* 1974. Supplement: *Notable American Women: The Modern Period.* 1980.
> *Webster's New Biographical Dictionary.* 1983.
> *Who's Who in America.* 1899 – .

ATLASES An atlas is a bound collection of maps. For current topics, make sure that you are working with an up-to-date atlas. For historical topics, consult an atlas covering the particular period. Following is a brief list of commonly used atlases.

> *National Geographic Atlas of the World.* 1981.
> *Rand McNally Cosmopolitan World Atlas.* 1984.
> *Rand McNally Historical Atlas of the World.* 1981.
> *The New York Times Atlas of the World.* 1980.

ALMANACS AND YEARBOOKS Almanacs and yearbooks are annual publications that record information about a year, often in the form of lists, charts, and tables. The information covers a range of subjects such as politics, world events, sports, economics, and even the weather. Here is a brief list of almanacs and yearbooks.

> *Americana Annual.* 1923 – .
> *Britannica Book of the Year.* 1938 – .
> *Facts on File.* 1941 – ,
> *Statistical Abstract of the United States.* 1878 – .
> *World Almanac and Book of Facts.* 1868 – .

UNABRIDGED DICTIONARIES An unabridged dictionary such as one of the following is more comprehensive than an ordinary college or desk dictionary.

> *The Oxford English Dictionary.* 13 vols. plus supplements.
> 1933 – 76.
> *The Random House Dictionary of the English Language.*
> Second Edition, Unabridged, 1987.
> *Webster's Third New International Dictionary.* 1981.

Books

Your library may have a traditional card catalog, a microform catalog, a computer catalog, or some combination of these. The card catalog files information about books on cards arranged alphabetically in drawers, and the microform catalog reprints the cards on microfilm or microfiche. The computer catalog allows you to call up the information using a keyboard.

THE CARD CATALOG The card catalog lists books alphabetically in three ways: by author's name, by the title of the book, and by subject. The cards in the catalog look like the example on page 363, though the top line might list an author or title instead of the subject.

If you know what to look for on the card, you can immediately select or reject a book, and you can use the "tracings" (lists of related headings) to lead you to more books. Keep the following points in mind as you look through the catalog for books most relevant to your topic.

Check the date to see when the book was published. For some topics, only the most recent books may be useful.

Check to see if the book has an index (for easy reference) and a bibliography (to suggest more books).

Check the tracings, lists of other places to look in the card catalog.

WHAT THE CARD CATALOG TELLS YOU

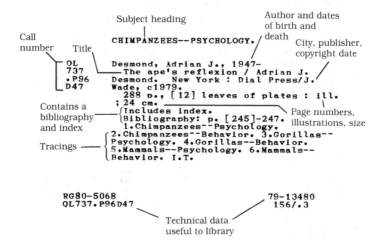

If the book looks useful, write down on a bibliography card the call number, author, title, and publishing information—details that you will need later when constructing your list of works cited (see 51e and 52g). If you just want to look at the book—to decide whether to use it—write down at least the call number and the title so that you can locate the book on the shelf.

If books on a subject are not listed under the first or second heading you try, consult the *Library of Congress Subject Headings* (discussed later in this section).

THE MICROFORM OR COMPUTER CATALOG Not all libraries list their holdings in drawers of 3″ × 5″ cards. In some libraries, card catalogs are presented on rolls of microfilm mounted on a machine with a large viewing screen (called a microfilm reader). This type of catalog is also called a COM (computer output microfilm) catalog. An alternative COM catalog is on microfiche: 4″ × 6″ pieces of film viewed on a machine called a microfiche reader. With either type of machine you can sometimes print a copy of the titles that appear on the screen, saving you the trouble of handcopying (and the possibility of miscopying) the information.

An on-line computer catalog uses a keyboard and a monitor to display the library's holdings. By following the simple directions and typing in the correct commands, you can see on the screen the same information that is contained on 3″ × 5″ cards in a drawer.

A complete copy of any catalog viewed on a screen may also be available as a printout.

THE LIBRARY OF CONGRESS SUBJECT HEADINGS   The headings under which you are likely to find books listed in the library's main catalog are contained in *The Library of Congress Subject Headings (LCSH)*. It consists of two large volumes usually placed near the card catalog. Though its listings are keyed to the Library of Congress system for classifying books, a system used in many libraries, it can be useful even if your library uses the Dewey decimal system, since many of the headings are the same. The headings are also likely to be similar to those used in magazine and newspaper indexes.

Because the library's catalog does not always list books under the most obvious headings, the *LCSH* is an extremely useful reference tool. If you are interested in researching senior citizens, for example, you would be frustrated by going directly to the card catalog and discovering nothing under "senior citizens." But by looking up "senior citizens" in *LCSH*, you would be referred to "aged," which covers two entire pages with subheadings. By looking up just one heading, "old age," you would learn that twenty-three different subheadings are used for books on the subject (see the example on page 365). From that one look into *LCSH*, you might also be able to restrict your topic. For example, you might limit your investigation to a pyschological aspect of growing old, to a disease that afflicts the elderly, or to employment opportunities after retirement.

OTHER INDEXES TO BOOKS *Books in Print* and *Paperbound Books in Print* list books by author, title, and subject; *Cumulative Book Index* lists books by author and subject.

WHAT THE LCSH TELLS YOU

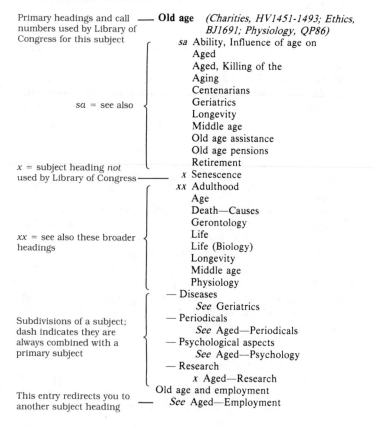

Primary headings and call numbers used by Library of Congress for this subject —— **Old age** *(Charities, HV1451-1493; Ethics, BJ1691; Physiology, QP86)*

sa = see also

    sa Ability, Influence of age on
    Aged
    Aged, Killing of the
    Aging
    Centenarians
    Geriatrics
    Longevity
    Middle age
    Old age assistance
    Old age pensions
    Retirement

x = subject heading *not* used by Library of Congress ——

    x Senescence

xx = see also these broader headings

    xx Adulthood
    Age
    Death—Causes
    Gerontology
    Life
    Life (Biology)
    Longevity
    Middle age
    Physiology

Subdivisions of a subject; dash indicates they are always combined with a primary subject

    — Diseases
        See Geriatrics
    — Periodicals
        See Aged—Periodicals
    — Psychological aspects
        See Aged—Psychology
    — Research
        x Aged—Research

This entry redirects you to another subject heading —

Old age and employment
    See Aged—Employment

Periodicals

Periodicals are publications issued at regular intervals, such as magazines, newspapers, and scholarly or technical journals. Articles in periodicals are useful reference tools because they often contain more up-to-date information than books and because they usually discuss in detail a specific aspect of a subject.

To track down useful articles, consult a magazine index, a newspaper index, or one of the many specialized indexes to scholarly or technical journals. Most libraries provide, in a conspicuous spot close to these indexes, a list of the periodicals they own. The list usually tells you the form in which the periodical has been preserved: on microfilm, on microfiche, in bound volumes, or in unbound files. It also tells you which years of the periodical the library owns. You will save yourself time if you check the periodicals list as you use the indexes. If your library doesn't have the periodical in which an article appears and if you don't plan to visit another library, there is no need to write down the name of the article.

MAGAZINE AND NEWSPAPER INDEXES Magazine indexes list articles in popular magazines such as *Time, Popular Mechanics, Science, Fortune,* and *Psychology Today.* Newspaper indexes list articles in major newspapers such as *The New York Times, The Washington Post,* and *The Christian Science Monitor.* Here is an annotated list of useful indexes to magazines and newspapers; a sample entry from one of these indexes, the *Readers' Guide to Periodical Literature,* is shown on page 367.

> *Magazine Index.* A microfilm machine that indexes magazine articles for the past five years. It is updated monthly.
> *Readers' Guide to Periodical Literature.* 1900 – . Volumes that index magazine articles by year of publication. For the current year, check the paperback supplements.

WHAT THE READERS' GUIDE TELLS YOU

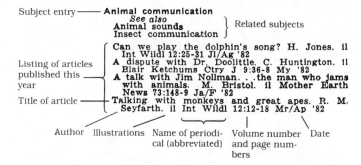

- *National Newspaper Index.* 1979 – . A microfilm compilation of articles in five newspapers: *The New York Times, The Christian Science Monitor, The Wall Street Journal, The Washington Post,* and *The Los Angeles Times.*
- *Newsbank.* 1970 – . A microfiche compilation of articles in more than one hundred city newspapers.
- *New York Times Index.* 1913 – . Volumes that list all of the articles printed in *The New York Times* — an excellent source of condensed and recent information. There are similar indexes for other major newspapers, such as *The Washington Post, The Christian Science Monitor, The Wall Street Journal,* and *The Times* (London).

SPECIALIZED PERIODICAL INDEXES To locate articles in technical and scholarly journals such as *Computer World* and *Communication Quarterly,* you'll need to turn to a specialized index. You can find specialized indexes easily in the library's main catalog. In the subject file, look for cards giving the subheadings "Abstracts" and "Periodicals and Indexes" (for example, "Biology — Periodicals and Indexes"). The catalog will provide the title and call number for the index, usually with REF as the top line, indicating that you will find it in the reference section. The librarian also can help you locate specialized indexes.

Following is a list of specialized indexes covering a variety of academic disciplines.

Applied Science and Technology Index. 1958 – . Formerly
    Industrial Arts Index, 1913 – 57.
Art Index. 1929 – .
Biological Abstracts. 1926 – .
Biological and Agricultural Index. 1964 – . Formerly
    Agricultural Index, 1916 – 64.
Business Periodicals Index. 1958 – . Formerly *Industrial Arts
    Index,* 1913 – 57.
Central Index to Journals of Education. 1969 – .
Education Index. 1929 – .
Engineering Index. 1884 – .
General Science Index. 1978 – .
Historical Abstracts. 1955 – .
Humanities Index, 1974 – . Formerly *International Index to
    Periodicals,* 1907 – 65, and *Social Sciences and
    Humanities Index,* 1965 – 74.
*MLA International Bibliography of Books and Articles in the
    Modern Languages and Literature.* 1921 – .
Monthly Catalog of United States Government Publications.
    1895 – .
Music Index. 1949 – .
Philosopher's Index. 1967 – .
Public Affairs Information Service Bulletin. 1915 – .
Psychological Abstracts. 1927 – .
Social Sciences Index. 1974 – . Formerly *International Index,*
    1907 – 65, and *Social Sciences and Humanities Index,*
    1965 – 74.

Other sources

A library's holdings are not limited to reference works, books, and periodicals. Look as well for pamphlets, usually located in a large file cabinet known as the vertical file, and for films, filmstrips, records, and tapes.

For some topics, you may want to look beyond the library for information. Many organizations, both public and private, willingly mail literature in response to a phone call or a letter. Consider also the possibility of learning more about your subject through interviews, questionnaires, or experiments that you conduct yourself.

51d Evaluate sources for relevance and reliability.

Even after you have narrowed your topic, your search for useful titles may supply you with many more books and articles than you have time to read, so you will need to be selective.

Often you can judge both the relevance and the reliability of a source without even reading it. You might reject a book with an irrelevant subtitle or a too-old date, or you might select one by a well-known expert in the field. The table of contents of a book may reveal a relevant chapter or two; the index at the back of the book as well as the preface and introduction can indicate the book's coverage. Periodical articles often express their purpose and coverage in the first several paragraphs. Sometimes you have to read only one paragraph to either reject an irrelevant article or decide to read the whole piece.

By reading book reviews, you can learn whether a book was well received by experts when it was published—an especially important strategy if your paper draws on only one or two books to establish its arguments. *Book Review Digest* is a good general survey of book reviews. *Book Review Index* covers fiction and books in the humanities and social sciences; *Technical Book Review Index* covers reviews in scientific and technical fields.

Biographical directories in many fields list the publications of well-known scholars; checking these will help establish the credentials of an author. A magazine publisher's reputation for checking facts closely and for objectivity can be discovered in *Magazines for Libraries*, a guide to the reputations of more than 6,500 magazines.

The preliminary judgments you make about the reliability of your sources need to be confirmed as you read them closely. Your best guide is your own critical intelligence. Are the author's assertions proved with valid evidence? Does the author present research data and not just a few anecdotes or emotional examples? Are the sources clearly documented? Is expert judgment cited? Does the author avoid logical fallacies and emotional language? (See 53.)

Primary and secondary sources

Research usually requires a reading of both primary and secondary sources. Primary sources are original documents such as novels, poems, plays, speeches, diaries, legislative bills, laboratory studies, field research reports, or eyewitness accounts. Secondary sources are commentaries on primary sources.

A primary source for Karen Shaw, whose sample research paper appears beginning on page 404, was an article by Allen and Beatrice Gardner reporting their experiments with the chimpanzee Washoe. Shaw also consulted Flora Davis's book *Eloquent Animals,* a secondary source that reports the studies of the Gardners and other researchers.

You should use primary sources as much as possible. Naturally, you can better evaluate what the secondary sources say if you have first read the primary source and are familiar with it. Reading the primary source will establish your credibility as a thorough researcher and an independent thinker.

51e Prepare bibliography cards.

The sources you have decided to consult should all be listed on separate $3'' \times 5''$ cards. These cards will be necessary later, when you compile the list of works cited in your paper. For books, take down carefully and completely the following information:

Call number

All authors; any editors or translators

Title and subtitle

Edition (if not the first)

Publishing information: city, publishing company, and date

For periodical articles you need this information:

All authors of the article

Title and subtitle of the article

Title of the magazine, journal, or newspaper

Date and page numbers

Volume and issue numbers, if relevant (see 52g)

NOTE: For the exact bibliographic form to be used in the final paper, see 52g.

SAMPLE BIBLIOGRAPHY CARD FOR A BOOK

QL776.D38 1978

Davis, Flora. *Eloquent Animals: A Study in Animal Communication: How Chimps Lie, Whales Sing and Slime Molds Pass the Message Along.* New York: Coward, McCann & Geoghegan, 1978.

- only first 6 chapters on apes and chimps
- discusses what grammar is (pages 24-26)
- interesting anecdotes, interviews

SAMPLE BIBLIOGRAPHY CARD FOR A PERIODICAL

Seyfarth, Robert M. "Talking with
Monkeys and Great Apes." *International
Wildlife* Mar./Apr. 1982: 12-18.

— good overview of the controversy
— discusses the author's own studies
   of apes in the wild

On the card you may want to write brief comments about the coverage of a book or article. Once you begin reading, you will take more specific notes on note cards.

51f As you read, take notes systematically. Avoid unintentional plagiarism.

Systematic notes on your reading will make it clear to you later, as you are drafting your paper, just which words and phrases belong to your sources and which are your own. This is a crucial matter, for if any language from your sources finds its way into your final draft without quotation marks and proper documentation, you will be guilty of plagiarism, a serious academic offense. (See 52d.)

You can take notes in a variety of ways, as long as they are accurate, but the following suggestions may help you make the most efficient use of your time. Have nearby a stack of blank, white cards (4″ × 6″ is customary). Write one note on each card so you can shuffle and reshuffle the cards in different orders later as you experiment with the organization of your paper. Put the last name of the author of your source in the upper right corner of the card, and put a subject label in the upper left corner. If you have read enough to form a preliminary outline, use the subdivisions of the outline as subject headings on your cards.

Next decide the most helpful way to preserve the information in a particular source: summarizing, paraphrasing, quoting word for word, or writing personal comments. As you take notes, be sure to include exact page references next to the information, since you will need the page numbers later if you use the information in your paper.

Note cards that summarize

Summarizing is the best kind of preliminary note taking because it is the fastest. A summary condenses information, perhaps capsulizing a chapter in a short paragraph or a paragraph in a single sentence. A summary should of course be written in your own words; if you do use apt phrases from the source, put them in quotation marks.

Here is a passage from an original source read by Karen Shaw in researching her essay on apes and language. Following the passage is Shaw's note card summarizing it.

ORIGINAL SOURCE

Public and scientific interest in the question of apes' ability to use language first soared some 15 years ago when Washoe, a chimpanzee raised like a human child by R. Allen Gardner and Beatrice Gardner of the University of Nevada, learned to make hand signs for many words and even seemed to be making short sentences.

Since then researchers have taught many chimpanzees and a few gorillas and orangutans to "talk" using the sign language of deaf humans, plastic chips or, like Kanzi, keyboard symbols. Washoe, Sarah, a chimpanzee trained by David Premack of the University of Pennsylvania, and Koko, a gorilla trained by the psychologist Francine Patterson, became media stars.   — Eckholm, "Pygmy," p. B7

SUMMARY

> Types of languages   Eckholm, "Pygmy"
>
> The ape experiments began about 15 years ago with Washoe, who learned sign language. In later experiments some apes learned to communicate using plastic chips or symbols on a keyboard. (p. 87)

Note cards that paraphrase

Like a summary, a paraphrase is written in your own words; but whereas a summary reports significant information in fewer words than the source, a paraphrase retells the information in roughly the same number of words. If you retain occasional choice phrases from the source, put quotation marks around them so that you'll know later which phrases are your own.

You will discover that it is amazingly easy to borrow too much language from a source as you paraphrase. Do not allow this to happen. You are guilty of plagiarism if you half-copy the author's sentences — either by mixing the author's well-chosen phrases with your own without quotation marks or by plugging your synonyms into the author's sentence structure. (For examples of this kind of plagiarism, see 52e.)

To prevent unintentional borrowing, resist the temptation to look at the source while you are paraphrasing. Keep

PARAPHRASE

Washoe   Eckholm, "Pygmy"

A chimpanzee named Washoe, trained 15
years ago by U. of Nevada professors
R. Allen and Beatrice Gardner, learned
words in the sign language of the deaf
and may even have created short
sentences. (p. 37)

---

the source close by — to check for accuracy — but don't try to
paraphrase with the source's sentences in front of you.

As you read the note card above, which paraphrases the
first paragraph of Shaw's original source (see p. 373), notice
that the language is significantly different from that in the
original. Working with this note card, Shaw was in no danger
of unintentional plagiarism.

Note cards that quote

A quotation consists of the exact words from a source. On
your note cards, put all quoted material in quotation marks;
do not trust yourself to remember later which words, phrases,
and passages you have quoted and which are your own. When
you quote, be sure to copy the words of your source exactly,
including punctuation and capitalization.

Quotations should be reserved for special purposes: to
use a writer's especially vivid or expressive wording, to allow

QUOTATION

```
Washoe                    Eckholm, "Pygmy"

Washoe, trained by R. Allen and Beatrice
Gardner, "learned to make hand signs
for many words and even seemed to
be making short sentences." (p. 87)
```

an expert to explain a complex matter clearly, or to let critics of an opinion object in their own words. If you find yourself quoting a great deal in your notes, you are probably wasting time, because your final essay should not contain excessive quotations (see 52e).

Above is an example of a note card containing a quotation from Shaw's original source (p. 373).

Personal note cards

At unexpected moments in your reading, you will experience the lucky accidents typical of the creative process: flashes of insight, connections with other reading, sharp questions, a more restricted topic, ways to set up the arguments of two opposing positions, a vivid scenario. Write these inspirations down before you forget them. An example of such a note card appears at the top of page 377.

PERSONAL COMMENT

> *Types of training*
>
> *Washoe (and I think Koko) were raised almost like children, not in a laboratory setting. Does the setting affect the apes' performance? What about scientific objectivity?*

Alternatives to note cards

Not every researcher uses note cards. For short research projects, some writers prefer to photocopy important material and underline or highlight key ideas, sometimes color coding the highlighted passages to reflect the major divisions in their outlines. In the margins they write personal comments or cross-references to other sources. Photocopying has the obvious advantage of saving time and labor. For extensive research projects, however, the technique is of limited value since there is no way of physically sorting the highlighted passages into separate batches of information.

A second alternative to note cards, the use of computer software, overcomes this disadvantage. With the appropriate software, you can type notes as you read, coding them to reflect the divisions of your outline. You can then print the notes in sorted batches. For example, Karen Shaw might have printed one batch of notes on the apes' sign language vocabularies, another on their creative uses of language, another on their mastery of grammar, and so on.

Although software programs can be time savers, their advantages should not be oversold. Any style of note taking demands that you read carefully, analyze what you read, and record information with care.

52

Writing the research paper

52a Focus on a tentative thesis and construct a preliminary outline.

A look through your note cards will probably suggest many ways to focus and organize your material. Before you begin writing, you should decide on a tentative thesis and construct a preliminary outline or you will flounder among the possibilities. Remain flexible, however, because you may need to revise your approach later. Writing about a subject is a way of learning about it; as you write, your understanding of your subject will almost certainly deepen.

Focusing on a tentative thesis

A thesis is a sentence asserting the main point of your essay (see 1c). If you are writing on a clearly argumentative topic, such as some aspect of the problem of nuclear waste, your thesis should state your informed opinion: that seabed disposal is not as safe as has been claimed, for example, or that because of politics and economics certain states have become dumping grounds for nuclear waste. You should avoid writing a paper that reports information for no apparent purpose. Few instructors want to read a paper that simply lists and describes the methods for disposing of nuclear waste. Most instructors want their students to take a stand.

Even if your subject is not so obviously controversial as nuclear waste, you can still assert a thesis. Nearly all subjects worth writing about contain some element of controversy; that is why scholars so often engage in polite — and sometimes not so polite — arguments. In researching the topic of apes and language, Karen Shaw, whose paper appears on pages 404–434, encountered a number of scholarly arguments. Early in her reading Shaw was impressed with the views of Francine Patterson, trainer of the gorilla Koko, who makes fairly dramatic claims about the linguistic abilities of apes. Later, after reading H. S. Terrace's criticisms of the ape language experiments, Shaw nearly reversed her earlier view. Finally, as she looked at all the arguments more closely, Shaw reached a conclusion: Patterson was right in insisting that the apes had used language spontaneously and creatively (despite Terrace's arguments to the contrary); Terrace was right in claiming that the apes' mastery of grammar has not yet been proved. For the exact wording of Shaw's final thesis, see her outline on pages 406–407.

Constructing a preliminary outline

Before committing yourself to a detailed outline, experiment with alternatives. Shuffle and reshuffle your note cards to get a feeling for the possibilities. With your tentative thesis in mind, plan a way to arrange your material in stages through a convincing argument. Rather than dividing your subject into static subdivisions, see the main body of your paper as a line of thought that moves step by step. What should be presented and analyzed first? Second? What is the most important evidence to save for the end?

Keep your preliminary outline as simple as possible, and construct it one step at a time. Put the thesis at the top and list your major points, leaving plenty of space between each one so that you can add minor ideas later. In her preliminary outline, Karen Shaw listed two major points in support of her thesis: first, that the apes have demonstrated significant language skills; second, that those skills do not extend to grammar. You might of course have more than two major points supporting your thesis, but you should rarely have more than five. If your list grows too long, you are probably not making enough connections among ideas.

Once you have decided on the thesis and the major points in support of the thesis, fill in the second level of organization by listing ideas supporting the major points. This is probably as much as you should attempt in a preliminary outline; a simple plan will be easier to adjust later as you gain new insights about your topic while writing the paper.

Many instructors require a formal outline with the final paper. For advice on constructing a formal outline, see 1d; for Karen Shaw's formal outline, see pages 406–407.

52b Draft the paper in your own voice.

With a restricted thesis, a preliminary outline, and stacks of note cards, you are ready to write a first draft. Keep it rough and keep it moving. Don't let your wish for perfect sentences stall you at this stage. First write down your ideas and their supporting details; polish your sentences later. Writing rapidly usually produces a more natural, individual voice and helps you avoid echoing the language of your sources.

A chatty, breezy voice is usually not welcome in academic papers, but neither is a stuffy, pretentious style or a timid, unsure one. If you believe in your main point and are interested in your subject, try to communicate that sense of conviction. Some writers find that they convey their tone more intensely if they imagine as they write that they are talking to a group of people or explaining their ideas to a television interviewer. To sound natural, Karen Shaw pretended that she was the guest lecturer in a psychology class.

Many researchers find that writing only from their outlines (rather than directly from their note cards) allows them to write in their own voices without mimicking the style of their sources. In writing their first draft, they refer to their note cards only for direct quotations and specific statistics. Other writers prefer to work more closely with their note cards, consulting them frequently as they write. Whichever method you use, it is crucial that your sentences be in your own words and not half-copied from your sources. (See 52d.)

Writing an introduction

In a research paper that refers to many other writers, it is especially important to establish your own voice in the introduction. Your opening paragraphs introduce you as well as your ideas to the reader.

One or two paragraphs are usually enough introduction for most papers in undergraduate courses. Most readers don't want a great deal of background; they want you to get right to the point.

Readers are accustomed to seeing the thesis statement — a one-sentence summary of the main point of the essay — at the beginning or at the end of the introduction. The advantage of beginning with the thesis is that readers can immediately grasp your purpose. The advantage of delaying the thesis is that you can provide a context for your point. You may first want to establish the importance of your topic, then review various attitudes toward it, and finally point to your view in your thesis statement.

In addition to stating the thesis and showing its importance, an introduction should hook readers. (See 2a.) Sometimes you can connect your topic to something recently in the news or bring your readers up to date about changing ideas.

Other strategies are to present a puzzling problem or to open with a startling statistic. Karen Shaw's sample paper (pages 404 – 434) begins with a series of vivid examples leading up to her thesis.

52c As you write, cite sources using a consistent system such as the MLA style of in-text citations.

In your paper you will be drawing on many sources. So that your readers will know where your information comes from, you will need to provide specific citations. Specific citations are required for summaries, paraphrases, quotations, and any ideas or facts that are not common knowledge (see also 52d).

The various academic disciplines use their own editorial styles both for citing sources and for listing the works that have been cited. The style used in this chapter is that of the Modern Language Association, contained in the *MLA Handbook for Writers of Research Papers* (2nd ed., 1984), which recommends that citations be given in the text of the paper rather than in footnotes. If your instructor prefers footnoting (also acceptable to MLA) or the American Psychological Association style of in-text citation, consult pages 436 – 445, where you will also find a list of style manuals used in various disciplines.

The MLA style of in-text citations

The Modern Language Association's in-text citations are made with a combination of signal phrases and parenthetical references. A signal phrase indicates that something taken from a source (such as a quotation, summary, or paraphrase) is about to be used; usually the signal phrase includes the author's name. The parenthetical reference includes at least a page number.

Citations in parentheses should be as concise as possible but complete enough so that readers can find the source in the list of works cited at the end of the paper, where works are listed alphabetically under the author's last name. The following models illustrate the form for the MLA style of citation.

AUTHOR IN SIGNAL PHRASE, PAGE NUMBER IN PARENTHESES
Ordinarily, you should introduce the material being cited with a signal phrase that includes the author's name. In addition to preparing readers for the source, the signal phrase allows you to keep the citation within the parentheses brief.

```
Flora Davis reports that a chimp at the Yerkes

Primate Research Center "has combined words into

new sentences that she was never taught" (67).
```

The signal phrase — "Flora Davis reports" — provides the name of the author; the parenthetical citation gives the page number where the quoted sentence may be found. By looking up the author's last name in the list of works cited, readers will find complete information about the work's title, publisher, and date of publication.

AUTHOR AND PAGE NUMBER IN PARENTHESES If the signal phrase does not include the author's name (or if there is no signal phrase), the author's last name must appear in parentheses along with the page number.

```
Although the baby chimp lived only a few hours,

Washoe signed to it before it died (Davis 42).
```

WHEN TO INCLUDE A TITLE Ordinarily the title of the work does not need to be included in either the signal phrase or the parentheses. However, if your paper cites two or more works by the same author (or by authors with the same last name), either mention the title in the signal phrase or use a short form of the title in parentheses.

In <u>Eloquent Animals</u>, Flora Davis reports that a chimp at the Yerkes Primate Research Center "has combined words into sentences that she was never taught" (67).

Flora Davis reports that a chimp at the Yerkes Primate Research Center "has combined words into sentences that she was never taught" (<u>Eloquent</u> 67).

In the rare case when both the author and a short title must be given in parentheses, the citation should appear as in the following example:

Although the baby chimpanzee lived only for a few hours, Washoe signed to it before it died (Davis, <u>Eloquent</u> 42).

A WORK WITH TWO OR MORE AUTHORS If your source has two or three authors, name them in the signal phrase or include them in the parenthetical reference.

Patterson and Linden agree that the gorilla Koko acquired language more slowly than a normal speaking child (83-90).

If your source has more than three authors, include only the first author's name followed by "et al." (Latin for "and others") in the signal phrase or in the parenthetical reference.

The study was extended for two years, and only after results were duplicated on both coasts did the authors publish their results (Doe et al. 137).

CORPORATE AUTHOR   Either name the corporate author in the signal phrase or include a shortened version in the parentheses.

> The Internal Revenue Service warns businesses that
> deductions for "lavish and extravagant entertain-
> ment" are not allowed (43).

UNKNOWN AUTHOR   If the author is not given, either use the complete title in a signal phrase or use a short form of the title in the parentheses.

> The UFO reported by the crew of a Japan Air Lines
> flight remains a mystery. Radar tapes did not
> confirm the presence of another craft ("Strange
> Encounter" 26).

A MULTIVOLUME WORK   If your paper cites more than one volume of a multivolume work, you must indicate in the parentheses which volume you are referring to.

> Terman's studies of gifted children reveal a pat-
> tern of accelerated language acquisition (2: 279).

If your paper cites only one volume of a multivolume work, the volume number will be mentioned in the list of works cited at the end of the paper. You will not need to include it in the parentheses.

A NOVEL, A PLAY, OR A POEM   In citing literary sources, include information that will enable readers to find the passage in various editions of the work. For a novel, put the page number first and then indicate the part or chapter in which the passage can be found.

> Fitzgerald's narrator captures Gatsby in a moment
> of isolation: "A sudden emptiness seemed to flow

```
now from the windows and the great doors, endowing
with complete isolation the figure of the host"
(56; ch. 3).
```

For a verse play, list the act, scene, and line numbers. Use arabic numerals unless your instructor prefers roman numerals.

```
In his famous advice to the players, Hamlet de-
fines the purpose of theater, "whose end, both at
the first and now, was and is, to hold, as 'twere,
the mirror up to nature" (3.2.21–23).
```

For a poem, cite the part (if there are a number of parts) and the line numbers.

```
When Homer's Odysseus came to the hall of Circe,
he found his men "mild / in her soft spell, fed on
her drug of evil" (10.209–11).
```

INDIRECT SOURCE When a writer's or speaker's quoted words appear in a source written by someone else, begin the citation with the abbreviation "qtd. in."

```
"We only used seven signs in his presence," says
Fouts. "All of his signs were learned from the
other chimps at the laboratory" (qtd. in Toner
24).
```

PARENTHETICAL CITATION OF TWO OR MORE WORKS You may want to cite more than one source to document a particular point. Separate the citations with a semicolon.

```
With intensive training, the apes in this study
learned more than 200 signs or signals (Desmond
229; Linden 173).
```

Multiple citations can be distracting to readers, however, so the technique should not be overused. If you want to alert your reader to several sources that discuss a particular topic, consider using a note instead (discussed next in this section).

Using footnotes or endnotes with parenthetical documentation

Researchers who use the MLA system of parenthetical documentation may also use footnotes or endnotes for one of two purposes:

1. to provide additional information that might interrupt the flow of the paper yet is important enough to include;
2. to refer readers to sources not included in the list of works cited.

Footnotes appear at the foot of the page; endnotes appear at the end of the paper, just before the list of works cited. For either style, the notes are numbered consecutively throughout the paper. The text of the paper contains a raised arabic numeral that corresponds to the number of the note.

TEXT

The apes' achievements cannot be explained away as the simple results of conditioning or unconscious cueing by trainers.[1]

NOTE

[1] For a discussion of the cueing of animals, see Wade 1349–51.

Notes used with parenthetical documentation (for the special purposes mentioned in this section) should not be confused with notes used as an alternative to parenthetical documentation (pp. 437–440).

52d Do not plagiarize: Cite all quotations and
borrowed ideas; avoid paraphrases that closely resemble
your sources.

Your research paper is a collaboration between you and your
sources. To be fair and ethical, you must acknowledge your
borrowing of other writers' ideas and words. To borrow without proper acknowledgment is a form of dishonesty known
as plagiarism (see also 51f).

The academic, business, and legal communities take plagiarism very seriously. Universities have been known to withdraw graduate degrees from students who have plagiarized.
Professional writers sue for (and get) thousands of dollars
when they discover that someone has plagiarized their work.

Two different acts are considered plagiarism: (1) to borrow someone's ideas, information, or language without citing
the source and (2) to cite the source but borrow choice words
and phrases without using quotation marks to indicate the
borrowing.

Citing quotations and borrowed ideas

You must of course cite all direct quotations. You must also
cite any specific ideas borrowed from a particular source: statistics and little-known facts; controversial data; paraphrases
of sentences; summaries of paragraphs or chapters; and tables, graphs, or diagrams.

The only exception is common knowledge — information
that your readers could find in any number of general sources
because it is commonly known. For example, the current population of the United States is common knowledge in such
fields as sociology and economics; Freud's theory of the unconscious is common knowledge in the field of psychology.

As a rule, when you have seen certain facts repeatedly in
your reading, you don't need to cite them. On the other hand,
when they have appeared in only one or two sources or when

they are controversial, you should cite them. If a topic is new to you and you are not sure what is considered common knowledge or what facts are a matter of controversy, ask someone with expertise. When in doubt, cite the source.

Avoiding close paraphrases

Close paraphrases are the most common form of plagiarism because if a researcher is sloppy at the note-taking stage, unacceptable borrowings can occur unintentionally (see 51f). When you paraphrase, it is not enough to name the source; you must restate the source's meaning completely in your own words. The following is an example of plagiarizing an author's wording even though the source is cited.

ORIGINAL VERSION
If the existence of a signing ape was unsettling for linguists, it was also startling news for animal behaviorists.

UNACCEPTABLE BORROWING OF WORDS, ALTHOUGH SOURCE IS CITED

An ape who knew sign language unsettled linguists and startled animal behaviorists (Davis 26).

Notice that "unsettling for linguists" and "startling news for animal behaviorists" have been barely changed.

It is also plagiarism to borrow the source's sentence structure but to substitute your own synonyms, even though the source is cited, as illustrated below.

UNACCEPTABLE BORROWING OF STRUCTURE, ALTHOUGH SOURCE IS CITED

If the presence of a sign–language–using chimp was disturbing for scientists studying language, it was also surprising to scientists studying animal behavior (Davis 26).

To avoid plagiarizing an author's wording, you should close the book, write down the ideas as you remember them, and then open the book to check for accuracy (see 51f). This technique prevents you from being captivated by the words on the page; it encourages you to write naturally, in your own voice, without plagiarizing. The following two paraphrases were written with the book closed.

ACCEPTABLE PARAPHRASES

According to Flora Davis, linguists and animal behaviorists were unprepared for the news that a
chimp could communicate with its trainers through
sign language (26).

When they learned of an ape's ability to use sign
language, both linguists and animal behaviorists
were taken by surprise (Davis 26).

52e Limit quotations and integrate them as smoothly as possible.

It is tempting to insert many long quotations in your paper and to use your own words only for connecting passages. This is an especially strong temptation if you feel that the authors of your sources are better writers than you are. But do not quote excessively. Long series of quotations give readers the impression that you cannot think for yourself.

The advice given earlier about note taking is relevant here: Use direct quotations only when the source is particularly clear or expressive or when it is important to let the debaters of an issue explain their positions in their own words. Except for this infrequent need for direct quotations, use your own words to summarize and paraphrase your sources and to explain your own ideas.

Integrating quotations

Integrate quotations smoothly enough for readers to move from your words to the words of a source without feeling a jolt. Avoid dropping quotations into the text without warning; instead, provide clear signal phrases, usually including the author's name, to prepare readers for the source.

DROPPED QUOTATION

Although the bald eagle is still listed as an endangered species, its ever-increasing population
is very encouraging.   "The bald eagle seems to
have stabilized its population, at the very least,
almost everywhere" (Sheppard 96).

QUOTATION WITH SIGNAL PHRASE

Although the bald eagle is still listed as an endangered species, its ever-increasing population
is very encouraging.   According to ornithologist
Jay Sheppard, "The bald eagle seems to have stabilized its population, at the very least, almost
everywhere" (96).

To avoid monotony, try to vary your signal phrases. The following models suggest a range of possibilities:

In the words of researcher Herbert Terrace, " . . . "
As Flora Davis has noted, " . . . "
The Gardners, Washoe's trainers, point out that " . . . "
" . . . ," claims linguist Noam Chomsky.
Psychologist H. S. Terrace offers an odd argument for this view: " . . . "
Terrace answers these objections with the following analysis: " . . . "

When the signal phrase includes a verb, choose one that is appropriate in the context. Is your source arguing a point, making an observation, reporting a fact, drawing a conclusion, refuting an argument, or stating a belief? By choosing an appropriate verb, such as one on the following list, you can make your source's stance clear.

acknowledges	comments	endorses	reasons
adds	compares	grants	refutes
admits	confirms	illustrates	rejects
agrees	contends	implies	reports
argues	declares	insists	responds
asserts	denies	notes	suggests
believes	disputes	observes	thinks
claims	emphasizes	points out	writes

It is not always necessary to quote full sentences from a source. At times you may wish to borrow only a phrase or to weave part of a source's sentence into your own sentence structure:

> Brian Millsap claims that the banning of DDT in 1972 was "the major turning point" leading to the eagles' comeback (2).

> The ultrasonography machine takes approximately 250 views of each breast, step by step. Mary Spletter likens the process to "examining an entire loaf of bread, one slice at a time" (40).

Using the ellipsis mark and brackets

Two useful marks of punctuation, the ellipsis mark and brackets, allow you to keep quoted material to a minimum and to integrate it smoothly into your text.

THE ELLIPSIS MARK   To condense a quoted passage, you can use the ellipsis mark (three periods, with spaces between) to indicate that you have omitted words. What remains must be grammatically complete.

> In a recent <u>New York Times</u> article, Erik Eckholm reports that "a 4-year-old pygmy chimpanzee . . . has demonstrated what scientists say are the most humanlike linguistic skills ever documented in another animal" (Al).

The writer has omitted the words *at a research center near Atlanta*, which appeared in the original.

On the rare occasions when you want to omit a full sentence or more, use a period before the three ellipsis dots.

> According to Wade, the horse Clever Hans "could apparently count by tapping out numbers with his hoof. . . . Clever Hans owes his celebrity to his master's innocence. Von Osten sincerely believed he had taught Hans to solve arithmetical problems" (1349).

Ordinarily, do not use an ellipsis mark at the beginning or at the end of a quotation. Your readers will understand that the quoted material is taken from a longer passage, so such ellipsis marks are not necessary. The only exception occurs when words at the end of the final quoted sentence have been dropped.

Obviously you should not use an ellipsis mark to distort the meaning of your source.

BRACKETS   Brackets (square parentheses) allow you to insert words of your own into quoted material. You can insert

words in brackets to explain a confusing reference or to keep
a sentence grammatical in your context.

> Robert Seyfarth reports that "Premack [a scientist at the
> University of Pennsylvania] taught a seven-year-old
> chimpanzee, Sarah, that the word for 'apple' was a small,
> plastic triangle" (13).

If your typewriter has no brackets, ink them in by hand.

Long quotations

When you quote more than four typed lines, set off the quotation by indenting it ten spaces from the left margin. Use
the normal right margin and do not single space. This format
displays your source's words more obviously than a set of
widely separated quotation marks.

Long quotations should be introduced by an informative
sentence, usually followed by a colon. Quotation marks are
unnecessary because the indented format tells readers that
the words are taken directly from the source.

```
Desmond describes how Washoe, when the Gardners

returned her to an ape colony in Oklahoma, tried

signing to the other apes:

            One particularly memorable day, a snake

            spread terror through the castaways on

            the ape island, and all but one fled in

            panic.  This male sat absorbed, staring

            intently at the serpent. Then Washoe was

            seen running over signing to him "come,

            hurry up." (42)
```

Notice that at the end of a block quotation the parenthetical
citation goes outside the final period.

52f Revise the paper.

When you are reworking the rough draft of a research paper, it is tempting to concentrate on documentation and ignore other important aspects of writing. The following checklist will help you review your draft thoroughly.

Content, focus, and organization

1. Is your topic restricted?
2. Is your thesis or purpose clearly stated in the introduction?
3. Does the body of the paper support the thesis with appropriate evidence such as facts, statistics, reasons, and expert testimony?
4. Can readers follow the organization? Are the ideas effectively arranged?

Paragraphing and coherence

5. Does each paragraph have a clear topic sentence stating a central idea related to the thesis?
6. Does each paragraph fully support its topic sentence?
7. Do the paragraphs read smoothly? Can readers move from one paragraph to another without feeling lost?

Style and correctness

8. Are the sentences clear, emphatic, and varied?
9. Is your style formal without being inflated?
10. Is the paper free of errors in grammar, punctuation, and mechanics?

Use of sources

11. Have you limited your use of quotations? Is each quotation used for a good reason? (See 52e.)
12. Have you acknowledged your sources (ideas, facts, summaries, paraphrases, quotations) with citations? Are you

certain that you have not paraphrased any sources too closely? (See 52d.)

13. Are quotations accurate word for word? If not, have changes been indicated with brackets or ellipsis marks? (See 52e.)

14. Are signal phrases and citations accurate and specific? (See 52c.)

When revising any paper, it is a good idea to focus first on the larger elements of writing — content, focus, organization, paragraphing, and coherence — and then to turn to matters of style and correctness. With the research paper, this strategy is especially important because reviewing your use of sources requires considerable attention to detail.

Once you have revised and edited your draft, type the final copy according to your instructor's guidelines, and proofread it carefully. Then only one task remains: compiling the list of works cited.

52g Prepare a list of works cited.

A list of works cited, which appears at the end of your paper, gives full publishing information for each of the sources you have cited in the paper. Start on a new page and title your list "Works Cited." Then, working from your bibliography cards (see 51e), list in alphabetical order all the sources that you have cited in the paper. Unless your instructor asks for them, sources not actually cited in the paper should not be given in this list, even if you may have read them. Alphabetize the list by the last name of the author (or editor); if there is no author or editor, alphabetize by the first word of the title other than *a, an,* or *the.*

Do not indent the first line of each bibliographic entry, but indent any additional lines. This technique highlights the names by which the list has been alphabetized (see, for example, the list of works cited at the end of Karen Shaw's paper on page 434).

The following models illustrate the form that the Modern Language Association (MLA) recommends for bibliographic entries.

BASIC FORMAT FOR A BOOK For most books, arrange the information into three units, each followed by a period: (1) the author's name, last name first; (2) the title and subtitle, underlined; and (3) the place of publication, the publisher, and the date.

Davis, Flora. Eloquent Animals: A Study in Animal

Communication. New York: Coward, 1978.

The information is taken from the title page of the book and from the reverse side of the title page (the copyright page), not from the outside cover. The complete name of the publisher (in this case Coward, McCann & Geoghegan, Inc.) need not be given. You may use a short form as long as it is easily identifiable; omit terms such as *Press, Inc.,* and *Co.* except when naming university presses such as Harvard UP. The date to use in your bibliographic entry is the latest copyright date.

TWO OR MORE AUTHORS Name the authors in the order in which they are presented on the title page; reverse the name of only the first author.

Fisher, Roger, and William Ury. Getting to Yes:

Negotiating Agreement Without Giving In.

Boston: Houghton, 1981.

The names of three authors are separated by commas: Smith, Margaret, Sharon Jones, and Harry Brown. For four or more authors, cite only the first one, followed by "et al." (the Latin abbreviation for "and others"): Doe, Jane, et al. The procedure for citing multiple authors of periodical articles is the same as for citing multiple authors of books.

EDITORS An entry for an editor is similar to that for an author except that the name is followed by a comma and the abbreviation "ed." for "editor." If there is more than one editor, use the abbreviation "eds." (for "editors").

Lenneberg, Eric H., and Elizabeth Lenneberg,

eds. <u>Foundations of Language Development</u>.

New York: Academic, 1975.

AUTHOR WITH AN EDITOR Begin with the author and title, followed by the name of the editor. In this case the abbreviation "Ed." means "edited by," so it is the same for one or multiple editors.

Shakespeare, William. <u>The Tragedy of Macbeth</u>.

Ed. Louis B. Wright and Virginia A. Lamar.

New York: Washington Square, 1959.

TRANSLATION List the entry under the name of the author, not the translator. After the title, write "Trans." (for "translated by") and the name of the translator.

Tolstoy, Leo. <u>Anna Karenina</u>. Trans. Constance

Garnett. Indianapolis: Bobbs, 1978.

CORPORATE AUTHOR Begin with the name of the corporate author, even if it is also the name of the publisher.

Maryland Commission for Women. <u>How to Translate</u>

<u>Volunteer Skills into Employment Credentials</u>.

Baltimore: MD Commission for Women, 1979.

UNKNOWN AUTHOR Begin with the title. Alphabetize the entry by the first word of the title other than *a, an,* or *the.*

> The Times Atlas of the World. 5th ed. New York:
>
> > New York Times, 1975.

EDITION OTHER THAN THE FIRST If you are citing an edition other than the first, include the number of the edition after the title: 2nd ed., 3rd ed., and so on.

> Spatt, Brenda. Writing from Sources. 2nd ed.
>
> > New York: St. Martin's, 1987.

MULTIVOLUME WORK Include the number of volumes before the city and publisher, using the abbreviation "vols." If your paper cites only one of the volumes, write the volume number after the date, using the abbreviation "Vol."

> Graves, Robert. The Greek Myths. 2 vols. New
>
> > York: Braziller, 1967. Vol. 2.

WORK IN AN ANTHOLOGY Present the information in this order, with each item followed by a period: author of the work; title of the work; title of the anthology; editor of the anthology, preceded by "Ed."; city, publisher, and date; page numbers on which the work appears.

> Abrams, M. H. "English Romanticism: The Spirit of
>
> > the Age." Romanticism Reconsidered. Ed.
> >
> > Northrop Frye. New York: Columbia UP, 1963.
> >
> > 63–88.

ENCYCLOPEDIA OR DICTIONARY Articles in well-known dictionaries and encyclopedias are handled in abbreviated form. Simply list the author of the article (if there is one), the title of the article, the title of the reference work, and the date of the edition.

```
Frankel, Mark S.   "Human Experimentation: Social
     and Professional Control."   Encyclopedia of
     Bioethics.   1978 ed.
```

Volume and page numbers are not necessary because the entries are arranged alphabetically and therefore are easy to locate.

If a reference work is not well known, provide full publishing information as well.

GOVERNMENT PUBLICATION   Treat the government agency as the author, giving the name of the government followed by the name of the agency.

```
United States.   Internal Revenue Service.   Tax
     Guide for Small Business.   Publication 334.
     Washington: GPO, 1983.
```

ARTICLE IN A MONTHLY MAGAZINE   In addition to the author, the title of the article, and the title of the magazine, list the month and year and the page numbers on which the article may be found. Abbreviate the names of months except for May, June, and July.

```
Lorenz, Wanda L.   "Problem Areas in Accounting for
     Income Taxes."   The Practical Accountant Feb.
     1984: 69–77.
```

If the article had appeared on pages 69 – 71 and 89 – 95, you would write "69 + " (not "69 – 95").

ARTICLE IN A WEEKLY MAGAZINE   Handle articles in weekly (or biweekly) magazines as you do those for monthly magazines, but give the exact date of the issue, not just the month and year.

Clark, Matt.   "Medicine: A Brave New World."

Newsweek 5 Mar. 1984: 64–70.

ARTICLE IN A JOURNAL PAGINATED BY VOLUME   Many professional journals continue page numbers throughout the year instead of beginning each issue with page 1; at the end of the year, all of the issues are collected in a volume. Interested readers can find the article if they know only the volume number, the year, and the page numbers.

Otto, Mary L.   "Child Abuse: Group Treatment for

Parents."   Personnel and Guidance Journal 62

(1984): 336–38.

ARTICLE IN A JOURNAL PAGINATED BY ISSUE   If each issue of the journal begins with page 1, you need to indicate the number of the issue. Simply place a period after the number of the volume, followed by the number of the issue.

Nichols, Randall G.   "Word Processing and Basic

Writers."   Journal of Basic Writing 5.2

(1986): 81–97.

ARTICLE IN A DAILY NEWSPAPER   Begin with the author, if there is one, followed by the title of the article. Next list the name of the newspaper, the date, the section letter or number, and the page number.

Gorney, Cynthia.   "When the Gorilla Speaks."

Washington Post 31 Jan. 1985: B1.

If the section is marked with a number rather than a letter, handle the entry as follows:

```
"Market Leaks: Illegal Insider Trading Seems to Be
    on Rise; Ethical Issues Muddled." Wall
    Street Journal 2 Mar. 1984, sec. 1: 1.
```

If an edition of the newspaper is specified on the masthead, name the edition after the date and before the page reference: eastern ed., late ed., natl. ed., and so on.

FILMS AND TELEVISION PROGRAMS Begin with the title and the director, and end with the distributor and the year. After the name of the director, include other information if you wish, such as the names of lead actors.

```
North by Northwest. Dir. Alfred Hitchcock. With
    Cary Grant. MGM, 1959.
```

LIVE PERFORMANCE OF A PLAY Begin with the title of the play, followed by the author. Then include specific information about the live performance: the director, the major actors, the theater company and its location, and the date of the performance.

```
Mother Courage. By Bertolt Brecht. Dir. Timothy
    Mayer. With Linda Hunt. Boston Shakespeare
    Company Theater, Boston. 20 Jan. 1984.
```

RECORDING Begin with the composer (or author, if the recording is spoken), followed by the title of the piece. Next list pertinent artists (for instance, the conductor, the pianist, or the reader). End with the company label, the catalog number, and the date.

```
Handel, George Frederick. Messiah. With Eliza-
    beth Harwood, Janet Baker, Paul Esswood, Rob-
    ert Tear, and Raimund Herincz. Cond. Charles
```

> Mackerras. English Chamber Orch. and the Am-
> brosian Singers. Angel, R 67–2682, 1967.

COMPUTER SOFTWARE Begin with the author of the program (if known), the title of the program, and the words "Computer software," each followed by a period. Then name the distributer and the year of publication. At the end of the entry you may add other pertinent information, such as the computer for which the program is designed or the form of the program.

> Childpace. Computer software. Computerose, 1984.
> Commodore 64, disk.

INTERVIEW Begin with the name of the person interviewed. Next write "Personal interview." End with the date of the interview.

> Shaw, Lloyd. Personal interview. 21 Mar. 1987.

TWO OR MORE WORKS BY THE SAME AUTHOR If your list of works cited includes two or more works by the same author, use the author's name only for the first entry. For subsequent entries use three hyphens followed by a period. List the titles in alphabetical order.

> Davis, Flora. Eloquent Animals: A Study in Animal
> Communication. New York: Coward, 1978.
> ---. Inside Intuition: What We Know About Nonver-
> bal Communication. New York: McGraw, 1973.

Somewhere Between the Word and the Sentence:

The Great Apes and the Acquisition of Language

1

By Karen Shaw

English 101, Section 30

Dr. Barshay

November 1, 1988

1. *Title page format.* Shaw uses a separate title page. She types the title about one-third down the page. One inch below the title Shaw types *By* and then her name, and one inch below that she types the name and section number of the course, her instructor's name, and the date. Each item is on a separate line, double-spaced. All the information is centered between the left and right margins.

Pages 406 – 407

2. *Outline.* Shaw begins the outline with her thesis, the main point of the paper: "The great apes resemble humans in language abilities more than researchers once believed, but it is as yet unknown to what extent apes can combine symbols in grammatical patterns." The outline has two major divisions corresponding to the two parts of the thesis.

   Shaw's outline is presented in standard form, with roman numerals for the major categories, capital letters indented for the next level, and arabic numerals indented further for the third level (see 1d).

   Shaw decided that a sentence outline was necessary to reflect the complexity of the ideas in her paper. She keeps the sentences as parallel and as simple as possible to make the relationships between and among ideas clear.

   The second page of the outline is numbered with a small roman numeral *ii.* The first page is left unnumbered.

Outline

Thesis: The great apes resemble humans in lan-   2
guage abilities more than researchers
once believed, but it is as yet unknown
to what extent apes can combine symbols
in grammatical patterns.

I. The great apes have demonstrated significant
language skills.

A. Chimpanzees and gorillas have acquired
large vocabularies in American sign language and in two artificial languages.

1. In sign language, chimpanzee Washoe
learned 160 signs, gorilla Koko possibly as many as 600.

2. In artificial languages, chimpanzees
Sarah and Lana learned more than 100
symbols each.

B. Despite charges that they are merely re-
sponding to their trainers' cues, apes
have used signs spontaneously.

1. They have performed well in experiments that eliminate the possibility
of cueing.

2. They initiate conversations with
other apes.

      3. Current experiments demonstrate con-
          clusively that apes can learn signs
          and symbols from one another.

   C. Apes appear to use their language skills
      creatively, although this is a matter of
      some dispute.

      1. They have invented creative names.

      2. There is some evidence that they
          lie, joke, and swear.

II. It has not yet been demonstrated that apes
    can combine signs in grammatical patterns to
    form sentences.

   A. The apes' sequences of signs are often
      confusing and repetitious.

   B. Lana's manipulation of stock sentences
      could be the result of conditioning.

   C. The Gardners' example is inconclusive.

   D. Even Patterson does not claim that her
      apes grasp grammar.

   E. Current research at Yerkes Primate Cen-
      ter, however, looks promising.

Somewhere Between the Word and the Sentence: 3
The Great Apes and the Acquisition of Language   4

Choosing from among the eighty signs in   5
American sign language that she had learned, a
chimpanzee named Lucy selected three and signaled
to her trainer, "Roger tickle Lucy." When Roger
failed to respond to her request and signaled instead, "No, Lucy tickle Roger," the chimpanzee
jumped onto his lap and began to tickle him (Des-   6
mond 43-44). One afternoon, Koko the gorilla,
who was often bored with language lessons, stub-
bornly and repeatedly signaled "red" when asked
the color of a white towel. She did this even
though she had correctly identified the color
white many times before. At last the gorilla
produced "a minute speck of red lint that had
been clinging to the towel" (Patterson and Linden
80-81). In Atlanta, when a two-and-a-half-year-
old pygmy chimpanzee's mother was taken away for
breeding, the young chimp amazed researchers by
revealing he had been learning "out of the corner

3. *Title.* The first part of Shaw's title is an evocative phrase introducing an idea that will be clarified at the end of the paper. The subtitle is an explicit description of her topic.

4. *Paper format.* The title is centered between the left and right margins, about two inches from the top of the page. The text begins four lines below the title. All pages are numbered with arabic numerals at the upper right-hand corner, about a half-inch from the top. (Traditionally, the first page was unnumbered, but the current *MLA Handbook* calls for numbering it.) The text is double-spaced, with a margin of one inch at the top, bottom, and sides of the paper.

   If your paper does not have a title page, put the following information on four separate lines, double-spaced, in the upper left corner of the first page: your name, your instructor's name, the name and section number of the course, and the date. Then center the title two lines below this information.

5. *Opening paragraph.* Karen Shaw decided to open her paper with three vivid examples that provide an overview of her subject.

6. *Author named in parentheses.* Because the name of the author is not included in a signal phrase, it must appear in parentheses along with the page number. (See 52c.)

of his eye" symbols that were being taught to his
mother. He hit the symbols for both apple and
ball on a computerized keyboard and pointed to
the objects (Eckholm, "Kanzi" C1).   **7**

          These and hundreds of similar scenes played   **8**
out over the past twenty years make it clear that
the great apes (chimpanzees, gorillas, and orangutans) resemble humans in language abilities more
than had previously been believed. Just how far
that resemblance extends, however, is a matter of
some controversy. Researchers agree that apes
have acquired large vocabularies, but they differ
sharply in interpreting the uses to which these
vocabularies have been put. On balance, the
evidence suggests--despite the opinions of some
skeptics--that apes have used symbols spontaneously and creatively. It is as yet unknown,
however, to what extent they can combine symbols
in grammatical patterns.

          Though apes lack the vocal ability to pro-
duce human sounds, they have acquired fairly
large vocabularies in American sign language, or
Ameslan, and in two artificial languages.
Washoe, an African-born chimpanzee trained by
psychologists Allen and Beatrice Gardner from
1966 to 1970, learned 160 signs in Ameslan.

7. *Author and short title in parentheses.* Because there are two works by Eckholm in the list of works cited, a short form of the title must be included in the parentheses. (See 52c.)

8. *Thesis.* Shaw's thesis is carefully articulated in her second paragraph. Ordinarily the thesis would appear in the opening paragraph, but Shaw decided to delay her thesis and begin with a series of vivid examples.

Shaw uses a full paragraph to express her thesis because her conclusions about the ape experiments are complex. Notice that the thesis paragraph surveys the organization of the paper, preparing readers for its two main parts and even for some of its subparts. The thesis sentence that appears in Shaw's outline presents the main point more succinctly.

The thesis of the paper is not as dramatic as Shaw thought it would be when she began the paper. Having seen several television shows and having read a few popular articles before fully researching her subject, Shaw was at first convinced that the apes' linguistic abilities were extensive. Later, as she read more widely, she began to doubt her preliminary thesis and even considered reversing it dramatically. On completing her reading, however, Shaw decided that the evidence for the apes' abilities was most convincing, even though their abilities were not as extensive as she had once thought.

Washoe began to learn signs by spontaneously imitating the Gardners, who used only sign language in her presence, but she learned more rapidly when the Gardners took her hands and molded the signs with them. To determine when Washoe truly knew a sign, the Gardners applied a rigid criterion: The sign had to be used "appropriately and spontaneously at least once a day for fourteen or **9** fifteen consecutive days" (Davis 21).

The largest Ameslan vocabulary claimed for an ape, 600 signs, is that of Francine Patterson's gorilla Koko, who has lived with Patterson since 1972. This figure is based on a simple count, not on the Gardners' strict criterion. But Patterson has also kept records showing that Koko has mastered nearly 200 signs as measured by the Gardners' criterion (Patterson and Linden **10** 83–84).

The first ape to acquire a vocabulary in an artificial language was Sarah, a chimpanzee trained by psychologist David Premack in the late 1960s. Sarah learned more than one hundred **11** "words" in a language of plastic tokens, each representing a different word or word combination in English. In the early 1970s, another chimp, Lana, learned over a hundred symbols in Yerkish,

9. *Importance of statistics and other numerical evidence.* Shaw uses statistics throughout to support her assertions. Here she provides a concrete explanation of what the Gardners mean by a rigid criterion.

10. *Two authors in a parenthetical reference.* When there are two authors, include both names either in a signal phrase or in the parenthetical reference. Linden did not help Patterson conduct her research, so his name could not be included in the signal phrase. He did, however, coauthor the source in which the statistics appear. Therefore his name must be included in the parentheses.

11. *Undisputed and common knowledge.* The vocabularies of the apes were mentioned in more than two general sources and they did not seem to be a matter of dispute, so Shaw did not provide citations for them. In the earlier paragraph about Koko's vocabulary, however, a citation was needed because those statistics have been challenged. (See 52d.)

an artificial language on a computerized keyboard
developed by psychologist Duane Rumbaugh.

In spite of claims made for Washoe, Koko,
and others, however, there is still skepticism
about whether the apes really learn signs or
whether they merely imitate or respond to the
cues of their trainers.[1] Psychologist H. S.   **12**
Terrace, the chief trainer of a chimp named Nim,
is one of the most formidable of the skeptics because he was once a believer. Ultimately Terrace
concluded that most of Nim's, Washoe's, and Koko's signs were responses to deliberate or nonde-
liberate cues given by trainers immediately
before the ape signed (Terrace et al. 899).   **13**

Although Terrace may be correct in asserting **14**
that a high percentage of the apes' signs have
been in response to cues, he and other critics
have not demonstrated that all of them are. The
Gardners and other researchers have performed
elaborate double-blind experiments that prevent
any possibility of cueing, and the apes have performed well in such tests.[2] But perhaps the most **15**
convincing evidence is that the apes have used
the signs spontaneously among themselves, even
without a trainer present.

When the Gardners returned Washoe to an ape
colony in Oklahoma, she desperately signaled to

12. *Use of endnotes.* The number at the end of this sentence refers to a note at the end of Shaw's paper. Shaw's rough draft contained a long discussion of cueing and the subtle ways it can occur, but the material had to be cut because Shaw was losing her focus on the thesis. She preserved a short passage by putting it in the note. (See 52c.)

13. *Use of "et al."* When a source has more than three authors, the last name of the first author followed by "et al." must appear either in the signal phrase or in the parentheses. (See 52c.)

14. *Addressing opposing arguments.* Shaw wisely addresses her opponents' arguments throughout the paper, showing that she knows both sides and that she believes her arguments stand up against the opposition. Here she counters Terrace's conclusion and offers evidence from concrete experiments to support her assertion.

15. *Use of endnotes.* The number at the end of this sentence refers to a note at the end of Shaw's paper. Shaw does not have the space to discuss the double-blind experiments but thinks some readers may want to read about them. The note at the end of the paper provides bibliographic information on a source that discusses these experiments in detail. (See 52c.)

humans from whom she was separated by a moat, and
from the start she signed to the other apes:

> Frustrated by lack of conversational-   **16**
> ists, she [Washoe] even tried talking
> to dogs. . . . One particularly memo-
> rable day, a snake spread terror
> through . . . the ape island, and all
> but one fled in panic. This male sat
> absorbed, staring intently at the ser-
> pent. Then Washoe was seen running
> over signing to him, "come, hurry up."
> (Desmond 42)

Patterson's gorillas Koko and Michael sign
to one another, with Michael occasionally using
signs that he could have learned only from Koko.
"Even more intriguing," writes Patterson, "is his
variation of the tickle sign depending on whom he
is conversing with" (Patterson and Linden 176).

The most dramatic and moving instances of
chimps signing to one another have involved
Washoe, now under the care of Roger Fouts at Central Washington University. When Washoe had a
baby in 1976, although the baby chimp lived only
a few hours, Washoe signed to it before it died
(Davis 42). Recently another baby chimpanzee   **17**
placed in the care of Washoe has mastered more

16. *Indented quotations, ellipsis marks, and brackets.* Quotations longer than four typed lines should be indented ten spaces from the left margin and typed double-spaced. Quotation marks are not used to enclose indented quotations because the format tells readers that the material is a quotation.

    It is a sacred rule of research that material should be quoted *exactly* as it appears in a source. Often, however, it is necessary to insert or omit material in a quoted passage. Brackets are used to insert words not in the original source, in this case the name Washoe. Bracketed information often clarifies the quotation or makes it fit grammatically within your text. Ellipsis dots indicate that words have been deleted. The first ellipsis in the quotation consists of a period (indicating the end of a sentence) and three dots. The second ellipsis appears within a sentence, so it consists simply of three dots. (See 52e.)

17. *Documentation of paraphrased material.* Shaw paraphrases the story of Washoe's baby instead of quoting Davis's account of the incident. But she still documents her source in a parenthetical reference. (See 52d.)

than fifty signs in American sign language without help from humans. "We only used seven signs
in his presence," says Fouts. "All of his signs
were learned from the other chimps at the laboratory" (qtd. in Toner 24).   **18**

In addition to showing that apes learn signs   **19**
and use them spontaneously, the studies suggest a
third important conclusion: Apes can use language, or something like it, creatively. Though
creative uses of language are difficult to prove,
there is evidence that apes have invented names
and that they have used signs to lie, joke, and
perhaps even swear.

One incident in particular has become a ral-
lying point for those who feel too much has been
claimed for the apes, however. Chimpanzee
Washoe, who knew the signs for "water" and
"bird," once signed "water bird" when in the
presence of a swan. H. S. Terrace legitimately
points out that although Washoe's answer may seem **20**
creative, there is "no basis for concluding that
Washoe was characterizing the swan as a 'bird
that inhabits water.'" Washoe may simply have
been "identifying correctly a body of water and a
bird, in that order" (Terrace et al. 895).

Other examples are not so easily explained   **21**
away. The precocious pygmy chimpanzee Kanzi,

18. *Indirect source.* When citing the words of a writer or speaker who has been quoted in a source, begin the citation with "qtd. in." (See 52c.)

19. *Use of summary as a transition.* Here Shaw summarizes the points she has made so far about the apes' language ability; the summary is an effective transition to the next part of her discussion.

20. *Acknowledging the opposition.* By presenting Terrace's interpretation of the "water bird" example, Shaw proves herself to be a fair researcher who listens to reasonable arguments even when they go against her own bias. In the next paragraphs, Shaw counters Terrace's conclusions with other examples of creative names that cannot be so easily explained away.

21. *Effective use of evidence.* Shaw draws on many different sources for evocative examples of creative names. Each example or series of examples is followed by a parenthetical reference to its source.

encouraged by his trainers to pick up language
the way a child does rather than through structured sessions with food rewards, has learned to
ask for particular films by combining symbols in
a creative way. For instance, to request <u>Quest
for Fire</u>, a film about early primates discovering
fire, Kanzi began to punch symbols for "campfire"
and "TV" (Eckholm, "Kanzi" C3). The Gardners'
Lucy is reported to have called an onion "cry
fruit" and a radish "cry hurt food" (Desmond 40).
And Patterson's Koko has a long list of creative
names to her credit: "elephant baby" to describe
a Pinocchio doll; "finger bracelet" to describe a
ring; "white tiger" to describe a toy zebra;
"bottle match" to describe a cigarette lighter;
"eye hat" to describe a mask (Patterson and Linden 146).

   If Terrace's analysis of the "water bird"
example were applied to the examples just mentioned, it would not hold. Surely Koko did not
see first an elephant and then a baby before
signing "elephant baby"—or a bottle and a match
before signing "bottle match."

   Apes who invent names are not simply learn-   **22**
ing by rote. They are adapting language for
their own purposes. And those purposes, it turns

22. *Transition.* Shaw provides a transition to signal that she has completed her discussion of creative naming and is ready to move on to three other creative uses of language: lying, joking, and swearing.

out, may include lying, joking, and even swearing.   Both Lucy and Koko have been reported to
lie (Desmond 201), and Lucy has been clever
enough to see through the lies of her trainers
(Desmond 102).   Ted Crail points out that lies   **23**
"fall within that part of language which is 'half
art.'   Lies are different from memorizing or
mimicking" (137).

    Francine Patterson is convinced that Koko   **24**
both appreciates jokes and jokes back in turn
with her trainers.   Patterson claims that many of
the apparent "mistakes" made by Koko in her lessons are really attempts to inject variety into
boring classroom drills.   For example, when one
trainer asked Koko where she wanted to put some
apple juice, Koko replied first "nose," then
"eye," and then "ear."   The trainer retorted,
"Okay, here it goes in your ear."   Koko laughed,
signed "drink," and opened her mouth, showing
that she knew very well where the drink belonged
(Patterson and Linden 142-43).   Patterson is
aware that many scientists find her anecdotal
evidence of humor unconvincing, but she doubts
whether an experiment that would satisfy them
could be designed for such a subjective activity
as joking (Patterson and Linden 207).

23. *Author named in signal phrase.* Because the author is named in the signal phrase, only the page number appears in the parentheses. (See 52c.)

24. *Development of an idea.* Shaw develops this paragraph through narration. The story about Koko follows the topic sentence describing Patterson's belief that apes can joke. Notice how Shaw develops her argument logically and coherently. For example, on page 6 Shaw states that there is evidence that apes invent creative names, swear, lie, and joke. In the next three pages she expands on each part of this assertion in order. She offers examples of creative naming, lying, joking, and swearing, and she interprets these examples using both sides of the argument about apes' language ability. She seems to have mastered the evidence, and she has a clear sense of how to develop a coherent argument.

Whether the apes can swear is debatable.
Patterson claims that Koko uses such swear words
as "rotten," "toilet," and "dirty." According to
Patterson, the sign for "dirty," which the trainers used to refer to feces, "became one of Koko's
favorite insults. Under extreme provocation she
will combine _dirty_ with _toilet_ to make her meaning inescapable" (Patterson and Linden 39).
Chimpanzee Nim also began to extend the use of
the sign _dirty_, which he was taught to use when
he wanted to go to the toilet, but his trainer
H. S. Terrace refuses to be convinced he was
swearing. He argues that Nim used the sign only
when what he really wanted was to be removed from
an uncomfortable situation (Terrace 154).

Although the great apes have demonstrated **25**
significant language skills, the question remains
whether they can combine signs in grammatical
patterns to form sentences. All human languages
have a grammar, a system through which relations
among words are conveyed. H. S. Terrace's de- **26**
scription of grammar echoes that of linguist Noam
Chomsky, after whom Terrace's chimp Nim was named:

> Unlike words, most sentences cannot be
> learned individually. Psychologists,
> psycholinguists, and linguists are in

25. *Restating the thesis as a transition.* Shaw shifts smoothly to the second part of her thesis by restating it. The last section of the paper, beginning with this paragraph, corresponds to the second half of Shaw's outline — II.A – D.

26. *Use of definition.* Shaw introduces this next section of the paper by defining *grammar*. The definition is a good strategy; if grammar is what distinguishes human beings from other species, then readers must have a clear understanding of what that distinction is.

> general agreement that using a human
> language indicates knowledge of a gram-
> mar. How else can one account for a
> child's ultimate ability to create an
> indeterminate number of meaningful sen-
> tences from a finite number of words?
> (Terrace et al. 891)

It is true that apes have strung together
various signs (for instance, "Roger tickle   **27**
Lucy"), but the sequences are often confusing and
repetitious. Nim's series of sixteen signs is a
case in point: "give orange me give eat orange me
eat orange give me eat orange give me you" (Terrace et al. 895).

Lana, the chimpanzee who communicates in an
artificial language, can tap out about six stock
sentences. For example, she might punch "please,"
then a name, then a verb (such as "tickle" or
"groom"), and then Lana. Such "sentences,"
however, could be conditioned responses involving
little or no understanding of grammar.

The Gardners were impressed by Washoe's
multisign sequences, seeing in them the beginnings
of some grasp of grammar, but these findings have
been disputed. In one frequently cited filmed
sequence, Washoe's teacher placed a baby doll in

27. *Repeated reference.* The phrase "Roger tickle Lucy" is not only a good example of how apes string together various signs; it also refers the reader back to the beginning of the paper where the phrase was first introduced. The repeated reference helps unify the paper.

a cup. Washoe signed "baby in baby in my drink,"
a series of signs that seemed to make grammatical
sense. Terrace points out, however, that Washoe   **28**
had previously been drilled in similar patterns
and that the teacher had pointed to the objects
(Terrace et al. 898).

Of all the apes, it is Patterson's Koko and
Michael for whom the most is claimed, but even
Patterson does not make large claims for her
apes' grasp of grammar. Many of Michael's and
Koko's short sequences make sense, but whether
one can conclude much from the longer sequences
seems doubtful. For instance, when Michael was
asked what "bird" meant, he signed the following:
"Bird good cat chase eat red trouble cat eat
bird." Patterson believes that Michael had seen
a cat catch a bird and was trying to describe the
scene (Patterson and Linden 173). It is certainly possible but, as Patterson herself would
probably admit, hardly proved.

More definite conclusions may come from the   **29**
Yerkes Primate Center and Language Research Center in Georgia, where the remarkable pygmy chimpanzee Kanzi is being studied by Duane Rambaugh
and Sue Savage-Rambaugh. Pygmy chimpanzees have
been little studied, and few are in captivity,

28. *Heavy reliance on one source.* Shaw relies heavily on Terrace throughout the paper; this is acceptable only because Terrace is one of the foremost authorities on the subject and because Shaw uses many other sources as well. A thesis that can be supported by only one main source should not be pursued.

29. *Current research.* Although Shaw is not convinced that apes can combine signs in grammatical patterns to form sentences, she acknowledges that current research might prove her wrong.

but the Atlanta scientists are convinced that
this species has a more "humanlike intelligence"
than the other apes. The Rambaughs are hesitant
to say that Kanzi creates sentences, but they do
report that Kanzi's "two and three word statements are often made without prompting, systematically add useful new information and represent
his own creative responses to novel situations"
(Eckholm, "Pygmy" B7) Chimps studied earlier
learned to ask to tickle or be tickled. Kanzi
can so skillfully manipulate symbols that he can
ask one person to tickle another while he
watches, then ask the second to tickle the first
(Eckholm, "Pygmy" B7).

     The best summation of the current state of
ape language studies comes from biologist Robert   **30**
Seyfarth, who writes that the line separating humans from other animals "remains hazily drawn,
somewhere between the word and the sentence"
(18). Apes have acquired large vocabularies and   **31**
they have used their "words" spontaneously and
creatively. But it is still to be discovered if
they can create a complex sentence with their vocabularies to say, for instance, "If I refuse to
eat this green banana, will I still be allowed to
watch the Bonzo rerun on television?"

30. *Revision.* The first draft of the paper included a long discussion of Seyfarth's studies of monkeys in the wild. Shaw wisely eliminated this discussion because it introduced a new kind of evidence (all the other examples involve apes learning language from human beings).

31. *Conclusion.* Shaw's conclusion summarizes her whole argument and satisfies the reader's desire to know where she stands on the issue of the apes' ability to learn language. Here the evocative phrase used for the title is seen in context; this phrase provides a memorable statement of Shaw's final position.

Notes **32**

[1] The most famous example of cueing involves **33**
a horse named Clever Hans whose owner sincerely
thought the horse could solve mathematical problems, tapping out the answers with his foot. It
was demonstrated that the horse was in fact re-
sponding to the involuntary jerks of the owner's
head at the point when the correct number of taps
had been reached.

[2] For a description of the Gardners' double- **34**
blind experiments, see Thomas A. Sebeok and Jean
Umiker-Sebeok, "Performing Animals: Secrets of
the Trade," Psychology Today Nov. 1979: 78–91.

32. *Format of endnotes.* Begin the endnotes on a separate page. Type the headings "Notes" one inch from the top of the page and center it between the left and right margins. Begin the notes two spaces below the heading. Double-space them and indent the first line of each note five spaces from the left margin. The number of the note (corresponding to the number used in the text of the paper) should be raised slightly above the note and separated from it by one space. The number should not be followed by a period or enclosed in parentheses.

33. *Use of endnotes.* The first note includes important information that Shaw wanted to make available to the reader but that did not belong in the text. The second note provides bibliographic information on a source that may be of interest to her readers. This source does not appear in Shaw's list of works cited, so she mentions it here.

34. *Format of the bibliographic reference.* Unlike in the list of works cited, the author's names are in normal order.

52 *title outline*

consulted

Works Cited   **35**

Crail, Ted. Apetalk and Whalespeak. Los Ange-   **36**
     les: Tarcher, 1981.

Davis, Flora. Eloquent Animals: A Study in Ani-
     mal Communication. New York: Coward, 1978.

Desmond, Adrian. The Ape's Reflexion. New
     York: Dial, 1979.

Eckholm, Erik. "Kanzi the Chimp: A Life in   **37**
     Science." New York Times 25 June 1985,
     local ed.: C1+.

---. "Pygmy Chimp Readily Learns Language Skill."
     New York Times 24 June 1985, local ed.: A1+.

Patterson, Francine, and Eugene Linden. The   **38**
     Education of Koko. New York: Holt, 1981.

Seyfarth, Robert M. "Talking with Monkeys and   **39**
     Great Apes." International Wildlife Mar.–
     Apr. 1982: 13–18.

Terrace, H. S. Nim. New York: Knopf, 1979.

Terrace, H. S., et al. "Can an Ape Create a   **40**
     Sentence?" Science 206 (1979): 891–902.

Toner, Mike. "Loulis, the Talking Chimp."
     National Wildlife Feb.–Mar. 1986: 24.

additional works consulted

machinary god, man, nature machine.
discribe an interesting machine.
about a machine that should exist.

35. *Format of the list of works cited.* Begin the list of works cited on a separate page. Type the heading "Works Cited" one inch from the top of the page, centered between the left and right margins and followed by two lines of space. Double-space the entries, with the first line of each entry beginning at the left margin; indent subsequent lines in an entry five spaces from the left margin. Begin each entry with the author's name (or names), giving the first author's name in inverted order and any additional names in normal order. Alphabetize the entire list. Anonymous works should be alphabetized by the title of the work.

   The title "Works Cited" tells readers that the list includes only the works that have been cited in the paper. If your instructor prefers a list of all the works you consulted, title the list "Works Consulted."

36. *Book by a single author.* The bibliographic entry has three parts: the author's name, the title of the book, and the publishing information. (See 52g.) Be careful to observe all details of punctuation.

37. *Two or more works by the same author.* In entries after the first, use three hyphens followed by a period instead of repeating the author's name.

38. *Work by two or three authors.* Invert the name of the first author only.

39. *Article in a magazine.* The bibliographic entry has five parts: the author's name, the title of the article, the name of the magazine, the date of the issue in which the article appears, and the page numbers of the article. (See 52g.)

40. *Article in a journal paginated by volume.* When a journal is paginated by volume rather than by issue, the volume number, in this case 206, is inserted immediately after the title of the journal.

52h Alternative systems for citing sources

To suit their special needs, the various academic disciplines have developed different editorial styles for citing sources in the text of the paper and for including them in the list of works cited. In your papers use the citation and bibliography style recommended by your instructor.

The style currently recommended by the Modern Language Association (MLA) is fully described in sections 52c and 52g. The section you are now reading presents a list of style manuals in various disciplines and descriptions of two alternative systems for citing sources: footnotes or endnotes (an MLA alternative); and the author-date style of in-text citation recommended by the American Psychological Association (APA).

A list of style manuals for various disciplines

American Chemical Society. *Handbook for Authors of Papers in American Chemical Society Publications.* Washington: American Chemical Soc., 1978.

American Institute of Physics. *Style Manual for Guidance in the Preparation of Papers.* 3rd ed. New York: American Inst. of Physics, 1978.

American Mathematical Society. *A Manual for Authors of Mathematical Papers.* 8th ed. Providence: American Mathematical Soc., 1980.

American Psychological Association. *Publication Manual of the American Psychological Association.* 3rd ed. Washington: American Psychological Assn., 1983.

Council of Biology Editors. *CBE Style Manual: A Guide for Authors, Editors, and Publishers in the Biological Sciences.* 5th ed. Bethesda: Council of Biology Editors, 1983.

Harvard Law Review. *A Uniform System of Citation.* 13th ed. Cambridge: Harvard Law Review Assn., 1981.

International Steering Committee of Medical Editors. "Uniform Requirements for Manuscripts Submitted to Biomedical Journals." *Annals of Internal Medicine* 90 (Jan. 1979): 95 – 99.

Linguistic Society of America. *LSA Bulletin*, Dec. issue,
    annually.
Modern Language Association. *MLA Handbook for Writers of
    Research Papers*. 2nd ed. New York: MLA, 1984.
Turabian, Kate L. *A Manual for Writers of Term Papers,
    Theses, and Dissertations*. 4th ed. Chicago: U of Chicago
    P, 1973.
United States Geological Survey. *Suggestions to Authors of the
    Reports of the United States Geological Survey*. 6th ed.
    Washington: GPO, 1978.

Footnotes or endnotes (an MLA alternative)

Until 1984 the *MLA Handbook* recommended footnotes or
endnotes instead of in-text citations. Although the current
MLA Handbook treats in-text citations as its preferred style
(see 52c), it also lists the traditional notes as an acceptable
alternative.

Notes provide complete publishing information, either at
the bottom of the page (footnotes) or at the end of the paper
(endnotes). A raised arabic numeral in the text indicates that
a quotation, paraphrase, or summary has been borrowed from
a source; to find the publishing information for that source,
readers consult the footnote or endnote with the corresponding number. Notes are numbered consecutively throughout
the paper.

TEXT

For instance, Lana once described a cucumber as
"banana which—is green."[9]

NOTE

[9] Flora Davis, <u>Eloquent Animals: A Study in
Animal Communication</u> (New York: Coward, 1978) 300.

The first time you cite a source in your paper, give the
full publication information for that work as well as the page

number of the specific quotation, paraphrase, or summary. The examples below cover the formats that are most frequently encountered.

BASIC FORMAT FOR A BOOK

[1] Eugene Linden, <u>Silent Partners: The Legacy of the Ape Language Experiments</u> (New York: Random, 1986) 87.

TWO OR MORE AUTHORS

[2] Roger Fisher and William Ury, <u>Getting to Yes: Negotiating Agreement Without Giving In</u> (Boston: Houghton, 1981) 108.

EDITOR OR TRANSLATOR

[3] Albert Camus, <u>Lyrical and Critical Essays</u>, trans. Ellen Conroy Kennedy, ed. Philip Thody (New York: Knopf, 1968) 8.

UNKNOWN AUTHOR

[4] <u>The Times Atlas of the World</u>, 5th ed. (New York: New York Times, 1975) 95.

EDITION OTHER THAN THE FIRST

[5] Brenda Spatt, <u>Writing from Sources</u>, 2nd ed. (New York: St Martin's, 1987) 78.

MULTIVOLUME WORK

[6] Robert Graves, <u>The Greek Myths</u>, 2 vols. (New York: Braziller, 1967) 2: 216.

WORK IN AN ANTHOLOGY

[7] M. H. Abrams, "English Romanticism: The Spirit of the Age," <u>Romanticism Reconsidered</u>, ed. Northrop Frye (New York: Columbia UP, 1963) 64.

ENCYCLOPEDIA OR DICTIONARY

[8] Mark S. Frankel, "Human Experimentation: Social and Professional Control," <u>Encyclopedia of Bioethics</u>, 1978 ed.

ARTICLE IN A MAGAZINE

[9] Matt Clark, "Medicine: A Brave New World," <u>Newsweek</u> 5 Mar. 1984: 65.

ARTICLE IN A JOURNAL PAGINATED BY VOLUME

[10] Mary L. Otto, "Child Abuse: Group Treat—ment for Parents," <u>Personnel and Guidance Journal</u> 62 (1984): 336.

ARTICLE IN A JOURNAL PAGINATED BY ISSUE

[11] Randall G. Nichols, "Word Processing and Basic Writers," <u>Journal of Basic Writing</u> 5.2 (1986): 93.

ARTICLE IN A NEWSPAPER

[12] Cynthia Gorney, "When the Gorilla Speaks," <u>Washington Post</u> 31 Jan. 1985: B1.

SUBSEQUENT REFERENCES TO THE SAME SOURCE Subsequent references to a work that has already been cited in a note should be given in shortened form. You need to give only enough information so that the reader can identify which work you are referring to — usually the author's last name and a page number. The abbreviations *ibid.* and *op. cit.* are no longer used.

> 13 Linden 129.
>
> 14 Fisher and Ury 16.

If you are using more than one work by one author or two works by authors with the same last name, cite the author's last name and a shortened title.

> 15 Linden, <u>Silent</u> 53.
>
> 16 Linden, <u>Apes</u> 136.

APA in-text citations

The American Psychological Association (APA) recommends in-text citations that provide at least the author's last name and the date of publication. For direct quotations, a page number is given as well.

BASIC FORMAT FOR A QUOTATION Ordinarily, introduce the quotation with a signal phrase that includes the author's last name followed by the date of publication in parentheses. Put the page number in parentheses at the end of the quotation.

> As Davis (1978) reports, "If the existence of a
> signing ape was unsettling for linguists, it was
> also startling news for animal behaviorists"
> (p. 26).

In the case when the author's name does not appear in the signal phrase, place the author's name, the date, and the page number in parentheses at the end. Use commas between items in the parentheses.

BASIC FORMAT FOR A SUMMARY OR A PARAPHRASE For a summary or a paraphrase, include the author's last name and the date either in a signal phrase or in parentheses at the end. A page number is not required.

> According to Davis (1978), when they learned of an ape's ability to use sign language, both linguists and animal behaviorists were taken by surprise.

> When they learned of an ape's ability to use sign language, both linguists and animal behaviorists were taken by surprise (Davis, 1978).

A WORK WITH TWO OR MORE AUTHORS If your source has two authors, name both in the signal phrase or parentheses each time cited; in the parentheses, use "&" (not "and").

> Patterson and Linden (1981) agree that the gorilla Koko acquired language more slowly than a normal speaking child.

If your source has three, four, or five authors, identify them all the first time you cite the source.

> The team of researchers also warned that the fishing industry on the Chesapeake Bay is threatened by pollution (Blake, Simon, & McCann, 1987).

In subsequent citations, use only the first author's name followed by "et al." in the signal phrase or parentheses.

> The team of researchers also warned that the fishing industry on the Chesapeake Bay is threatened by pollution (Blake et al., 1987).

If your source has six or more authors, use only the first author's name followed by "et al." in all citations.

AUTHOR UNKNOWN   If the author is not given, either use the complete title in a signal phrase or use the first two or three words of the title in the parenthetical citation.

> The UFO reported by the crew of a Japan Air Lines
>
> flight remains a mystery. Radar tapes did not
>
> confirm the presence of another craft ("Strange
>
> Encounter," 1987).

If "Anonymous" is specified as the author, treat it as if it were a real name: (Anonymous, 1987). In the bibliography, also use the name Anonymous as author.

CORPORATE AUTHOR   If the author is a government agency or other corporate organization with a long and cumbersome name, spell out the name the first time you use it in your paper followed by an abbreviation in brackets. In later citations, simply use the abbreviation.

> First citation: (National Institute of Mental Health
>   [NIMH], 1981)
>
> Later citations: (NIMH, 1981)

TWO OR MORE WORKS IN THE SAME PARENTHESES   When your parenthetical citation names two or more works, put them in the same order that they appear in the bibliography, separated by semicolons.

AUTHORS WITH THE SAME LAST NAME   To avoid confusion, use initials with the last names if your bibliography lists two or more authors with the same last name.

> Research by J. A. Smith (1987) revealed that . . .

PERSONAL COMMUNICATION   Conversations, memos, letters, and similar unpublished person-to-person communications should be cited by initials, last name, and precise date.

L. Smith (personal communication, October 12,

1987) predicts that government funding of this

type of research will end soon.

Do not include personal communications in the bibliographic references at the end of your paper.

APA references (list of works cited)

In APA style, the alphabetical list of works cited is entitled "References." The general principles are as follows:

1. Invert *all* authors' names, and use initials instead of first names. With two or more authors, use an ampersand (&) rather than the word "and."
2. Use all authors' names; do not use "et al."
3. Place the date in parentheses immediately after the last author's name.
4. Underline titles and subtitles of books; capitalize only the first word of the title and subtitle (as well as all proper nouns).
5. Do not place titles of articles in quotation marks, and capitalize only the first word of the title and subtitle (and all proper nouns). Capitalize names of periodicals as you would capitalize them ordinarily (see 45c). Underline the volume number of periodicals.
6. Use the abbreviation "p." (or "pp." for plural) before page numbers of magazine and newspaper articles and works in anthologies, but do not use them before page numbers of articles appearing in scholarly journals.
7. You may use a short form of the publisher's name as long as it is easily identifiable.

BASIC FORMAT FOR A BOOK

Linden, E. (1986). Silent partners: The legacy of

the ape language experiments. New York: Ran-

dom House.

TWO OR MORE AUTHORS

Patterson, F., & Linden, E. (1981). The education of Koko. New York: Holt, Rinehart and Winston.

EDITORS

Sebeok, T. A., & Umiker-Sebeok, J. (Eds.). (1980). Speaking of apes. New York: Plenum Press.

EDITION OTHER THAN THE FIRST

Falk, J. S. (1978). Linguistics and language: A survey of basic concepts and implications (2nd ed.). New York: Wiley.

WORK IN AN ANTHOLOGY

Basso, K. H. Silence in western Apache culture. (1970). In P. Giglioli (Ed.), Language and social context (pp. 67-86). Harmondsworth, England: Penguin.

ARTICLE IN A JOURNAL PAGINATED BY VOLUME

Otto, M. L. (1984). Child abuse: Group treatment for parents. Personnel and Guidance Journal, 62, 336-338.

ARTICLE IN A JOURNAL PAGINATED BY ISSUE

Nichols, R. G. (1986). Word processing and basic writers. Journal of Basic writing, 5(2), 81-97.

ARTICLE IN A MAGAZINE

Seyfarth, R. M. (1982, March–April) Talking with
monkeys and great apes. <u>International Wild-
life</u>, pp. 13–18.

TWO OR MORE WORKS BY THE SAME AUTHOR Use the author's name for first and subsequent entries. Arrange the entries by date, the earliest first.

Davis, F. (1973). <u>Inside intuition: What we know
about nonverbal communication</u>. New York:
McGraw–Hill.

Davis, F. (1978). <u>Eloquent animals: A study in
animal communication</u>. New York: Coward,
McCann & Geoghegan.

53

Logic in argumentative essays

Nearly all writing involves argument; that is, the attempt to
back up some claims (called conclusions) with others (called
premises), which are in turn supported by more specific evidence. When you write an essay or term paper for a course or
a memo, business letter, research report, or proposal for a
job, part of your task is persuading readers to agree with your
conclusions. Choosing your evidence carefully is essential.
Equally important is knowing how to structure the supporting evidence so that the conclusion follows logically from it.

A valid argument depends not only on evidence but on logic — the way you reason from that evidence.

An understanding of logic will help you both to construct and to evaluate an argument. This chapter includes only the essentials: a brief discussion of inductive and deductive reasoning; practical suggestions for constructing an effective argument; and a list of logical fallacies, the most common mistakes writers make in moving from premises to conclusions.

53a Use inductive reasoning with care.

When you reason inductively, you draw a conclusion from an array of facts. For example, you might conclude that a professor is friendly because he or she smiles frequently and talks to students after class or that fifty-five miles per hour is a safer speed limit than sixty-five miles per hour because there are fewer deaths per accident at that speed.

For inductive reasoning to be valid, the conclusion must be based on a sufficient number of specific, representative cases. Consider, for example, the following brief argument:

> According to our survey, 434 of the 500 households questioned say they would like to subscribe to cable television. Therefore, the majority of households in our city would subscribe if cable were available.

Is the evidence sufficient? That depends. In a city of 5,000, the 500 households are a ten percent sample, sufficient for the purposes of marketing research. But in a city of one million, the households would amount to less than one percent of the population, an inadequate sample on which to base an important decision. Is the evidence representative? Again, that depends. The cable company would trust the survey if it knew that the sample had been carefully constructed to reflect the age, race, sex, and income of the city's population as a whole.

53b Use deductive reasoning with care.

When you reason deductively, you draw a conclusion from two or more assertions (called premises).

> The police do not give speeding tickets to people driving less than five miles per hour over the limit. Sam is driving fifty-nine miles per hour in a fifty-five-mile-per-hour zone. Therefore, the police will not give Sam a speeding ticket.

The conclusion is true only if the premises are true. If the police sometimes give tickets for less than five-mile-per-hour violations or if the speedometer is inaccurate, Sam cannot safely conclude that he will avoid a ticket.

Deductive reasoning can often be structured in a three-step argument called a *syllogism*. The three steps are the major premise, the minor premise, and the conclusion:

1. Anything that increases radiation in the environment is dangerous to public health. (major premise)
2. Nuclear reactors increase radiation in the environment. (minor premise)
3. Therefore, nuclear reactors are dangerous to public health. (conclusion)

The major premise is a generalization. The minor premise is a specific case. The conclusion follows from applying the generalization to the specific case.

Many deductive arguments do not state one of the premises but rather leave the reader to infer it. In the preceding example, the conclusion would still sound plausible without the major premise: *Nuclear reactors increase radiation in the environment; therefore, they are dangerous to public health.* A careful reader, however, will see the missing premise and will question the whole argument if the premise is debatable.

Deductive arguments break down if one of the premises is not true or if the conclusion does not logically follow from them. For example, consider this argument:

> The deer population in our state should be preserved. During hunting season hundreds of deer are killed. Therefore, the hunting season should be discontinued.

To challenge this argument, the state's wildlife commission might agree with both the major and minor premises but question whether the conclusion follows logically from them. True, the deer population should be preserved; true, deer are killed during hunting season. However, in a state where deer have no natural enemies, herds become too large for the natural forest vegetation to support them. The overpopulated herds strip the leaves from the young trees, killing the trees, before dying of starvation themselves. The commission might conclude, therefore, that a limited hunting season helps preserve a healthier and more stable population of deer.

53c Structure a convincing argument.

Readers who already agree with you need no persuasion, although a well-argued case for their own point of view is always welcome. But indifferent and skeptical readers will tend to resist your argument because they have minds of their own. To convince such readers, you will need to anticipate objections, refute opposing arguments, establish credibility, and maintain a reasonable tone.

Anticipating objections; refuting opposing arguments

To give up a position that seems reasonable, a reader has to see that there is an even more reasonable one. In addition to presenting your own case, review the chief arguments of the other side and explain what you think is wrong with them.

There is no best place in an essay to deal with the other

side. Often it is useful to summarize the opposing position early in your essay. After stating your thesis but before developing the detailed reasons, you might have a paragraph beginning "Critics of this view argue that. . . ." But sometimes a better plan is to anticipate objections as you develop your case paragraph by paragraph. Wherever you decide to deal with opposing arguments, do your best to refute them. Show readers why they are not as persuasive as your critics believe.

As you refute opposing arguments, try to establish common ground with readers who are not in initial agreement with your views. If you can show that you share your readers' values, they may be able to switch to your position without giving up what they feel is important. For example, to persuade people emotionally opposed to shooting helpless deer, a state wildlife commission would have to show that it too cares about preserving deer and does not want them to die needlessly. Having established these values in common, the commission might be able to persuade critics that a carefully controlled hunting season is good for the deer population because it prevents starvation caused by overpopulation. By the same token, if those opposed to hunting want to persuade the commission to ban the hunting season, they would need to show that the commission could achieve its goals by some other feasible means, such as expanding the deer preserve or allowing the deer and the food supply to come into a natural balance.

People believe that intelligence and decency support their side of an argument. To change sides, they must continue to feel intelligent and decent. Otherwise they will persist in their opposition.

Establishing credibility

Readers will not listen to you if they don't trust you. You can establish your credibility by showing that you have considered both sides and that you are knowledgeable. To demonstrate your knowledge, cite relevant facts and statistics and if possible quote respected experts. For example, the state wildlife commission should provide data on the size of the deer population, the amount of forest acreage needed for that number of deer, and the number of deer dying of starvation compared with the number killed by hunters. The commission might also quote one or more environmentalists who support its view. If the statistics and quotations come from respected neutral sources, such as a university research study, they will of course be more persuasive than if they come from a self-interested group such as the National Rifle Association or a hunting club.

Maintaining a reasonable tone

Build goodwill by sounding reasonable and likable. Most readers are put off by overemotional language or strident complaining. Strongly worded outbursts might express an arguer's feelings well, but they have the disadvantage of arousing equally strong feelings on the other side. If your goal is persuading the other side, maintain a reasonable tone (see also 3d).

53d Avoid logical fallacies.

Logical fallacies are errors in reasoning that occur frequently enough, either alone or in combination, to deserve special attention.

Hasty generalization

A *hasty generalization* is a conclusion based on insufficient or unrepresentative evidence.

> Deaths from drug overdoses in Metropolis have doubled in the past three years. More Americans than ever are dying from drug abuse.

Data from one city do not justify a conclusion about the whole United States.

Many hasty generalizations contain words like *all, every, always,* and *never,* when *most, many, usually,* or *seldom* would be more accurate. Go over your writing carefully for such general statements and make sure that you have enough data to verify your position or that you qualify the statement.

A *stereotype* is a hasty generalization (usually derogatory) about a group. Examples: Women are bad bosses; politicians are corrupt; yuppies are self-centered. Stereotyping is common because of our human tendency to perceive selectively. We tend to see what we want to see; that is, we notice evidence confirming our already formed opinions and fail to notice evidence to the contrary. For example, if you have concluded that politicians are corrupt, your stereotype will be confirmed by occasional news reports of legislators being indicted — even though every day the newspapers describe conscientious officials serving the public honestly and well. Generalizations about people must be based on numerous typical cases and not contradicted by many exceptions. And even conclusions that are generally valid — that Americans tend to place a high value on individual rights, for example — will have significant exceptions because what is generally true about groups of people will not be true of all individuals within that group.

Either . . . or fallacy

The *either . . . or* fallacy is the suggestion that only two alternatives exist when in fact there are more.

> Either learn how to operate a computer or you won't be able to get a decent job after college.

Many occupations do not require knowledge of computers.

Non sequitur

A *non sequitur* (Latin for "does not follow") is a conclusion that does not follow logically from preceding statements.

> Mary loves good food; therefore, she will be an excellent chef.

Mary's love of good food does not guarantee that she will be able to cook it well.

Post hoc

Careless thinkers often assume that because one event follows another, the first is the cause of the second. This common fallacy is known as *post hoc*, from the Latin *post hoc, ergo propter hoc*, meaning "after this, therefore because of this." Like a non sequitur, it is a leap to an unjustified conclusion.

> Governor Smoot has reduced unemployment among minorities. Since he took office, employment of minorities in the state has increased by seven percent.

The writer must show that Governor Smoot's policies are responsible for this increase; it is not enough to show that the increase followed the governor's taking office.

False analogy

An analogy points out a similarity between two things that are otherwise dissimilar. Analogies can be an effective means of illustrating a point (see 6b), but they are not proof. In a *false analogy*, a writer falsely assumes that because two things are alike in one respect, they must be alike in others.

> If we can put humans on the moon, we should be able to find a cure for the common cold.

Putting humans on the moon and finding a cure for the common cold are both scientific challenges, but the technical problems confronting medical researchers are quite different from those solved by space scientists.

Circular reasoning and begging the question

Suppose you go to see a doctor about a rash you suddenly developed. "I have a rash," you say to the doctor. "What is your diagnosis?" The doctor answers, "You have allergitis." When you ask, "What's that?" the doctor replies, "It's a rash." This is an example of circular reasoning: No real information has been introduced; by a trick of semantics you have wound up back where you started.

Like circular reasoning, *begging the question* is a way of ducking the issue. Instead of supporting the conclusion with evidence and logic, the writer simply restates the conclusion in different language.

> Faculty and administrators should not be permitted to come to student council meetings because student council meetings should be for students only.

The writer has given no reason for this position but has merely repeated the point.

Appeals to emotion

Many of the arguments we see in the media strive to win our sympathy rather than our intelligent agreement. A TV commercial suggesting that you will be thin, tan, and sexy if you drink a certain diet beverage is making a pitch to emotions. So is a political speech that recommends electing John D'Eau because he is a devoted husband and father who fought for his country in Vietnam.

The following passage illustrates several types of emotional appeals.

> This progressive proposal to build a large ski resort in the state park has been carefully researched by Fidelity, the largest bank in the state; furthermore, it is favored by a majority of

the local merchants. The only opposition comes from narrow-minded, do-gooder environmentalists who care more about trees than they do about people; one of their leaders was actually arrested for disturbing the peace several years ago.

Words with strong positive or negative connotations, such as *progressive* and *do-gooders*, are examples of *biased language.* Attacking the persons who hold a belief (environmentalists) rather than refuting their argument is called *ad hominem*, a Latin term meaning "to the man." Associating a prestigious name (Fidelity) with the writer's side is called *transfer.* Claiming that an idea should be accepted because a large number of people are in favor (the majority of merchants) is called the *bandwagon appeal.* Bringing in irrelevant issues (the arrest) is a *red herring*, named after a trick used in fox hunts to mislead the dogs by dragging a smelly fish across the trail.

In examining your own and other people's writing for errors of logic, you will find that logical fallacies are frequently not so clear-cut that a casual reader can spot them immediately. Often they show up in combination. To recognize such fallacies in your own writing takes discipline, but you can do it if you train yourself to become a skeptical and demanding reader — the kind of person who measures all claims against the evidence.

EXERCISE 53–1

Explain what is illogical in each of the following brief arguments. It may be helpful to identify the logical fallacy or fallacies by name. Answers to lettered sentences appear in the back of the book.

a. A mandatory five-cent deposit on bottles and cans will eliminate litter because everyone will return the containers for the money rather than throw them away.

b. Soliciting money to save whales and baby seals is irresponsible when thousands of human beings can't afford food and shelter.

c. Whenever I wash my car, it rains. I have discovered a way to end droughts — get all the people to wash their cars.

d. If you're old enough to vote, you're old enough to drink. The drinking age should be lowered to eighteen.

e. This country has been run too long by old, out-of-date, out-of-touch, entrenched politicians protecting the special interests that got them elected.

1. If the president had learned the lesson of Vietnam, he would realize that sending U.S. troops into a foreign country can only end in disaster.

2. Although Ms. Bell's observations about Constable's iconography are impressive, one wonders if a critic born and educated in Australia can do full justice to the painter's intimacy with the English landscape.

3. If you're not part of the solution, you're part of the problem.

4. Marijuana wouldn't be illegal if it weren't hazardous to health.

5. It was possible to feed a family of four on $50 a week before Governor Leroy took office and drove up food prices.

6. Most Americans never heard of blues musician Robert Johnson until the Rolling Stones recorded his song "Love in Vain" or of Sonny Boy Williamson until the Who recorded "Eyesight to the Blind." We can't appreciate our own music unless the British introduce it to us.

7. If professional sports teams didn't pay athletes such high salaries, we wouldn't have so many kids breaking their legs at hockey and basketball camps.

8. It's never wise to buy the first used car you look at because finding a used car takes time.

9. All of the students I interviewed are opposed to a tuition increase; therefore, the board of trustees should not pass the proposed increase.

10. Michael Jackson's impact on popular music is comparable to that of other major figures in the past — Buddy Holly, the Beatles, Bob Dylan — in that he both epitomizes the ideals of a particular period and pushes the musical scene in new directions. Jackson is a better musician, however, because he doesn't smoke, drink, or use drugs.

54

Business letters and résumés

54a Business letters

In writing a business letter be direct, clear, and courteous, but do not hesitate to be firm if the situation calls for it. State your purpose or request at the beginning of the letter and include only pertinent information in the body. Follow conventions of form and usage, and avoid spelling errors.

Business letters usually follow one of three patterns: full block, block, and semiblock. In full block form, letterhead stationery, giving the return address of the writer (or of the writer's company), is used. Every element of the letter (including date, inside address, salutation, body, close, and signature) is typed flush with the left margin. In block form, the return address of the writer, the close, and the signature are moved to the right. Paragraphs are not indented but begin flush with the left margin. In semiblock form, considered the least formal of the three patterns, the return address, close, and signature are moved to the right, and the beginning of each paragraph is indented five spaces from the left margin.

Type business letters on letterhead stationery or on unlined paper that is at least $5\frac{1}{2}'' \times 8\frac{1}{2}''$. Type on only one side of the paper, single-spacing the body of the letter and double-spacing between paragraphs. The sample letter on the next page, in block form, illustrates the proper placement of each part of a business letter. The return address is followed by the date. (Note that the writer's name is not part of this heading.) The inside address includes the full name, title, and complete address of the person to whom the letter is written. (This information is repeated as the address on the envelope.) The inside address is typed flush left, a few lines below the return address heading. The salutation, or greeting, is typed

14 Closter Road
Langdon, ND 58249
March 12, 1988

Personnel Manager
Minnesota Public Radio
45 East 8th Street
St. Paul, MN 55101

Dear Sir or Madam:

I am applying for the summer internship you
listed with the Job Information and Placement
Center at North Dakota State University. I am
currently a sophomore at North Dakota State University, with a major in mass communication and a
minor in English.

As the enclosed résumé shows, I have had a variety of experiences in radio. In addition to
producing the weekly debate show "The Forum" for
the university radio station, KDSU, I have also
taken several upper-level courses in broadcast
journalism and audio production. My job last
summer at KDSU provided an overview of the administrative aspects of radio, and I believe the internship you offer will give me an opportunity to
acquire specific experience in the production
area of broadcasting.

I would be happy to send you a transcript of "The
Forum." I am available for an interview almost
anytime and can be reached at (701) 256-7011.

I look forward to hearing from you.

Sincerely,

Barbara C. Hansen

Barbara C. Hansen

Enc.

two lines below the inside address. A colon follows the salutation, and the body of the letter begins two lines below the greeting.

In the salutation use *Ms.* if you are writing to a woman whose title or marital status you do not know or if the woman prefers this form of address. If you are not writing to a particular person, you can use the salutation *Dear Sir or Madam* or you can address the company itself — *Dear Solar Technology.*

In block form the close is lined up with the return address and typed two lines below the end of the letter. Common closes are *Yours truly, Very truly yours,* and *Sincerely.* (Note that only the first word of the close is capitalized.) The name of the writer is typed four lines below the close, leaving room for the written signature between the close and the typed name. The name of the writer should not be prefaced by a title or followed by an abbreviation for a title or position. This information can be included in a separate line under the typed name (for example, *Director* or *Sales Manager*).

Other information can be included below the signature and flush with the left margin (for example: *Enc.*, indicating that something is enclosed with the letter; *cc: Mr. Theodore Jones*, indicating that a copy of the letter is being sent to Mr. Jones, a third party; or *JEF:njl*, indicating that JEF [the writer's initials] wrote the letter and njl typed it).

The name and return address of the writer is typed in the upper left-hand corner of the envelope. The addressee's name, title, and complete address are typed just right of the center of the envelope. The letter (which should be about the same width as the envelope) is folded in thirds.

54b Résumés

An effective résumé presents relevant information in a clear and concise form. Every résumé should include name, address, and telephone number; a history of education and em-

RÉSUMÉ

Barbara C. Hansen
14 Closter Road
Langdon, ND 58249
(701) 256-7011

Position Desired   Internship in News Department

Education
1986 to present   North Dakota State University,
                         Fargo, ND. B.A. in mass communi-
                         cation expected May 1990. Minor
                         in English.

1982-1986   Langdon High School, Langdon, ND.

Experience
1986 to present   Producer of "The Forum," a weekly
                         broadcast on KDSU, the university
                         radio station. Responsibilities
                         include selecting the issues and
                         the participants, moderating the
                         debates.

May-Sept. 1987   Receptionist, KNDK Radio Station,
                         Langdon, ND. Answered telephones;
                         performed various clerical duties.

Related Interests   Volunteer tutoring in the Moorhead
and Activities   area public schools; basketball;
                         reading.

References   Academic references available from
                         the Job Information and Placement
                         Office at North Dakota State Uni-
                         versity, Fargo, ND 58105.

                         Employment   Ms. Kimberly Quinlan
                         Reference   KNDK Radio Station
                                        Langdon, ND 58249

                         Personal   Mr. Stephen Hurley
                         Reference   45 Main Street
                                        Langdon, ND 58249

ployment; a list of special interests or related activities; and information about how to obtain references. You may also include personal information such as date of birth or marital status, but such information is not necessary. Some résumés name the specific position desired. If you are applying for a number of different positions, you may find it more useful to name a broader employment goal.

In the education history, begin with the institution you are currently attending and work backward to your high school, listing degrees and dates of attendance. If you have won special honors, include them. In the employment history, again list your most recent job first and then work backward. Give the dates of employment and the company name and address. You can also list your supervisors. Describe your responsibilities, highlighting those tasks or skills related to the position you are seeking. In listing special interests, concentrate on those related to your employment goal. Instead of listing the names and addresses of references, you can state that references are available on request.

In a résumé, present yourself in the best possible light, but do not distort any of the facts about your experience or qualifications. Select details wisely and your résumé will be a valuable tool.

When you send your résumé, you should include a letter that tells what position you seek and where you learned about it. The letter should also summarize your education and past experience, relating them to the job you are applying for. You may want to highlight a specific qualification and refer the reader to your résumé for more information. End the letter with a suggestion for a meeting, and tell your prospective employer when you will be available.

Glossary of Usage

This glossary addresses an assortment of specific problems that do not fit neatly under more general headings. If an item is not listed here, consult the index. For irregular verbs (such as *sing, sang, sung*), see 27a. For idiomatic use of prepositions, see 18d.

a, an   Use *an* before a vowel sound, *a* before a consonant sound: *an apple, a peach*. Problems sometimes arise with words beginning with *h*. If the *h* is silent, the word begins with a vowel sound, so use *an: an hour, an heir, an honest senator, an honorable deed*. If the *h* is pronounced, the word begins with a consonant sound, so use *a: a hospital, a hymn, a historian, a hotel*.

accept, except   *Accept* is a verb meaning "to receive." *Except* is usually a preposition meaning "excluding." *I will accept all the packages except that one. Except* is also a verb meaning "to exclude." *Please except that item from the list*.

advice, advise   *Advice* is a noun, *advise* a verb: *We advise you to follow John's advice*.

affect, effect   *Affect* is usually a verb meaning "to influence." *Effect* is usually a noun meaning "result." *The drug did not affect the disease, and it had several adverse side effects. Effect* can also be a verb meaning "to bring about": *Only the president can effect such a dramatic change*.

aggravate   *Aggravate* means "to make worse or more troublesome": *Overgrazing aggravated the soil erosion*. In formal writing, avoid the colloquial use of *aggravate* meaning "to annoy or irritate": *Her babbling annoyed* (not *aggravated*) *me.*

agree to, agree with   *Agree to* means "to give consent." *Agree with* means "to be in accord" or "to come to an understanding": *He agrees with me about the need for change, but he won't agree to my plan.*

ain't   *Ain't* is nonstandard. Use *am not, are not* (*aren't*), or *is not* (*isn't*): *I am not* (or *I'm*; not *ain't*) *going home for spring break.*

all ready, already   *All ready* means "completely prepared." *Already* means "previously." *Susan was all ready for the concert, but her friends had already left.*

all right   *All right* is always written as two words. *Alright* is nonstandard.

all together, altogether   *All together* means "everyone gathered." *Altogether* means "entirely." *We were not altogether certain that we could bring the family all together for the reunion.*

allusion, illusion   An *allusion* is an indirect reference. An *illusion* is a misconception or false impression. *Did you catch my allusion to Shakespeare? Mirrors give the room an illusion of depth.*

a lot   *A lot* is two words. Do not write *alot. We have had a lot of rain this spring.* See also *lots, lots of.*

A.M., P.M., a.m., p.m.   Use these abbreviations with numerals: *6 P.M., 11 a.m.* Do not substitute them for the words *morning* and *evening: I worked until late in the evening* (not *p.m.*) *yesterday.*

among, between   Ordinarily, use *among* with three or more entities, *between* with two: *The prize was divided among several contestants. You have a choice between carrots and beans.*

amount, number   Use *amount* with quantities that cannot be counted; use *number* with those that can: *This recipe calls for a large amount of sugar. We have a large number of toads in our garden.*

an   See *a, an.*

and etc.   *Et cetera* (*etc.*) means "and so forth"; therefore, *and etc.* is redundant. See also *etc.*

ante-, anti-   The prefix *ante-* means "earlier" or "in front of"; the prefix *anti-* means "against" or "opposed to." *William Lloyd Garrison was one of the leaders of the antislavery movement during the antebellum period. Anti-* should be used with a hyphen when it is followed by a capital letter or a word beginning with *i.*

anymore Reserve the adverb *anymore* for negative contexts, where it means "any longer." *Moviegoers are rarely shocked anymore by profanity.* Do not use *anymore* in positive contexts. Use *now* or *nowadays* instead. *Interest rates are so high nowadays* (not *anymore*) *that few people can afford to buy homes.*

anyone, any one *Anyone*, an indefinite pronoun, means "any person at all." *Any one*, the pronoun *one* preceded by the adjective *any*, refers to a particular person or thing in a group. *Anyone from Chicago may choose any one of the games on display.*

anyplace *Anyplace* is informal for *anywhere*.

anyways, anywheres *Anyways* and *anywheres* are nonstandard for *anyway* and *anywhere*.

as *As* is sometimes used to mean "because." But do not use it if there is any chance of ambiguity: *We canceled the picnic because* (not *as*) *it began raining.* The *as* here could mean "because" or "when."

as, like See *like, as*.

awful The adjective *awful* means "awe-inspiring." Colloquially it is used to mean "terrible" or "bad." The adverb *awfully* is sometimes used in conversation as an intensifier meaning "very": *I was very* (not *awfully*) *upset last night.* In formal writing, avoid these colloquial uses.

awhile, a while *Awhile* is an adverb; it can modify a verb, but it cannot be the object of a preposition such as *for*. The two-word form *a while* is a noun preceded by an article and therefore can be the object of a preposition. *Stay awhile. Stay for a while.*

bad, badly *Bad* is an adjective, *badly* an adverb. (See 26.) *They felt bad about being late and ruining the surprise. Her arm hurt badly after she slid headfirst into second base.*

being as, being that *Being as* and *being that* are nonstandard expressions. Write *because* or *since* instead. *Because* (not *being as*) *I slept late, I had to skip breakfast.*

beside, besides *Beside* is a preposition meaning "at the side of" or "next to." *Annie Oakley slept with her gun beside her bed. Besides* is a preposition meaning "except" or "in addition to." *No one besides Terrie can have that ice cream. Besides* is also an adverb meaning "in addition." *I'm not hungry; besides, I don't like ice cream.*

between See *among, between*.

bring, take Use *bring* when an object is being transported toward you, *take* when it is being moved away: *Please bring me a glass of water. Please take these flowers to Mr. Scott.*

burst, bursted; bust, busted *Burst* is an irregular verb meaning "to come open or fly apart suddenly or violently." Its principal parts are *burst, burst, burst.* The past-tense form *bursted* is nonstandard. *Bust* and *busted* are slang for *burst* and, along with *bursted*, should not be used in formal writing.

can, may The distinction between *can* and *may* is fading, but many careful writers still observe it in formal writing. *Can* is traditionally reserved for ability, *may* for permission. *Can you ski down the advanced slope without falling? May I help you?*

capital, capitol *Capital* refers to a city, *capitol* to a building where lawmakers meet. *Capital* also refers to wealth or resources. *The capitol has undergone extensive renovations. The residents of the state capital protested the development plans.*

censor, censure *Censor* means "to remove or suppress material considered morally or otherwise objectionable." Censure means "to criticize severely." *The library's new policy of censoring controversial books has been censured by the media.*

center around *Center on* and *center in* are considered more logical than *center around*. *His talk centered on the global buildup of arms in the last five years.*

climactic, climatic *Climactic* is derived from *climax*, the point of greatest intensity in a series or progression of events. *Climatic* is derived from *climate* and refers to meteorological conditions. *The climactic period in the dinosaurs' reign was reached just before severe climatic conditions brought on an ice age.*

compare to, compare with *Compare to* means "to represent as similar": *She compared him to a wild stallion. Compare with* means "to examine the ways in which two things are similar": *The study compared the language ability of apes with that of dolphins.*

complement, compliment *Complement* is a verb meaning "to go with or complete" or a noun meaning "something that completes." *Compliment* as a verb means "to flatter"; as a noun it means "flattering remark." *Her skill at rushing the net complements his skill at volleying. Mother's flower arrangements receive many compliments.*

conscience, conscious *Conscience* is a noun meaning "moral principles." *Conscious* is an adjective meaning "aware or alert": *Let your conscience be your guide. Were you conscious of his love for you?*

continual, continuous *Continual* means "repeated regularly and frequently." *She grew weary of the continual telephone calls. Continuous* means "extended or prolonged without interruption." *The broken siren made a continuous wail.*

could care less *Could care less* is a nonstandard expression. Write *couldn't care less* instead. *He couldn't* (not *could*) *care less about his psychology final.*

could of *Could of* is nonstandard for *could have. We could have* (not *could of*) *had steak for dinner if we had been hungry.*

criteria *Criteria* is the plural of *criterion,* which means "a standard, or rule, or test on which a judgment or decision can be based." *The only criterion for the scholarship is ability.*

data *Data* is the plural of *datum,* which means "a fact or proposition." *The new data suggest* (not *suggests*) *that our theory is correct.* The singular form *datum* is rarely used.

deal *Deal* is a colloquial expression for "bargain," "business transaction," or "agreement": *We made a deal.* Avoid such colloquial use in formal writing.

different from, different than Ordinarily, write *different from: Your sense of style is different from Jim's.* However, *different than* is acceptable to avoid an awkward construction: *Please let me know if your plans are different than* (to avoid *from what*) *they were six weeks ago.*

differ from, differ with *Differ from* means "to be unlike"; *differ with* means "to disagree." *She differed with me about the wording of the agreement. My approach to the problem differed from hers.*

disinterested, uninterested *Disinterested* means "impartial, objective"; *uninterested* means "not interested." *We sought the advice of a disinterested counselor to help us solve our problem. He was uninterested in anyone's opinion but his own.*

don't *Don't* is the contraction for *do not: I don't want any.* *Don't* should not be used as the contraction for *does not,* which is *doesn't. He doesn't* (not *don't*) *want any.* See also 28c.

double negative See 31d.

due to *Due to* is an adjective phrase and should not be used as a preposition meaning "because of." *The trip was canceled because of* (not *due to*) *lack of interest. Due to* is acceptable as a subject complement and usually follows a form of the verb *be: His success was due to hard work.*

effect See *affect, effect.*

elicit, illicit *Elicit* is a verb meaning "to bring out" or "to evoke." *Illicit* is an adjective meaning "unlawful." *The reporter was unable to elicit any information from the police about illicit drug traffic.*

emigrate from, immigrate to *Emigrate* means "to leave one country or region to settle in another": *In 1900, my grandfather emigrated from Russia to escape the religious pogroms. Immigrate* means "to enter another country and reside there": *Many Mexicans immigrate to the United States to find work.*

enthused Many people object to the use of *enthused* as an adjective. Use *enthusiastic* instead. *The children were enthusiastic* (not *enthused*) *about going to the circus.*

-ess Many people find the *-ess* suffix demeaning. Write *poet*, not *poetess; Jew*, not *Jewess; author*, not *authoress.*

etc. Avoid ending a list with *etc.* It is more emphatic to end with an example, and in most contexts readers will understand that the list is not exhaustive. When you don't wish to end with an example, *and so on* is more graceful than *etc.* See also *and etc.*

everyone, every one *Everyone* is an indefinite pronoun. *Every one*, the pronoun *one* preceded by the adjective *every*, means "each individual or thing in a particular group." *Every one* is usually followed by *of. Everyone wanted to go. Every one of the missing books was found.*

exam *Exam* is informal for *examination.*

except See *accept, except.*

expect Avoid the colloquial use of *expect* meaning "to believe, think, or suppose." *I think* (not *expect*) *it will rain tonight.*

explicit, implicit *Explicit* means "expressed directly" or "clearly defined"; *implicit* means "implied, unstated." *I gave him explicit instructions not to go swimming. My mother's silence indicated her implicit approval.*

farther, further   *Farther* describes distances: *Chicago is farther from Miami than I thought. Further* suggests quantity or degree: *You extended the curfew further than you should have.*

fewer, less   *Fewer* refers to items that can be counted; *less* refers to general amounts. *Fewer people are living in the city, so real estate is less expensive.*

finalize   *Finalize* is jargon meaning "to make final or complete." Avoid using it in formal writing.

firstly   *Firstly* sounds pretentious, and it leads to the ungainly series *firstly, secondly, thirdly, fourthly,* and so on. Write *first, second, third* instead.

flunk   *Flunk* is colloquial for *fail* and should be avoided in formal writing.

folks   *Folks* is an informal expression for "parents" or "relatives" or "people" in general. Use a more formal expression instead.

further   See *farther, further.*

get   *Get* has many colloquial uses. Avoid using *get* to mean the following: "to evoke an emotional response" (*That music always gets to me*); "to annoy" (*After a while his sulking got to me*); "to take revenge on" (*I got back at him by leaving the room*); "to become" (*He got sick*); "to start or begin" (*Let's get going*). Avoid using *have got to* in place of *must: I must* (not *have got to*) *finish this paper tonight.*

good, well   *Good* is an adjective, *well* an adverb. See 26. *He hasn't felt good about his game since he sprained his wrist last season. She performed well on the uneven parallel bars.*

hardly   Avoid expressions such as *can't hardly* and *not hardly,* which are considered double negatives. *I can* (not *can't*) *hardly describe my elation at getting the job.* See 31d.

has got, have got   *Got* is unnecessary and awkward in such constructions. It should be dropped. *We have* (not *have got*) *three days to prepare for the opening.*

he   At one time it was acceptable to use *he* to mean "he or she." Today such usage is inappropriate. See 22a for alternative constructions.

hisself   *Hisself* is nonstandard. Use *himself.*

hopefully   *Hopefully* means "in a hopeful manner": *We looked hope-*

fully to the future. Do not use *hopefully* in constructions such as the following: *Hopefully, your daughter will recover soon.* Indicate who is doing the hoping: *I hope that your daughter will recover soon.*

if, whether Use *if* in a statement of condition and *whether* to express alternatives. *If you go on a trip, whether it be to Nebraska or New Jersey, remember to bring traveler's checks.*

illusion See *allusion, illusion.*

imply, infer *Imply* means "to suggest or state indirectly"; *infer* means "to draw a conclusion." *John implied that he knew all about computers, but the interviewer inferred that John was inexperienced.*

in, into *In* indicates location or condition; *into* indicates movement or a change in condition. *They found the lost letters in a box after moving into the house.*

in regards to *In regards to* confuses two different phrases: *in regard to* and *as regards.* Use one or the other: *In regard to* (or *as regards*) *the contract, ignore the first clause.*

irregardless *Irregardless* is nonstandard. Use *regardless.*

is when, is where These mixed constructions are often incorrectly used in definitions: *A run-off election is* (not *is when*) *a second election held to break a tie.* See 11c.

its, it's *Its* is a possessive pronoun; *it's* is a contraction for *it is.* See 36c, 36e. *The dog licked its wound whenever its owner walked into the room. It's a perfect day to walk the twenty-mile trail.*

kind(s) *Kind* is singular and should be treated as such in constructions in which it occurs. Don't write *These kind of chairs are rare.* Write instead *This kind of chair is rare. Kinds* is plural and should be used only when you mean more than one kind: *These kinds of chairs are rare.*

kind of, sort of Avoid using *kind of* or *sort of* to mean "somewhat": *The movie was kind of boring.* Do not put *a* after either phrase: *That kind of* (not *kind of a*) *salesclerk annoys me.*

learn, teach *Learn* means "to gain knowledge"; *teach* means "to impart knowledge." *I must teach* (not *learn*) *my sister to read.*

lie, lay *Lie* is an intransitive verb meaning "to recline or rest on a surface." Its principal parts are *lie, lay, lain. Lay* is a transitive verb meaning "to put or place." Its principal parts are *lay, laid, laid.* See 27b.

like, as *Like* is a preposition, not a subordinating conjunction. It is followed only by a noun or a noun phrase. *As* is a subordinating conjunction that introduces a subordinate clause. In casual speech you may say *She looks like she hasn't slept* or *You don't know her like I do.* But in formal writing, use *as: She looks as if she hasn't slept. You don't know her as I do.* See prepositions and subordinating conjunctions, 47f, 47g, 49b.

likely, liable *Likely* means "plausible or probable"; *liable* means "obligated": *You're likely* (not *liable*) *to trip if you don't tie your shoelaces.*

loan Some readers object to the use of *loan* as a verb. Use *lend* instead: *Please lend* (not *loan*) *me five dollars.*

loose, lose *Loose* is an adjective meaning "not securely fastened." *Lose* is a verb meaning "to misplace" or "not win." *Did you lose your only loose pair of work pants?*

lots, lots of *Lots* and *lots of* are colloquial substitutes for *many, much,* or *a lot.* Avoid using them in formal writing.

mankind Avoid *mankind* whenever possible. It offends many readers because it excludes women. Use *humanity, humans, the human race,* or *humankind* instead.

may See *can, may.*

maybe, may be *Maybe* is an adverb meaning "possibly." *May be* is a verb phrase. *Maybe the sun will shine tomorrow. Tomorrow may be a brighter day.*

may of, might of *May of* and *might of* are nonstandard for *may have* and *might have. We may have* (not *may of*) *had too many cookies.*

media, medium *Media* is the plural of *medium. Of all the media covering the Olympics, television is the medium that best captures the spectacle of the events.*

most *Most* is colloquial when used to mean "almost": *Almost* (not *most*) *everyone went to the parade.*

must of See *may of.*

myself *Myself* is a reflexive or intensive pronoun. See 47b. Reflexive: *I cut myself.* Intensive: *I will drive you myself.* Do not use *myself* in place of *I* or *me: He gave the flowers to Melinda and me* (not *myself*). See 24a and 24b.

nowheres *Nowheres* is nonstandard for *nowhere.*

number See *amount, number.*

off of *Off* is sufficient. Omit *of. The ball rolled off* (not *off of*) *the table.*

OK, O.K., okay All three spellings are acceptable, but in formal speech and writing avoid these colloquial expressions for consent or approval.

percent, per cent, percentage *Percent* (also spelled *per cent*) and *percentage* refer to numbers and actual statistics. *Percent* is always preceded by a number and should be spelled out in formal writing (do not use %). *The candidate won 80 percent of the primary vote.* When preceded by *the, percentage* is singular: *The percentage of engineering students was high.* When preceded by *a, percentage* is either singular or plural depending on the number of the noun in the prepositional phrase that follows. Plural noun: *A small percentage of workers want to quit.* Singular: *A small percentage of the work force wants to quit.*

phenomena *Phenomena* is the plural of *phenomenon,* which means "an observable occurrence or fact." *Strange phenomena occur at all hours of the night in that house, but last night's phenomenon was the strangest of all.*

plus *Plus* should not be used to join independent clauses. *This raincoat is dirty; moreover* (not *plus*), *it has a hole in it.*

principal, principle *Principal* is a noun meaning "the head of a school or organization" or "*a sum of money.*" It is also an adjective meaning "most important." *Principle* is a noun meaning "a basic truth or law." *The principal expelled her for three principal reasons. We believe in the principle of equal justice for all.*

quote, quotation *Quote* is a verb; *quotation* is a noun. Avoid using *quote* as a shortened form of the noun. *Her quotations* (not *quotes*) *from Shakespeare intrigued us.*

raise, rise *Raise* is a transitive verb meaning "to move or cause to move upward." It takes a direct object. *I raised the shades. Rise* is an intransitive verb meaning "to go up." It does not take a direct object. *Heat rises.*

real, really *Real* is an adjective; *really* is an adverb. *Real* is sometimes used informally as an adverb, but avoid this use in formal writing. *She was really* (not *real*) *angry.* See 26a.

reason is because   Use *that* instead of *because: The reason I'm late is that* (not *because*) *my car broke down.* See 11c.

respectfully, respectively   *Respectfully* means "showing or marked by respect." *He respectfully submitted his opinion to the judge. Respectively* means "each in the order given." *John, Tom, and Larry were a butcher, a baker, and a lawyer, respectively.*

sensual, sensuous   *Sensual* means "gratifying the physical senses," especially those associated with sexual pleasure. *Sensuous* means "pleasing to the senses," especially those involved in the experience of art, music, and nature. *The sensuous music and balmy air led the dancers to more sensual movements.*

set, sit   *Set* is a transitive verb meaning "to put" or "to place." Its principal parts are *set, set, set. Sit* is an intransitive verb meaning "to be seated." Its principal parts are *sit, sat, sat. She set the dough in a warm corner of the kitchen. The cat sat in the warmest part of the room, directly over the furnace.* See 27a.

shall, will   *Shall* was once used as the helping verb with *I* or *we: I shall, we shall, you will, he/she/it will, they will.* Today, however, *will* is generally accepted even when the subject is *I* or *we.* The word *shall* occurs primarily in polite questions (*Shall I find you a pillow?*) and in legalistic sentences suggesting duty or obligation (*The applicant shall file form 1080 by December 31*).

should of   *Should of* is nonstandard for *should have. They should have* (not *should of*) *been home an hour ago.*

since   Do not use *since* to mean *because* if there is any chance of ambiguity: *Since we won the game, we have been celebrating with a pitcher of beer. Since* here could mean "because" or "from the time that."

sit   See *set, sit.*

sometime, some time, sometimes   *Sometime* is an adverb meaning "at an indefinite or unstated time": *I'll see you sometime soon. Some time* is the adjective *some* modifying the noun *time* and is spelled as two words to mean "a period of time": *I haven't lived there for some time. Sometimes* is an adverb meaning "at times, now and then": *Sometimes I run into him at the library.*

sure and   *Sure and* is nonstandard for *sure to. We were all taught to be sure to* (not *and*) *look both ways before crossing a street.*

take   See *bring, take.*

than, then   *Than* is a conjunction used in comparisons; *then* is an adverb denoting time. *That pizza is more than I can eat. Tom laughed, and then we recognized him.*

that, which   Many writers reserve *that* for restrictive clauses, *which* for nonrestrictive clauses. See 32e.

theirselves   *Theirselves* is nonstandard for *themselves*. *The two people were able to push the Volkswagen out of the way themselves* (not *theirselves*).

there, their, they're   *There* is an adverb specifying place; it is also an expletive. Adverb: *Sylvia is lying there unconscious.* Expletive: *There are two plums left.* *Their* is a possessive pronoun: *Fred and Jane finally washed their car.* *They're* is a contraction of *they are*: *They're later than usual today.*

this kind   See *kind(s)*.

to, too, two   *To* is a preposition; *too* is an adverb; *two* is a number. *Too many of your shots slice to the left, but the last two were right on the mark.*

toward, towards   *Toward* and *towards* are generally interchangeable, although *toward* is preferred.

try and   *Try and* is nonstandard for *try to*. *The teacher asked us all to try to* (not *and*) *write an original haiku.*

unique   Avoid expressions such as *most unique, more straight, less perfect, very round*. Something either is unique or it isn't. It is illogical to suggest degrees of uniqueness. See 26g.

use, utilize   *Utilize* means "to make use of." It often sounds pretentious; in most cases *use* is sufficient: *I used* (not *utilized*) *the best workers to get the job done fast.*

use to, suppose to   *Use to* and *suppose to* are nonstandard for *used to* and *supposed to*. See 29.

wait for, wait on   *Wait for* means "to be in readiness for" or "await." *Wait on* means "to serve." *We're only waiting for* (not *waiting on*) *Ruth before we can leave.*

ways   *Ways* is colloquial when used to mean "distance": *The city is a long way* (not *ways*) *from here.*

where   Do not use *where* in place of *that*. *I heard that* (not *where*) *the crime rate is increasing.*

which   See *that, which*.

while   Avoid using *while* ambiguously: *While Gloria lost money in the slot machine, Tom won it at roulette.* Here *while* could mean either "although" or "at the same time that."

who, which   Use *who* to refer to people, *which* to refer to things: *She was the guard who* (not *which*) *told me which stairway to use.*

who's, whose   *Who's* is a contraction of *who is; whose* is a possessive pronoun. *Who's ready for more popcorn? Whose coat is this?*

will   See *shall, will.*

would of   *Would of* is nonstandard for *would have. She would have* (not *would of*) *had a chance to play if she had arrived on time.*

you   In formal writing, avoid *you* in an indefinite sense meaning "anyone." See 23d. *Any spectator* (not *you*) *could tell by the way John caught the ball that his throw would be too late.*

your, you're   *Your* is a possessive pronoun; *you're* is a contraction of *you are. Is that your new motorcycle? You're on the list of finalists.*

(Continued from page iv)

Barnaby Conrad III, from " 'Train of Kings, the King of Trains' Is Back on Track," *Smithsonian*, December 1983. Reprinted by permission of *Smithsonian*.

Earl Conrad, from *Harriet Tubman*. Reprinted by permission of Paul S. Eriksson, Publisher.

James Underwood Crockett, Oliver E. Allen, and the Editors of Time-Life Books, from *The Time-Life Encyclopedia of Gardening*. © 1977 Time-Life Books Inc. Reprinted by permission of Time-Life Books Inc.

Erik Eckholm, from "Pygmy Chimp Readily Learns Language Skill," *The New York Times*. Copyright © 1985 by The New York Times Company. Reprinted by permission.

Stephen Jay Gould, from "Were Dinosaurs Dumb?" *The Panda's Thumb: More Reflections in Natural History*. Copyright © 1980 by Stephen Jay Gould. Reprinted by permission of W. W. Norton & Company, Inc.

Hillary Hauser, from "Exploring a Sunken Realm in Australia," *National Geographic*, January 1984. Reprinted by permission of the National Geographic Society.

Richard Hofstadter, from *America at 1750: A Social Portrait*. Copyright © 1971 by Beatrice K. Hofstadter, executrix of the estate of Richard Hofstadter. Reprinted by permission of Alfred A. Knopf, Inc.

Martin Luther King, Jr., from "I Have a Dream." Reprinted by permission of Joan Daves. Copyright © 1963 by Martin Luther King, Jr.

Margaret Mead, from "New Superstitions for Old," *A Way of Seeing*. Reprinted by permission of William Morrow & Company, Inc.

Gloria Naylor, from *Linden Hills*. Copyright © 1985 by Gloria Naylor. Reprinted by permission of Houghton Mifflin Company.

Flannery O'Connor, from "The King of the Birds," *Mystery and Manners*. Copyright © 1969. Reprinted by permission of Farrar, Straus and Giroux, Inc.

Saul K. Padover, from *Jefferson*. Copyright 1942, 1970 by Saul K. Padover. Reprinted by permission of Harcourt Brace Jovanovich, Inc.

Readers' Guide to Periodical Literature, March 1982 – February 1983, from entries under "Animal Communications." Copyright © 1982, 1983 by The H. W. Wilson Company. Material reproduced by permission of the publisher.

Paul Reps, from "The Moon Cannot Be Stolen" *Zen Flesh, Zen Bones*. Reprinted by permission of Charles E. Tuttle, Co., Inc., of Tokyo, Japan.

Arthur M. Schlesinger, Jr., from *The Age of Roosevelt: The Crisis of the Old Order*. Copyright © 1957 by Arthur M. Schlesinger, Jr. Reprinted by permission of Houghton Mifflin Company.

Lewis Thomas, from "On Societies as Organisms," *The Lives of a Cell*. Copyright © 1974 by Lewis Thomas. All rights reserved. Reprinted by permission of Viking Penguin, Inc.

James Thurber, from "University Days," *My Life and Hard Times*. Copyright © 1933, 1961 by James Thurber. Published by Harper & Row, Publishers, Inc. Reprinted by permission.

Olivia Vlahos, from *Human Beginnings*. Published by Viking Penguin Inc. Reprinted by permission of the author.

Answers to Lettered Exercises

EXERCISE 8 – 1, page 76

Possible revisions:

a. After a couple of minutes went by, the teacher walked in smiling.
b. Although Mary will graduate from high school in June, she has not yet decided on a college.
c. Some major companies exert an overwhelming influence on their employees by dictating where they may live and determining where their children should go to school.
d. The aides help the younger children with reading and math, their weakest subjects.
e. My first sky dive, from an altitude of 12,500 feet, was the most frightening experience of my life.

EXERCISE 8 – 2, page 79

Possible revisions:

a. This highly specialized medical training, called a "residency," usually takes four years to complete.
b. His starting salary of roughly $15,000 will increase by 10 to 15 percent yearly until it reaches $25,000.
c. When I presented the idea of job sharing to my supervisors, to my surprise they were delighted with the idea.
d. Although outsiders have forced changes on them, the Hawaiians try to preserve their ancestors' sacred customs.
e. Sharon's country kitchen, formerly a lean-to porch, overlooks a field where horses and cattle graze among old tombstones.

EXERCISE 9 – 1, page 84

Possible revisions:

a. Karen was a friend of many years who helped us through some rough times.
b. The personnel officer told me that I would answer the phone, welcome visitors, distribute mail, and do some typing.

c. This summer I want a job more than a trip to Disney World.
d. I quit Weight Watchers not because I didn't want to continue but because my friend stopped going with me.
e. Nancy not only called the post office but checked with the neighbors to see if the package had come.

EXERCISE 10 – 1, page 89

Possible revisions:

a. Dip the paint brush into the paint remover and spread a thick coat on a small section of the door.
b. Some say that Ella Fitzgerald's renditions of Cole Porter's songs are better than any other singer's.
c. SETI (the Search for Extraterrestrial Intelligence) has excited and will continue to excite interest among space buffs.
d. The study showed that tenth graders are more polite to strangers than to ninth graders. [*or* . . . than ninth graders are.]
e. Gunther Gebel-Williams, whom we watched today and who is a star of the Ringling Brothers and Barnum & Bailey Circus, is well known for his training of circus animals.

EXERCISE 11 – 1, page 93

Possible revisions:

a. My instant reaction was anger and disappointment.
b. I brought a problem into the house that my mother wasn't sure how to handle.
c. It is through the misery of others that old Harvey has become rich.
d. One controversial application of the polygraph is its use by employers to screen job applicants.
e. Encouraging the players to excel may help them learn to overcome obstacles later in life.

EXERCISE 12 – 1, page 96

Possible revisions:

a. This form is required only when the traveler is receiving an advance.
b. Within the next few years, orthodontists will be using as standard practice the technique Kurtz developed.
c. Celia received a flier from a Japanese nun about a workshop on making a kimono.
d. Marie played almost the whole game, but she was taken out in the last ten minutes.
e. Each state would set into motion a program of recycling all reusable products.

EXERCISE 12 – 2, page 99

Possible revisions:

a. To protest the arms buildup, demonstrators set bonfires throughout the park.

b. When I was nestled in the cockpit, the pounding of the engine was muffled only slightly by my helmet.

c. Feeling unprepared for the exam, June found the questions as hard as her instructor had suggested they would be.

d. While my sister was still a beginner at tennis, the coaches recruited her to train for the Olympics.

e. Dr. Curtis recommends striding rather than strolling for those who want to get the most from walking.

EXERCISE 13 – 1, page 101

Possible revisions:

a. On behalf of the team, I want to thank you for this award.

b. Despite horrid weather, poor equipment, and long odds, the prospectors found gold.

c. Some of these friends have received degrees since being employed, but their degrees have not led to advancement.

d. Jurors are encouraged to sift through the evidence carefully and thoroughly.

e. Even to tie her shoes was difficult for the girl with the sprained wrist.

EXERCISE 14 – 1, page 106

Possible revisions:

a. We waited in the emergency room for about an hour. Finally, the nurse came in and told us that we were in the wrong place.

b. Newspapers put the lurid details of an armed robbery on page 1 and relegate the warm, human-interest stories to page G-10.

c. Ministers often have a hard time because they have to please so many different people.

d. We drove for eight hours until we reached the South Dakota Badlands. We could hardly believe the eeriness of the landscape at dusk.

e. The interviewer asked if we had brought our proof of birth and citizenship and our passports.

EXERCISE 16 – 1, page 118

Possible revisions:

a. When visitors come, Grandmother just stares at the wall.

b. The colors of the reproductions were exact.

c. Bloom's race for the governorship is futile.

d. Even ten terry cloth towels stuffed under the door did nothing to stop the flow.

e. In Biology 10A a faculty tutor will assign you eight taped modules and clarify any information on the tapes.

EXERCISE 17 – 1, page 123

Possible revisions:

a. It is a widely held myth that middle-aged people can't change.

b. All work-study students must prove that they are currently enrolled.

c. Dan's early work hours leave his afternoons free for errands and for helping the children with their homework.

d. When our father was laid off from his high-paying factory job, we learned what it was like to be poor.

e. You must make sure that correspondence meets our guidelines. You must also prepare the agenda for each staff meeting, making sure to include time for questions that have arisen since the last meeting.

EXERCISE 18 – 2, page 133

Possible revisions:

a. The processor automatically develops, fixes, washes, and dries the film.
b. The producer overlooks the entire operation.
c. Active
d. Escaping into the world of drugs, I rebelled against anything and everything laid down by the establishment.
e. Players were fighting on both sides of the rink.

EXERCISE 18 – 3, page 134

Possible revisions:

a. Many of us are not persistent enough to make a change for the better.
b. Hours of long practice often distinguish an excellent musician from a sloppy one.
c. Sam Brown began his career as a lawyer, but now he is a real estate mogul.
d. When Robert Frost died at age eighty-eight, he left a legacy of poems that will make him immortal.
e. This patient is kept in isolation to prevent her from catching our germs.

EXERCISE 18 – 4, page 136

a. I was so angry with the salesperson that I took her bag of samples and emptied it on the floor in front of her.
b. Correct
c. Try to come up with the rough outline, and we will find someone who can fill in the details.
d. "Your prejudice is no different from mine," she shouted.
e. The parade moved off the street and onto the beach.

EXERCISE 18 – 5, page 139

Possible revisions:

a. John stormed into the room like a tornado.
b. The president thought that the scientists were using science as a means of furthering their political goals.
c. I told Al that he was taking a terrible risk when I learned that he intended to spy on the trustees' meeting.
d. We ironed out the wrinkles in our relationship.
e. Mel told us that he wasn't willing to take the chance.

EXERCISE 19 – 1, page 146

Possible revisions:

a. Sam told us that he would soon be getting out on work release and that he might be able to come home for a visit on certain weekends.
b. It has been said that there are only three indigenous American art forms: jazz, musical comedy, and soap opera.
c. Correct
d. Myra did not tell us about her new job for six weeks, although she saw one or the other of us every day.
e. While on a tour of Italy, Maria and Kathleen sneaked away from their group to spend some quiet minutes with Leonardo da Vinci's *Last Supper,* a stunning fresco painted in the fifteenth century in a Milan monastery.

EXERCISE 20 – 1, page 153

Possible revisions:

a. The city had one public swimming pool that stayed packed with children all summer long.
b. Most babies come down with a high temperature at some point, and mine was no exception.
c. Why should we pay taxes to support public transportation? We prefer to save energy dollars by carpooling.
d. Charles was like any of us; he resisted having an idea pulled from under him.
e. The experience taught Marianne that she could not always rely on her parents to bail her out of trouble.

EXERCISE 20 – 2, page 154

Possible revisions:

a. Because the trail up Mount Finegold was declared impassable, we decided to return to our hotel a day early.
b. Correct
c. Residents have a variety of complaints about the windmills. For instance, the noise keeps people awake at night, the vibrations have been known to break windows, television reception is affected, and the windmills themselves are just plain ugly.
d. Researchers studying the fertility of Texas land tortoises X-rayed all the female tortoises to see how many eggs they had.
e. The Chevy Chase swimmers were determined to win this medley relay for one reason: It was their last chance to beat their archrivals from Kensington.

EXERCISE 21 – 1, page 164

a. Subject: friendship and support; verb: have; b. Subject: rings; verb: are; c. Subject: Neither; verb: was; d. Subject: source; verb: is; e. Subject: people; verb: are

EXERCISE 21 – 2, page 165

a. Correct
b. At the back of the room are an aquarium and a terrarium.
c. Correct
d. Crystal chandeliers, polished floors, and a new oil painting have transformed Sandra's apartment.
e. Either Alice or Jan usually works the midnight shift.

EXERCISE 22 – 1, page 170

Possible revisions:

a. Employees on extended leave may continue their life insurance.
b. Correct
c. When I looked out the window of our tenement during these periods of insomnia, I sometimes saw a priest or a brother entering the side door of the church, his face silhouetted briefly in the moonlight.
d. When parents have been drinking or using drugs, they are more likely to abuse their children.
e. If you have any students attending class who are still not on your roster, please send them to the registration office.

EXERCISE 23 – 1, page 176

Possible revisions:

a. The detective photographed the body after removing the blood-stained shawl.
b. In Professor Johnson's class, students are lucky to earn a C.
c. I am proud of all my children, three of whom have become legislators.
d. The Comanche braves lived violent lives; they gained respect for their skill as warriors.
e. All students can secure parking permits from the campus police office, which is open from 8 A.M. until 8 P.M.

EXERCISE 24 – 1, page 183

a. The most traumatic experience for her father and me occurred long after her operation.
b. Correct
c. Correct
d. The winners, Julie and he, were unable to attend the awards ceremony.
e. My father always tolerated our whispering after the lights were out.

EXERCISE 25 – 1, page 186

a. In his first production of *Hamlet,* whom did Laurence Olivier replace?
b. Correct
c. Correct
d. Some group leaders cannot handle the pressure; they give whoever makes the most noise most of their attention.
e. Correct

EXERCISE 26 – 1, page 193

a. My mechanic showed me exactly where to wrap the wire firmly around the muffler.
b. Bill's apple fritters taste really good.
c. My mother thinks that Carmen is the more pleasant of the twins.
d. Correct
e. Last Christmas was the most wonderful day of my life.

EXERCISE 27 – 1, page 199

a. Last June my cousin Albert swam the length of the lake in forty minutes.
b. When I get the urge to exercise, I lie down until it passes.
c. Correct
d. The team of engineers watched in horror as the newly built dam burst and flooded the small valley.
e. Correct

EXERCISE 27 – 2, page 205

a. Correct
b. Watson and Crick discovered the mechanism that controls inheritance in all life: the workings of the DNA molecule.
c. Marion would write more if she weren't distracted by a house full of children.
d. Sharon told me that she had gone to the meeting the day before.
e. Correct

EXERCISE 27 – 3, page 208

Possible revisions:

a. The research assistant reported the results.
b. Parents do not use enough discretion in deciding which television programs their children may watch.
c. As the patient undressed, we saw scars on his back, stomach, and thighs. Child abuse was what we suspected.
d. We noted right away that the taxi driver had been exposed to Americans because he knew all the latest slang.
e. The tailor replaced the buttons, lengthened or shortened the hems, and cleaned and pressed all of the costumes.

EXERCISE 28 – 1, page 214

a. Correct
b. Does he have enough energy to hold down two jobs while going to night school?
c. The whooping crane has been an endangered species since the late 1930s.
d. Our four children play one or two instruments each.
e. Even though Maria is in her late twenties, her mother treats her like a child.

EXERCISE 29 – 1, page 217

a. Our captain talked so much at meals that we learned to ignore him.
b. Correct
c. That line of poetry can be expressed more dramatically.
d. Our church has a closed-circuit television.
e. England, France, and the United States had already signed a treaty before the war intensified.

EXERCISE 31 – 1, page 225

a. The children in my neighborhood all walked to school.
b. They skate swiftly, waving and dodging as they drive the pucks toward the opposing team's goal.
c. Chris didn't know about Marlo's death because he never listens. He is always talking.
d. Correct
e. With the budget deadline approaching, our office has hardly had time to handle routine correspondence.

EXERCISE 32 – 1, page 231

a. Correct
b. The man at the next table complained loudly, and the waiter stomped off in disgust.
c. Correct
d. Nursing is physically and mentally demanding, yet the pay is low.
e. After I won the hundred-yard dash, I found a bench in the park and collapsed.

EXERCISE 32 – 2, page 234

a. She wore a black silk cape, a rhinestone collar, satin gloves, and army boots.
b. Correct
c. He was an impossible, demanding guest.
d. Juan walked through the room with casual, elegant grace.
e. Correct

EXERCISE 32 – 3, page 238

a. We bought a home in Upper Marlboro, where my husband worked as a mail carrier.
b. Ms. Taylor, who works in accounting, will be joining our carpool.
c. Correct
d. Shakespeare's tragedy *King Lear* was given a splendid performance by the actor Laurence Olivier.
e. The man whom you recommended to us is an excellent addition to our staff.

EXERCISE 32 – 4, page 243

a. Each morning the seventy-year-old woman cleans the barn, shovels manure, and spreads clean hay around the milking stalls.
b. Good technique does not guarantee, however, that the power you develop will be sufficient for Kyok Pa competition.
c. Correct
d. We pulled into the first apartment complex we came upon and slowly patrolled the parking lots.
e. We wondered how our overweight grandmother could have been the pretty bride in the picture, but we kept our wonderings to ourselves.

EXERCISE 33 – 1, page 249

a. We'd rather spend our money on blue-chip stocks than speculate on pork-bellies.
b. Being prepared for the worst is one way to escape disappointment.
c. Correct
d. My father said that he would move to California if I would agree to transfer to UCLA.
e. I quickly accepted the fact that I was literally in third-class quarters.

EXERCISE 34 – 1, page 253

a. If fifty million people say a foolish thing, it is still a foolish thing.
b. When I get a little money, I buy books; if any is left, I buy food and clothes.
c. Don't talk about yourself; it will be done when you leave.
d. The only sensible ends of literature are first, the pleasurable toil of writing; second, the gratification of one's family and friends; and lastly, the solid cash.
e. All animals are equal, but some animals are more equal than others.

EXERCISE 35 – 1, page 256

a. The second and most memorable week of survival school consisted of five stages: orientation, long treks, POW camp, escape and evasion, and return to civilization.
b. Among the canceled classes were calculus, physics, advanced biology, and English 101.
c. I entered this class feeling jittery and incapable; I leave feeling poised and confident.
d. Do not volunteer for any leadership position unless you are certain that you can fulfill all the responsibilities.
e. Correct

EXERCISE 36 – 1, page 261

a. In a democracy anyone's vote counts as much as mine.
b. Correct
c. The puppy's favorite activity was chasing its tail.

d. Correct
e. A crocodile's life span is about thirteen years.

EXERCISE 37 – 1, page 266

a. "Fire and Ice" is one of Robert Frost's most famous poems.
b. As Emerson wrote in 1849, "I hate quotations. Tell me what you know."
c. Joggers have to run up the hills and then back down, but bicyclers, once they reach the top of a hill, get a free ride back down.
d. Correct
e. Historians Segal and Stineback tell us that the English settlers considered these epidemics "the hand of God making room for His followers in the 'New World.' "

EXERCISE 39 – 1, page 275

a. We lived in Davenport, Iowa, during the early years of our marriage.
b. Pat helped Geoff put the tail on his kite, which was made of scraps from old dresses, and off they went to the park.
c. Correct
d. Cancer — a disease that strikes without regard to age, race, or religion and causes dread in the most stalwart person — had struck my family. [*or* Cancer, . . . person, . . .]
e. The class stood, faced the flag, placed hands over hearts, and raced through "I pledge allegiance . . . liberty and justice for all" in less than sixty seconds.

EXERCISE 40 – 1, page 283

a. Correct
b. My grandmother told me that of all the subjects she studied, she found political science the most challenging.
c. Correct
d. Julius Caesar was born in 100 B.C. and died in 44 B.C.
e. Turning to page 195, Marion realized that she had finally reached the end of chapter 22.

EXERCISE 41 – 1, page 286

a. On a normal day I spend at least four to five hours working on computers.
b. Correct
c. Correct
d. We ordered three 4-door sedans for company executives.
e. In 1987, only 112 male high school students in our state planned to make a career of teaching.

EXERCISE 42 – 1, page 289

a. Howard Hughes commissioned the *Spruce Goose*, a beautifully built but thoroughly impractical wooden aircraft.
b. The old man screamed his anger, shouting to all of us, "I will not leave my money to you worthless lay-abouts!"

c. Even though it is almost always hot in Mexico in the summer, you can usually find a cool spot on one of the park benches in the town's *zócalo*.

d. Correct

e. One of my favorite novels is George Eliot's *Middlemarch*.

EXERCISE 44 – 1, page 304

a. Correct

b. The swiftly moving tugboat pulled alongside the barge and directed it away from the oil spill in the harbor.

c. Many states are adopting laws that limit property taxes for homeowners.

d. Two-thirds of the House voted for the amendment.

e. Correct

EXERCISE 45 – 1, page 309

a. District Attorney Johnson was disgusted when the jurors turned in a verdict of not guilty after only one hour of deliberation.

b. Correct

c. Correct

d. Refugees from Central America are finding it more and more difficult to cross the Rio Grande into the United States.

e. I want to take Environmental Biology 103, one other biology course, and one English course.

EXERCISE 47 – 1, page 317

a. cat, gloves, mice; b. Repetition, lie, truth; c. flower, concrete (noun/adjective), cloverleaf; d. censorship, flick, dial; d. Figures, liars

EXERCISE 47 – 2, page 320

a. your (pronoun/adjective), them; b. those, who; c. I, some (pronoun/adjective), that, I, myself; d. who, his (pronoun/adjective); e. No one

EXERCISE 47 – 3, page 322

a. have been; b. can be savored; c. are, is; d. flock; e. Do scald

EXERCISE 47 – 4, page 325

a. Adjectives: Useless, necessary; b. Adjectives: The (article), American, toler-
ant; adverb: wonderfully; c. Adverbs: too, historically; d. Noun/adjective: work; e. Adjective: the (article); adverb: faster

EXERCISE 48 – 1, page 331

a. Complete subject: A spoiled child; simple subject: child; b. Complete subject: all facts; simple subject: facts; c. (You); d. Complete subject: nothing except change; simple subject: nothing; e. Complete subject: hope

EXERCISE 48 – 2, page 334

a. lead (intransitive); b. is (linking); c. have lived and loved (intransitive); d. hate (transitive), love (transitive); e. can be (linking)

EXERCISE 48 – 3, page 337

a. Direct object: a hundred fathers; subject complement: an orphan; b. Direct object: another; c. Direct objects: your door, your neighbors; object complement: honest; d. Direct object: Jack; object complement: a dull boy; e. Indirect object: her father; direct object: forty whacks

EXERCISE 49 – 1, page 340

a. with no side effects (adjective phrase modifying *tranquilizer*); b. on its back (adverbial phrase modifying *carries*); c. of money (adjective phrase modifying *love*), of all evil (adjective phrase modifying *root*); d. in a graveyard (adverbial phrase modifying begins), in a river (adverbial phrase modifying *ends*); e. with words (adverbial phrase modifying *can stroke*)

EXERCISE 49 – 2, page 344

a. Though you live near a forest (adverb clause modifying *do waste*); b. who help themselves (adjective clause modifying *those*); c. What is whispered (noun clause used as subject of the sentence); d. that trots (adjective clause modifying *dog*); e. unless it is practiced on clever persons (adverb clause modifying *is*)

EXERCISE 49 – 3, page 348

a. being sixteen (gerund phrase used as subject complement); b. made in storms (participial phrase modifying *Vows*); c. To help a friend (infinitive phrase used as subject of the sentence), to give ourselves pleasure (infinitive phrase used as subject complement); d. bearing gifts (participial phrase modifying *Greeks*); e. being dead (gerund phrase used as object of the preposition *by*)

EXERCISE 50 – 1, page 352

a. complex; who always speaks the truth (adjective clause); b. compound; c. simple; d. complex; If you don't go to other people's funerals (adverb clause); e. complex; who sleep like a baby (adjective clause)

EXERCISE 53 – 1, page 454

a. hasty generalization; b. *non sequitur;* c. *post hoc;* d. false analogy; e. biased language

Index

CORRECTION SYMBOLS

Boldface numbers refer to sections of the handbook.

abbr	faulty abbreviation **40**	p	error in punctuation
ad	misuse of adverb or adjective **26**	⩓	comma **32**
agr	faulty agreement **21, 22**	no ,	no comma **33**
appr	inappropriate language **17**	;	semicolon **34**
art	article **30**	:	colon **35**
awk	awkward	∀	apostrophe **36**
cap	capital letter **45**	" "	quotation marks **37**
case	error in case **24, 25**	. ? !	period, question mark, exclamation point **38**
coh	coherence **7**	— () [] ... /	dash, parentheses, brackets, ellipsis, slash **39**
coord	faulty coordination **8b**	par, ¶	new paragraph **5–7**
cs	comma splice **20**	pass	ineffective passive **27g**
dev	inadequate development **2, 6**	plan	faulty planning **1**
dm	dangling modifier **12c**	ref	error in pronoun reference **23**
-ed	error in -ed ending **29**	rev	revise **3, 4**
exact	inexact language **18**	-s	error in -s ending **28, 31b**
frag	sentence fragment **19**	sep	awkward separation of words **13**
fs	fused sentence **20**	shift	distracting shift **14**
gl/us	see glossary of usage	sp	misspelled word **43**
gr	grammar **47–50**	sub	faulty subordination **8c–d**
hyph	error in use of hyphen **44**	t	error in verb tense **27c–e**
inc	incomplete construction **10**	trans	transition needed **7c**
irreg	error in irregular verb **27a**	v	voice **27g**
ital	italics (underlining) **42**	var	lack of variety in sentence structure **8, 15**
lc	use lowercase letter **45**	vb	error in verb form **27**
log	faulty logic **53**	w	wordy **16**
mixed	mixed construction **11**	//	faulty parallelism **9**
mm	misplaced modifier **12a–b**	∧	insert
mood	error in mood **27f**	X	obvious error
ms	manuscript form **46**	#	insert space
nonst	nonstandard usage **28–31**	⌒	close up space
num	error in use of numbers **41**		
om	omitted word **10, 31a**		